THE FOUR GOSPELS

AN EXEGETICAL TRANSLATION

by

Boyce W. Blackwelder, MA., TH.D.

Published by
Warner Press, Inc.
Anderson, Indiana

To

All the persons, men, women, children, ministers, and scholars whose lives have touched mine and who have been an influence in helping me to seek the will of God for my life.

To

All who have helped me better to proclaim the gospel of Jesus Christ.

**Books by
Boyce W. Blackwelder**

Light from the Greek New Testament
Toward Understanding Paul
Toward Understanding Romans
Toward Understanding Thessalonians
Letters from Paul

Contents

Preface   7

Introduction   9

Matthew 13

Mark 73

Luke 111

John 171

Preface

Our word *gospel,* from the Anglo-Saxon *godspell,* which means the good story, good tidings, or God's story, renders the Greek *euaggelion,* the good news.

It is the good news about Jesus Christ (objective genitive), or the good news from Jesus Christ (subjective genitive). It is good news because it proclaims the life, death, and resurrection of Jesus of Nazareth who is declared to be the Son of Man and the Son of God, the ultimate revelation of God, the Savior of the world, and the Founder and Builder of the Church. All Scripture points to Him.

There is only one gospel—the message from God which sets forth the way of salvation through faith in His Son. In the Greek New Testament, there is only one passage in which an adjective is used with the gospel of Christ—Revelation 14:6, where we read of "the everlasting gospel."

The gospel is not confined to events or activities and teachings that happened in Palestine nineteen hundred years ago. It has a basis in history, of course, but it is changless in character, timeless in relevance, universal in scope, powerful in its nature, and judgmental in its imperativeness (Cf. John 12:48).

The gospel is not an explanation—it is an affirmation, a proclamation. It is the message of life and hope for every person who believes it, in this present generation as well as in every succeeding one. It is the objective standard of faith and experience. If received and practiced, it will meet the needs and challenges of every age.

Luke says there are many accounts of the life and work of Jesus (Cf. Luke 1:1). Four canonical Gospels have been preserved for us: the declarations of Matthew, Mark, Luke and John.

These accounts are more than records of the experiences of the first disciples. They are part of the Scriptures—literature which is *Theopneustos* —God-breathed (2 Timothy 3:16). They contain four separate accounts of the life and work of Jesus. These words of love and life were written by men who were primarily evangelists. Each one gave the particular information suited for his express purpose in writing.

Our sources are more reasonable and reliable than is sometimes realized. Matthew and John wrote of the things which they had seen and heard. John must have received much information from Mary, the mother of Jesus, during the time she spent in his home after the crucifixion, resurrection, and ascension of Jesus.

Mark received a great deal of information from Peter. It is said that Mark wrote Peter's Gospel. Luke, well known for his accuracy as a historian, made a thorough investigation of the "things which are most surely believed among us, even as they delivered them unto us, which from the beginning were eyewitnesses and ministers of the word" (Luke 1:1-2). And with the close relationship he had with Paul, the great Apostle to the Gentiles, there must have been rich times of sharing.

This translation of the four Gospels attempts to present to readers some of the insights which are the reward of diligent study of the written Word. It is my hope that students, ministers, and Christians in general will feel the heartthrob experienced by the first disciples, who in the long ago, heard and received the message, placed faith in Jesus as their Christ and Savior, and who went forth to proclaim their newfound joy to the people of their generation.

This is an exegetical translation—not a paraphase. The aim of biblical exegetics is to make as clear as possible the meaning of the scriptural text. The term *exegesis,* formed from two Greek words, the preposition *ek,* "out of," and the verb *hegeomai,* "to lead, guide, unfold, narrate," refers to the process of getting out of a literary composition the truth contained therein. Thus an interpreter tries to discover what each statement meant to the original writer and to render it accurately into the language at hand.

It is impossible in every instance, to translate the same Greek word by the same English word. Translation is more than a mere word-for-word rendering of the one language into another language. Transferring the idiom characteristic of the Greek into the corresponding idiom characteristic of contemporary English becomes a challenging task.

Words inserted, in an effort to convey deeper meanings implied by the Greek vocabulary and sentence structure are marked by brackets, and explanatory footnotes are used to help clarify the meaning of the scriptural text.

I have closely followed the Greek text edited by Professor Eberhard Nestle, fourth edition, 1904 (London: British and Foreign Bible Society, 1934). The Nestle text is the result of a collation of three of the principal recensions of the Greek New Testament prepared in the latter half of the nineteenth century—those of Tischendorf, Wescott and Hort, and Bernhard Weiss.

The purpose of the Apostle John in writing, remains the object of every Christian preacher and writer: "These stand written in order that you might believe that Jesus is the Christ, the Son of God, and that by believing you may go on enjoying life in His Name."

—Boyce W. Blackwelder

INTRODUCTION

The publication of this book, the last work of the late Dr. Boyce W. Blackwelder, reflects the love and appreciation of his many friends. As pastor, evangelist, conference leader, seminary professor, and friend he influenced the life of the Church of God movement. There was no question about his personal commitment. It was first to Christ, then to the Church which Christ loved and purchased with his own blood. He has left to all of us a legacy in exemplary living that we would do well to emulate. His standard of excellence in Christian scholarship placed him in a field of biblical knowledge that is respected by the academician and appreciated by the uneducated. The honesty and humility with which he handled the Scriptures enabled him to communicate the gospel both in the classroom and from the pulpit. We thank God for his life and this legacy of revealed truth in this bound volume.

To make possible the printing of this book, Warner Press has joined with the First Church of God in Middletown, Ohio and the Mass Communications Board of the Church of God to underwrite the initial cost of publication. We are happy to recognize on these opening pages two of Dr. Blackwelder's dear friends: the late Dr. R. C. Caudill and the present pastor of the First Church of God in Middletown, J. Herschel Caudill. Dr. Blackwelder found in this congregation the loving support and acceptance that made him an annual speaker at conferences and indoor camp meetings. His close relationship to the Caudill family endeared his ministry to the congregation and throughout the Miami Valley of Ohio.

It is our prayer that the influence of Dr. Blackwelder and of these dynamic pastors of God's Church will encourage others to a standard of excellence as they serve the Lord.

Do your best to present yourself to God as one approved, a workman who has no need to be ashamed, rightly handling the word of truth (2 Tim. 2:15).

Arlo F. Newell
Editor in Chief
Warner Press, Inc.

Dr. R. C. Caudill
Pastor 1926-1966
First Church of God
Crawford & Logan Streets
Middletown, Ohio

J. Herschel Caudill
Pastor 1963-1980
First Church of God
Breiel Boulevard
Middletown, Ohio

The Church of God reformation movement in Middletown was started in the winter of 1909-10 in the humble home of John Alexander on Baltimore Street.

The small group soon moved to a storefront in 1911 where Claude Black was the first pastor. In 1914 S. D. Steenbergen became the pastor, and under his leadership a new church was constructed on Young Street. In 1918 B. F. Lawson was called as pastor. The church grew rapidly through his ministry. Many revivals with R. C. Caudill, W. Dale Oldham, W. F. Chappel, and John Chappel enlarged the numbers.

It was in 1924 that a site was purchased at Crawford and Logan Streets, and a new church was dedicated in May 1925. R. C. Caudill became pastor August 1, 1926. Several additions were made to the church building to accommodate the people.

In February 1946 Dr. Caudill took a leave from the church, and Dr. A. Leland Forrest became pastor until 1948. At that time Dr. Caudill returned and remained until his death in 1966.

J. Herschel Caudill, his son, came as co-pastor in 1956 and as pastor in 1963 when his father retired. He served the church well, leading them into relocating to their present new facilities at 2000 North Breiel Boulevard where they have worshiped since May 1975. Herschel and his father served the church for a total of sixty-two and a half years.

This congregation was once the only Church of God in Middletown, but there are now ten congregations there. The church has sent more than sixty ministers and their spouses into the "harvest field of service" and has been instrumental in starting some thirty-seven new congregations.

Matthew

Chapter 1

A record of the ancestry of Jesus Christ,[a] a descendant of David, a descendant of Abraham. ²Abraham was the father of Isaac, and Isaac was the father of Jacob, and Jacob was the father of Judah and his brothers. ³Judah was the father of Perez and Zerah by Tamar. Perez was the father of Hezron, and Hezron was the father of Aram. ⁴Aram was the father of Amminadab, and Amminadab was the father of Nahshon, and Nahshon was the father of Salmon. ⁵Salmon was the father of Boaz by Rahab. Boaz was the father of Obed by Ruth. Obed was the father of Jesse, ⁶and Jesse was the father of King David.

David was the father of Solomon by Uriah's wife.[b] ⁷Solomon was the father of Rehoboam, and Rehoboam was the father of Abijah, and Abijah was the father of Asa. ⁸Asa was the father of Jehoshaphat, and Jehoshaphat was the father of Joram, and Joram was the father of Uzziah. ⁹Uzziah was the father of Jotham, and Jotham was the father of Ahaz, and Ahaz was the father of Hezekiah. ¹⁰Hezekiah was the father of Manasseh, and Manasseh was the father of Amon, and Amon was the father of Josiah. ¹¹Josiah was the father of Jechoniah and his brothers about the time of the deportation to Babylon.

¹²After the deportation to Babylon, Jechoniah became the father of Salathiel, and Salathiel became the father of Zerubbabel. ¹³Zerubbabel was the

---

[a]The term *Christ,* from the Greek *Christos,* equivalent to the Hebrew *Mashiach, Messiah,* means *Anointed One.*

[b]The reference is to Bathsheba. Cf. 2 Sam. 11:1-27; 12:24.

father of Abiud, and Abiud was the father of Eliakim, and Eliakim was the father of Azor. [14]Azor was the father of Zadok, and Zakok was the father of Achim, and Achim was the father of Eliud. [15]Eliud was the father of Eleazar, and Eleazar was the father of Matthan, and Matthan was the father of Jacob. [16]Jacob was the father of Joseph the husband of Mary. Of her was born Jesus who is called Christ.

[17]So, in all, there were fourteen generations from Abraham until David, and fourteen generations from David until the deportation to Babylon, and fourteen generations from the deportation to Babylon until the Christ.

[18]Now the birth of Jesus Christ took place in the following manner: Mary His mother was promised in marriage[c] to Joseph, but before they began to live together it was learned that she was going to have a child by the Holy Spirit. [19]Joseph her husband was a man who respected the Law,[d] yet he did not want to make a public accusation of disgrace against her. So he decided to dissolve the marital contract secretly.[e]

[20]But while he was thinking about these things, behold, an angel of the Lord appeared to him in a dream and said, "Joseph, son of David, do not be afraid to take home Mary as your wife, for it is by the Holy Spirit that she has conceived this child. [21]She will give birth to a son, and you are to name Him Jesus[f] because He will save His people from their sins."

[22]All this happened in order to fulfill what the Lord had spoken through the prophet, "Behold, the virgin will conceive and bear a son, and they will name Him Emmanuel,"[g] which may be translated, "God is with us."

[24]And Joseph awoke from sleep, and did as the angel of the Lord had directed him. He took his wife to his home, [25]but he had no intimate relations with her until she had given birth to a son.[h] And he named Him Jesus.

Chapter 2

Now after Jesus was born at Bethleham in Judaea, during the reign of King

---

[c]Engagement was practically equivalent to marriage, and required divorce to terminate it. After the betrothal there was an interval, approximately a year, before the bride took residence in her husband's house and the union was consummated. During such an interval Mary was found with child, ordinarily a circumstance punishable by death. Cf. Deut. 22:20-21.

[d]Literally, "was a righteous man."

[e]Cf. Deut. 24:1.

[f]Our word *Jesus* is based on *Iesous,* Greek form of the Hebrew *Yehoshua* (contracted to *Joshua*) which means *Yahweh (Jehovah) saves.*

[g]Isa. 7:14.

[h]Thus Mary's child might be considered Joseph's legal son, and therefore heir of David's throne. Cf. Acts 2:29-30.

Herod,[a] behold, Magi from the East arrived in Jerusalem [2]asking, "Where is He who has been born king of the Jews? For we saw His star when it rose, and have come to worship Him."

[3]When King Herod heard about this he was disturbed, and all Jerusalem with him. [4]So he gathered together all the chief priests and Law-experts[b] of the people, and sought to learn from them where the Messiah was to be born. [5]They told him, "At Bethlehem in Judaea; for thus it stands written by the prophet, [6]'And you, Bethlehem, in the land of Judah, are by no means least among the princely towns of Judah, for from you will come a Leader who is to shepherd My people Israel.' "[c]

[7]Then Herod secretly summoned the Magi, and learned from them exactly what time the star had appeared. [8]And he sent them to Bethlehem, saying, "Go and search carefully for the child. And when you find Him, report to me so that I, too, may come and worship Him."

[9]After listening to the king, [the Magi] started [on their] way and, behold, the star which they had seen when it rose kept going ahead of them until it reached and stood over [the place] where the child was. [10]When they saw the star, they rejoiced with very great joy.

[11]And having entered the house, they saw the child with Mary His mother, and they knelt down and worshipped Him. Then they opened their treasure-chests and presented to Him gifts: gold and frankincense and myrrh. [12]And, being divinely warned in a dream not to return to Herod, they returned to their own country by a different road.

[13]After the Magi left, behold, an angel of the Lord appeared to Joseph in a dream and said, "Arise, take the child and His mother, and escape to Egypt, and remain there until I notify you; because Herod is about to make an extended search for the child in order to destroy Him." [14]So Joseph arose and took the child and His mother by night, and withdrew into Egypt. [15]There he remained until Herod's death, so that what the Lord had spoken through the prophet was fulfilled, "Out of Egypt I called My Son."[d]

[16]When Herod realized that the Magi had tricked him, he became highly enraged and sent and massacred all the little boys in Bethlehem and its neighborhood who were two years of age or under, according to the extension of the time which he had carefully ascertained from the Magi. [17]Then were

---

[a]Designated by historians as Herod the Great. He ruled over Judaea from 40 B.C. until his death in 4 B.C. This means that Jesus was born about 5 or 6 B.C., according to our present calendar.

[b]The Law-experts or scribes were the professional interpreters of the Jewish sacred writings.

[c]Mic. 5:2.

[d]Hos. 11:1.

fulfilled the words spoken through the prophet Jeremiah, [18]"A cry was heard in Ramah, weeping and bitter mourning—Rachel sobbing for her children, and refusing to be comforted because they are no more."[e]

[19]But after Herod died, behold, an angel of the Lord appeared in a dream to Joseph in Egypt [20]and said, "Arise, take the child and His mother and return to the land of Israel, for those who were seeking the child's life are dead." [21]So he rose, took the child and His mother, and went to the land of Israel. [22]But when he heard that Archelaus[f] had succeeded his father Herod as ruler of Judaea, he was afraid to go back there. And being divinely directed in a dream, he withdrew to the region of Galilee. [23]And he came and made his home in a town called Nazareth, so that what was spoken through the prophets was fulfilled: "He shall be called a Nazarene."

Chapter 3

In those days John the Baptizer appeared, preaching in the wilderness of Judaea. [2]"Repent,"[a] he declared, "for the kingdom of heaven has come near." [3]Indeed, this is he of whom Isaiah the prophet spoke when he said, "The voice of one exclaiming in the wilderness, 'Prepare the way for the Lord,[b] make His paths straight.' "[c]

[4]This John wore clothing made of camel's hair, with a leather belt around his waist; and his food was locusts and wild honey. [5]Then the people of Jerusalem, and of all Judaea, and from the whole Jordan valley began going out to him, [6]and they were being baptized by him in the Jordan River, as they made thorough confession[d] of their sins.

[7]But when John saw many of the Pharisees and Sadducees coming to be baptized,[e] he said to them, "You brood of vipers! Who gave you the idea that you can escape the wrath that is coming? [8]You must produce fruit indicative of repentance, [9]and do not presume to say to yourselves, 'We have Abraham as our forefather.' For I tell you that from these stones God is able to raise up descendants for Abraham. [10]Even now the axe is lying at the root of the trees.

---

[e]Jer. 31:15.

[f]Archelaus was ethnarch of Idumea, Samaria, and Judaea from 4 B.C. until A.D. 6 when, on account of his cruelty, he was deposed by the Roman emperor.

[a]The Greek verb means to *think differently*. It indicates a change of mind which is reflected in conduct. Cf. v. 8.

[b]Objective genitive.

[c]Isa. 40:3

[d]Or, public confession. Literally, "confessing out their sins."

[e]Literally, "coming to the baptism." Cf. Luke 3:7.

Therefore, every tree which does not yield good fruit will be cut down and thrown into the fire. [11]I, on my part, baptize you with water on the basis of[f] [your] repentance, but the One who is coming after me is mightier than I, whose sandals I am not worthy to carry. He will baptize you with the Holy Spirit and with fire. [12]His winnowing-shovel is in His hand, and He will thoroughly cleanse His threshing-floor. He will gather His wheat into the granary, but the chaff He will consume with unquenchable fire."

[13]Then Jesus came[g] from Galilee to John at the Jordan to be baptized by him. [14]John tried to prevent[h] Him, saying, "I myself need to be baptized by You, and do You come to me?" [15]But Jesus answered him, "Permit it now, for in this manner it is proper for us to fulfill all [the requirements of] righteousness." Then John consented. [16]So Jesus was baptized, and the moment He came up out of the water, behold, the heavens were opened and He saw the Spirit of God descending like a dove, and coming upon Him. [17]And, behold, a voice from heaven said, "This is My Son, the Beloved, with whom I am[i] well pleased."

Chapter 4

Then Jesus was led up by the Spirit into the wilderness, to be tempted by the devil. [2]And after fasting for forty days and forty nights He was hungry. [3]The tempter approached and said to Him, "Since you are the Son of God,[a] command these stones to become loaves of bread." [4]Jesus answered, "It stands written,[b] 'Man shall not live by bread alone but by every command that comes from the mouth of God.' "[c]

[5]Then the devil took Him into the Holy City and placed Him on the highest point of the Temple, [6]and said to Him, "Since You are the Son of God, throw Yourself down. For it stands written, 'He will give His angels instruction concerning You, and they will uphold You by their hands, to prevent You from ever striking Your foot against a stone.' "[d] [7]Jesus declared to him, "Also it stands written, 'You shall not test the Lord your God.' "[e]

---

[f]Casual use of Greek preposition, *eis*. Cf. Matt. 12:41.
[g]Historical present.
[h]Conative imperfect.
[i]Timeless aorist.

[a]A condition of the first class, which in the mind of the speaker assumes the reality of the premise. Same construction in vs. 6. Cf. 8:31; Phil. 2:1.
[b]*Gegraptai*, perfect passive indicative. The Greek perfect tense expresses the idea of an action which has been completed and the results of which remain.
[c]Cf. Deut. 8:3.
[d]Cf. Ps. 91:11-12.
[e]Deut. 6:16.

[8]Next the devil took Him to a very high mountain, pointed out to Him all the kingdoms of the world and their splendor, [9]and said to Him, "These things—all of them—I will give You if You kneel and make an act of homage to me." [10]Then Jesus said to him, "Be gone, Satan! For it stands written, 'You shall worship the Lord your God, and Him only shall you serve.' "[f] [11]At that the devil left Him and angels came and began ministering[g] to Him.

[12]Now when Jesus heard that John had been imprisoned, He withdrew into Galilee. [13]And leaving Nazareth[h] He went to live in Capernaum the [city] beside the lake, on the borders of Zebulon and Naphtali, [14]so that what was spoken through Isaiah the prophet was fulfilled. [15]"Land of Zebulon and land of Naphtali, [along the] way of the sea, [the land] beyond the Jordan, Galilee of the Gentiles![i] [16]The people who were sitting in darkness have seen a great light, and for those who were dwelling in the region and shadow of death, light has dawned."[j]

[17]From that time Jesus began to preach and to say, "Repent, for the kingdom of heaven has come near." [18]As He was walking beside the Lake of Galilee, He saw two brothers, Simon who is called Peter, and his brother Andrew, throwing a circular drag-net into the lake, for they were fishermen. [19]He said to them, "Come, follow Me, and I will make you fishers of men." [20]And at once they left the nets and followed Him.[k]

[21]As Jesus went on from there He saw two other brothers, James the son of Zebedee, and his brother John, in the boat with Zebedee their father, adjusting their nets. He called them, [22]and immediately they left the boat and their father, and followed Him.

[23]And Jesus went about in all Galilee, teaching in their synagogues, proclaiming the good news about the kingdom,[l] and healing every [kind of] disease and every [kind of] illness among the people. [24]The report about Him spread through the whole of Syria; and they brought to Him all those with terrible afflictions[m]—people suffering from various diseases and torments—demoniacs, and epileptics[n] and paralytics; and He healed them. [25]Great crowds followed Him from Galilee and from the ten towns,[o] from Jerusalem and Judaea, and from beyond the Jordan.

---

[f]Cf. Deut. 6:13.

[g]Inchoative imperfect.

[h]He was rejected in Nazareth where he grew up. Cf. Luke 4:16-31.

[i]Or nations. Galilee was noted for its diversity of population.

[j]Cf. Isa. 9:1-2.

[k]Earlier Andrew and Peter had become disciples of Jesus. Cf. John 1:35-42. Now they are called to full-time service with Him.

[l]Objective genitive.

[m]Literally, "all those having it bad."

[n]Or, lunatics. Literally, "moon-struck persons." A popular theory was that the moon influenced epilepsy.

[o]Greek, *Decapolis*.

Chapter 5

When Jesus saw the multitudes He went up on the mountain-side, and when He had sat down His disciples came to Him. [2]And He opened His mouth and began to teach[a] them, saying, [3]"How fortunate[b] are those who are aware of their spiritual need, for theirs is the kingdom of heaven! [4]How fortunate are those who mourn, for they will be comforted! [5]How fortunate are the gentle, for they shall inherit the earth! [6]How fortunate are those who continually hunger and thirst for righteousness, for they will be completely satisfied! [7]How fortunate are those who show mercy, for mercy will be shown to them! [8]How fortunate are the pure in heart, for they will see God! [9]How fortunate are the peacemakers, for they will be called God's sons! [10]How fortunate are those who have endured persecution on account of righteousness, for theirs is the kingdom of heaven! [11]How fortunate are you when people reproach you and persecute you and say every [kind of] evil against you falsely, on account of Me! [12]Be glad and keep rejoicing exceedingly, because great is your reward in heaven. For in the same manner they persecuted the prophets [who were] before you.

[13]"You yourselves are the earth's salt. But if the salt loses its distinctive quality as salt,[c] in what way can it regain that quality?[d] It is good for nothing but to be thrown out and walked on by men.

[14]"You yourselves are the world's light. A city situated on a hill cannot be hidden. [15]Neither do men light a lamp and place it under a measuring-container[e] but on the lampstand, and it gives light for everyone in the house. [16]Thus let your light shine before men, that they may see your excellent works and give glory to your Father who is in heaven.

[17]"Do not suppose that I came to destroy the Law or the Prophets. I did not come to destroy but to fulfill.[f] [18]Indeed, I say to you that until heaven and earth pass away, not one iota[g] or one particle[h] of a letter will in any wise pass away from the Law until all things are accomplished. [19]Therefore whoever sets aside one of the least of these requirements and teaches men to do so, will

---

[a]Inchoative imperfect.

[b]The Greek word, *makarioi* is difficult to translate into English. It includes such ideas as "blessed," "fortunate," "joyful," "truly happy," "privileged."

[c]Or, becomes tasteless or insipid.

[d]Or, how can it be re-salted?

[e]Greek, *modios,* an earthen-ware bowl used for measuring grain.

[f]Or, bring them to completion. Apparently this fulfillment involves Christ's complete atoning work and all its implications.

[g]The smallest Greek vowel, in size equivalent to the little Hebrew letter, *yod.*

[h]Greek, *keraia,* "little horn," or "small stroke." Used of the minute projection on certain Hebrew letters which distinguishes them from similar letters.

be called least in the kingdom of heaven. But whoever observes and teaches them will be called great in the kingdom of heaven. [20]"Indeed I tell you that unless your compliance to God's will[i] far surpasses that of the Law-experts and Pharisees, you certainly will never enter the kingdom of heaven.

[21]"You have heard that it was said to the men of long ago, 'You shall not commit murder,[j] and 'Whoever commits an act of murder will be held guilty of a crime.[k] [22]But I tell you that anyone who is enraged against his brother is guilty of a crime.[k] Whoever uses insulting language against his brother will [have to] answer to the Sanhedrin.[l] And whoever expresses contempt [for a human being] will be liable to the Gehenna[m] characterized by fire.[n] [23]So if are presenting your offering at the altar, and there you remember that your brother has some grievance against you, [24]leave your offering there in front of the altar, and go [and] first be reconciled to your brother; then come and present your offering.

[25]"Come to terms quickly with your accuser while you have the opportunity to do so,[o] or he may hand you over to the magistrate, and the magistrate to the officer and you will be thrown into prison. [26]I solemnly tell you that you will certainly not get out until you have paid the last cent!

[27]"You have heard that it was said, 'You shall not commit adultery.'[p] [28]But I tell you that anyone who gazes at a woman with a lustful motive has already in his heart committed adultery with her. [29]So if your right eye is a stumbling-block for you, tear it out and throw it away from you. It is to your advantage to be deprived of one of your [bodily] members than for your entire body to be cast into Gehenna. [30]And if your right hand is a stumbling-block for you, cut it off and throw it away from you. It is better to be deprived of one of your [bodily] members than for your entire body to go into Gehenna. [31]"Also it was said, 'Whoever divorces his wife, let him give her a certificate

---

[i]The Greek term, *dikaiosune,* "righteousness," in its widest sense, means conformity of God's will in thought and conduct.

[j]Exod. 20:13; 21:12; Lev. 24:17; Deut. 5:17.

[k]Or, liable to the judgment, Or, subject to [action by] the court of justice. Cf. Deut. 16:18.

[l]The Sanhedrin was the supreme tribunal of the Jews during the Greek and Roman periods. It was composed of 70 members, plus the high priest who was its president.

[m]Gehenna was the Valley of Hinnom, located southwest of Jerusalem, where fires were kept burning to consume the refuse and rubbish deposited there. It is the word rendered *hell* in traditional English versions. Jesus uses *Gehenna* to symbolize the destiny which awaits persons who reject the gospel. Cf. Matt. 5:29, 30; 10:28; 18:9; 23:15; 23:33; Luke 12:5.

[n]Descriptive genitive.

[o]Literally, "while you are with him on the way."

[p]Exod. 20:14; Deut. 5:18.

of dismissal.[q] [32]But I tell you that anyone who divorces his wife for any cause except unchastity causes her to be considered an adulteress,[r] and whoever marries a woman who has been [thus] divorced commits adultery.

[33]"Again you have heard that it was said to the ancients, 'Do not break an oath, but keep the vows you have made to the Lord.'[s] [34]But I tell you not to swear at all—not by heaven, because it is God's throne; [35]not by the earth, because it is His footstool; not by Jerusalem, because it is the city of the great King; [36]nor shall you swear by your head, because you cannot make one hair white or black. [37]But let your speech be simply 'Yes' [if you mean] 'Yes,' and 'No' [if you mean] 'No.'[t] Anything in excess of these comes from evil.[u]

[38]"You have heard that it was said, 'An eye [shall be exacted] for an eye, and a tooth for a tooth.'[v] [39]But I tell you not to take personal revenge.[w] If someone strikes you on the right cheek, turn to him the other also. [40]And if anyone wants to go to law with you to take away your shirt,[x] let him have your cloak as well.[y] [41]And if any person [in authority] compels you to go one mile, go with him two. [42]Give to the man who begs from you, and when someone wishes to borrow from you, do not turn [him] away.

[43]"You have heard that it was said, 'You shall love your neighbor and hate your enemy.'[z] [44]But I tell you, Love[a] your enemies, and pray for those who persecute you, [45]so that you may be sons of your Heavenly Father; for He causes His sun to rise on evil persons and on good persons, and He sends rain upon the righteous and the unrighteous. [46]If indeed you love [only] those who love you, what reward have you? Even the tax collectors do that much, do they not? [47]And if you greet only your brothers, what is remarkable about that? Do not even the pagans practice the same? [48]So then, you be complete [in this way], as your Heavenly Father is complete."

---

[q]A written statement that she is no longer his wife. Cf. Deut. 24:1.

[r]The Greek aorist infinitive is passive, hence expresses the idea of being sinned against, rather than committing sin. The reference seems to be to a woman whose marriage has been terminated without wrong on her part.

[s]Cf. Num. 30:2; Deut. 23:23.

[t]Literally, *Yes, Yes; No, No.*

[u]Or, from the evil one.

[v]Cf. Exod. 21:24.

[w]Or, not to use force against a wicked person.

[x]Greek *chiton,* "under-garment" or "tunic."

[y]Greek, *himation,* "outer-garment." Also used by the poor as a covering at night. Cf. Exod. 22:26-27; Deut. 24:12-13.

[z]This was the popular attitude toward anyone regarded as an enemy.

[a]Jesus sets up a new ethical standard. Love (*agape,* "purposive good-will") is to be shown to all peoples, foes as well as friends.

Chapter 6

"Be careful not to practice your righteous deeds in front of men, for the purpose of being seen by them. If you do good just to attract the attention of people,[a] you have no reward from your Father who is in heaven. ²Therefore, when you are doing [acts of] charity, do not sound a trumpet in front of you, like the hypocrites do in the synagogues and on the streets, in order that they may be applauded by men. Truly I tell you, they have received all the reward they will ever get.[b] ³But when you give money to the poor, do not let your left hand know what your right hand is doing, ⁴so that your benevolence may be done in secret. Then your Father, who sees in secret, will reward you.

⁵"And when you pray, do not be like the hypocrites. They like to pray standing in the synagogues and on the corners of the open streets, so that they may be seen by men. Truly I tell you, they have received all the reward they will ever get.[c] ⁶But you, when you pray, go into your inner room, close the door, and pray to your Father who is in secret; and your Father who sees in secret will reward you.

⁷"Furthermore, when you are praying, do not babble like the pagans,[d] for they imagine that they will be heard because of[e] their much speaking. ⁸Do not be like them. Your Father knows what things you need before you ask Him. ⁹Therefore pray in the following manner:

'Our Father who art in heaven,

May Thy name be held in reverence.

¹⁰May Thy kingdom come.

May Thy will be done on earth as it is in heaven.

¹¹Give us today our daily bread.[f]

¹²And forgive us the wrongs we have done, as we ourselves

have also forgiven those who have wronged us.

¹³And do not bring us into testing, but deliver us from evil.[g]

For Thine is the kingdom and the power and the glory forever.

Amen.'[h]

¹⁴"Indeed, if you forgive the misdeeds of others, your Heavenly Father will also forgive you. ¹⁵But if you do not forgive others, neither will your Father forgive your misdeeds.

---

[a]Literally, *otherwise*.

[b]The Greek idiom means they have been paid off in full. Perfective force of preposition *apo* in composition with verb *echo*.

[c]See note on vs. 2.

[d]Cf. 1 Kings 18:26; Acts 19:34.

[e]Causal use of Greek preposition, *en*.

[f]Or, our bread for the coming day.

[g]Or, from the evil one.

[h]The doxology is not found in our oldest Greek manuscripts, hence it is placed in the margin by Nestle.

[16]"When you fast, do not be gloomy in appearance like the hypocrites, for they disfigure their faces so that people may notice that they are fasting. Truly I tell you, they have received all the reward they will ever get.[i] [17]But you,[j] when you fast, anoint your head and wash your face, [18]so that you may not appear to men [to be] fasting, but to your Father who is in secret. And your Father who sees in secret will reward you.

[19]"Do not store up for yourselves treasures upon the earth, where moth and rust consume [them], and where thieves dig through and steal. [20]But store up for yourselves treasures in heaven, where neither moth nor rust consumes [them] and where theives do not dig through and steal. [21]Indeed, where your treasure is, there will your heart be also.

[22]"The body's lamp is the eye. So if your eye is healthy, your entire body will be full of light. [23]But if your eye is defective, your entire body will be full of darkness. So if your source of light is itself darkness, how great is the darkness!

[24]"No one is able to serve two masters, for he will either hate the one and love the other, or he will devote himself firmly to one and despise the other. You cannot serve God and Mammon.[k]

[25]"Therefore I tell you, Stop worrying about your life, what you are going to eat or what you are going to drink, or about your body, what you are going to wear. Is not life more [important] than food, and the body [more important] than clothing? [26]Look at the birds of the sky! They neither sow nor reap, nor gather [anything] into storehouses, yet your Heavenly Father feeds them. Are you not more valuable than they?

[27]"Furthermore who among you, by means of worry, can prolong the span of his life?[l] [28]Then why worry about clothing? Consider carefully the lilies of the field, how they grow. They do not toil nor do they spin, [29]yet I tell you that not even Solomon in all his splendor ever clothed himself like one of these. [30]Now if God in such a manner enrobes the grass of the field, [which] today exists and tomorrow is thrown into an oven, [will He] not much more certainly [clothe] you, men of little faith?

[31]"So do not worry at all, asking, 'What are we going to eat?' or 'What are we going to drink?' or 'What are we going to wear?' [32]For all these the pagans seek after. Certainly your Heavenly Father knows that you need all these

---

[i]Same expression as in vv. 2 and 5.

[j]Singular.

[k]The term *mammon* is probably of Aramaic origin and conveys the idea of money, riches, or earthly goods. Here it is personified as that which is allowed to take the place of God in an individual's life. Cf. Luke 16:9, 11, 13.

[l]Or, add one cubit to his height? The Greek word *helikia* means "age" or "life-span" in John 9:21; Heb. 11:11; and "stature" in Luke 19:3.

things. [33]But you seek first [God's] kingdom and the righteousness He requires, and all these things will be provided for you. [34]Therefore, do not worry in the least about tomorrow. Let tomorrow worry about itself. Each day has enough trouble of its own.''[m]

Chapter 7

''Do not be judging[a] [others], so that you may not be judged.[b] [2]For with what judgment you judge you will be judged, and with what measure you measure it will be measured to you. [3]And why do you keep looking[c] at the minute particle in your brother's eye but never notice the beam of timber in your own eye? [4]Or how can you say to your brother, 'Let me remove the splinter from your eye,' while the beam of timber remains in your eye? [5]You hypocrite! First remove the beam of timber from your eye, and then you will see clearly to remove the minute particle from your brother's eye.

[6]''Do not at any time give that which is sacred to dogs, and do not cast your pearls in front of swine, or they may trample them beneath their feet, then turn and tear you to pieces.

[7]''Continue asking,[d] and it will be given to you. Continue seeking, and you will find. Continue knocking, and [the door] will be opened for you. [8]For everyone who keeps asking[e] keeps receiving,[f] and he who keeps seeking, keeps finding, and to him who keeps knocking, [the door] will be opened. [9]What man is there among you who, if his son asks for bread, will give him a stone? [10]Or if he asks for a fish, will give him a serpent? [11]If you, then, imperfect as you are,[g] know how to give good gifts to your children, how much more will your Heavenly Father give excellent things to those who consistently ask[h] Him! [12]All things, therefore, whatever you wish men to do to you, you yourselves do likewise to them. For this is [the essence of] the Law and the Prophets.

[13]''Enter in through the narrow gate; for wide is the gate and broad is the road that leads to destruction, and there are many who travel it. [14]Narrow is the gate and difficult is the road that leads to life, and only a few find it.

---

[m]Literally, *Sufficient for the day is the evil of it.*

[a]Linear force of the present imperative.

[b]The aorist passive subjunctive expresses a summary act, and may refer to the retributive character of the world, or to God's judgment.

[c]Present active indicative.

[d]Present imperative.

[e]Present participle.

[f]Present indicative.

[g]Or, you whose nature is selfish. Literally, *you who are evil.*

[h]Present active participle, or present active indicative.

[15]"Keep on your guard against false prophets, who come to you in the garments of sheep but inwardly they are ravenous wolves. [16]You will recognize them by their deeds.[i] People certainly do not gather grapes from thorn-bushes, or figs from thistles, do they? [17]So every sound tree produces good fruit, but a decayed tree produces bad fruit. [18]A sound tree cannot bear bad fruit, nor can a decayed tree bear good fruit. [19]Every tree that does not produce good fruit is cut down and thrown into the fire. [20]And so it is—you will recognize people by what they do.[j]

[21]"Not every one who addresses Me, 'Lord, Lord,' will enter the kingdom of heaven, but [only] he who does consistently the will of My Father who is in heaven. [22]On that Day many will say to Me, 'Lord, Lord' did we not preach in Your name, and in Your name cast out demons, and in Your name perform many mighty works?' [23]Then I will declare to them, 'Never at any time did I recognize you. Depart from Me, you workers of lawlessness.'

[24]"Therefore, everyone who hears these sayings of Mine and acts accordingly[k] will be like a sensible man who built his house upon rock.[l] [25]The rain came down, and the floods rose, and the winds blew, and beat against that house; yet it did not fall, for it was built upon the [mighty] rock. [26]But everyone who hears these sayings of Mine and does not act accordingly will be like a foolish man who built his house on sand. [27]The rain came down, and the floods rose, and the winds blew, and struck against that house, and it collapsed; and great was its fall."

[28]Now when Jesus had finished these sayings, the crowds were amazed at His doctrine. [29]For He was teaching them as one who had authority and not like their Law-teachers.[m]

Chapter 8

After Jesus came down from the mountain, great crowds followed Him. [2]And behold, a leper came forward, knelt before Him, and said, "Lord, if you are willing, Your are able to make me clean." [3]Jesus stretched out His hand and touched him, saying, "I am willing. Be cleansed." And instantly he was

---

[i]Literally, *fruits.*

[j]Literally, *by their fruits.*

[k]Literally, *and practices them.*

[l]Greek, *petra,* a massive, immovable rock. Cf. v. 25; 16:18; 27:51, 60; Rev. 6:15, 16.

[m]Literally, *scribes.* See note on 2:4.

cured of his leprosy. [4]Then Jesus told him, "Be sure that you tell no one; but go and show yourself to the priest [that he may examine you and pronounce you clean]. Then present the offering which Moses commanded,[a] for the certification of a cure."[b]

[5]When Jesus had entered Capernaum, a centurion came to Him entreating Him, [6]and saying, "Lord, my servant-boy[c] is at home lying ill with paralysis [and he is] suffering terribly." [7]Jesus answered, "I, Myself, will come and heal him." [8]But the centurion replied, "Lord, I am not worthy for You to come under my roof. Just say the word, and my servant-boy will be cured. [9]for even I, myself, am a man having some authority, with soldiers under my command.[d] To this one I say, 'Go!' and he goes; to another 'Come!' and he comes; and to my servant, 'Do this!' and he does it."

[10]When Jesus heard that, He marvelled and He said to those who were following, "Truly I tell you, from no one in Israel have I found such faith. [11]And I say to you, that many will come from east and west and recline at table with Abraham and Isaac and Jacob in the kingdom of heaven. [12]But the sons of the kingdom will be banished into the outer darkness, where there will be weeping and grinding of teeth."

[13]Then Jesus said to the centurion, "Go [on home].[e] As you have believed, [so] let it be [done] for you." And in that very hour the servant-boy was cured.

[14]When Jesus came into Peter's house, He saw Peter's mother-in-law lying ill with fever. [15]He took hold of her hand, and the fever left her. And she rose and began to minister[f] to Him.

[16]When evening came, they brought to Him many demon-possessed persons. He drove out the [evil] spirits, by means of a word, and healed all the people who were ill.[g] [17]Thus was fulfilled what was spoken through the prophet Isaiah, "He Himself took our infirmities and bore our diseases."[h]

[18]Now when Jesus saw a crowd around Him, He gave [the disciples] orders to cross over to the other side [of the lake]. [19]And a certain Law-teacher approached and said to Him, "Teacher, I will follow You wherever you may go." [20]Jesus replied, "The foxes have dens and the birds of the sky have lodging places, but the Son of Man has nowhere to lay His head."

[21]Another man, who was a disciple, said to Him, "Lord, permit me first to go home and bury my father." [22]But Jesus said to him, "Keep following Me, and let the dead bury their own dead."

---

[a]Cf. Lev. 14:1ff.
[b]Literally, *for a witness to them.*
[c]Cf. Luke 7:1-10.
[d]Literally, *Under myself.*
[e]Cf. vs. 6.
[f]Inchoative imperfect.
[g]Literally, *all those having it bad.*
[h]Isa. 53:4.

²³As He entered the boat, His disciples followed Him. ²⁴Suddenly, a violent storm struck the lake, so that the boat was being buried under the waves. But He Himself was sleeping. ²⁵So they came and awoke Him, saying, "Lord save us! We are perishing!" ²⁶He said to them, "Why are you frightened, men of little faith?" Then Jesus stood up and rebuked the winds and the waves; and there came a great calm. ²⁷The men were amazed, and exclaimed, "What sort of person is this, that even the winds and the sea obey Him?"

²⁸When He landed on the other shore, in the country of the Gadarenes, He was met by two demon-possessed men coming out of the tombs. The men were so exceedingly fierce that no one was able to travel along that road. ²⁹Suddenly, they cried out, saying, "What relationship is there between us and You,ⁱ Son of God? Did You come here to torture us before [the appointed] time?"

³⁰Now some distance away from them a large herd of swine was feeding. ³¹And the demons began beggingʲ Jesus, saying, "If You cast us out,ᵏ send us into the herd of swine." ³²He said to them, "Be going!" So they came out and went forth into the swine. And quickly all the herd rushed down the precipice into the lake, and were drowned in the water.

³³At that the swine-keepers fled, and went into the city, and reported everything, including what happened to the demon-possessed men. ³⁴And immediately the entire town came out to meet Jesus; and when they saw Him, they asked Him to depart from their borders.

Chapter 9

So He stepped into a boat, crossed over [the lake], and came into His own city.ᵃ ²And at once they brought to him a paralyzed man, who was lying on a mat. When Jesus saw their faith, He said to the paralytic. "Be of good cheer, son; your sins are forgiven!" ³At that, some of the Law-teachers said among themselves, "This fellow is speaking blasphemy." ⁴Jesus, aware of their thoughts, said, "Why are you entertaining wicked ideas in your hearts? ⁵Which is easier: to say, 'Your sins are forgiven,' or to say, 'Stand up and walk'? ⁶But to let you know that the Son of Man has authority on earth to

---

ⁱOr, Why are you interfering with us? Literally, *What to us and to you?* Cf. Mark 1:24; 5:7.

ʲInchoative imperfect.

ᵏA condition of the first class, which indicates that the demons expected to be cast out. See note on 4:3.

ᵃThat is, Jesus returned to Capernaum, His base of operation during His ministry in Galilee. Cf. 4:13; Mark 2:1.

forgive sins"—He then said to the paralytic—"Arise, take up your mat, and go home." [7]So the man stood up, and went home. [8]When the crowds saw it, they were afraid; and they praised God for granting such authority to men.

[9]As Jesus passed along from there, He saw a man named Matthew sitting at the tax office, and He said to him, "Follow Me." And Matthew rose up, and followed Him. [10]Afterward, when Jesus was at dinner in the house, behold, many tax collectors and social outcasts[b] came and were reclining at table with Jesus and His disciples. [11]When the Pharisees saw this they said to His disciples, "Why does your Teacher eat with tax collectors and social outcasts?" [12]Jesus heard [their question] and replied, "It is not healthy people who need a physician, but those who are ill.[c] [13]Go and learn what is [meant by the saying] 'I desire mercy and not sacrifice.'[d] Indeed, I did not come to call righteous persons, but sinners."

[14]At that time the disciples of John came to Jesus and asked, "Why do we and the Pharisees fast, but Your disciples do not?" [15]Jesus said to them, "The bridegroom's attendants cannot mourn as long as the bridegroom is with them, can they? But the days will come when the bridegroom will be taken away from them, and then they will fast."

[16]"No one sews a patch of unshrunk cloth on an old garment; for such a patch[e] [as it shrinks] pulls away from the garment and makes the tear worse. [17]Nor do people pour new wine into old wineskins; if they do, the wineskins burst, the wine is spilled, and the wineskins are ruined. But new wine is put into fresh wineskins, and both are preserved."

[18]While Jesus was speaking these things to them, behold, a certain magistrate approached and knelt before Him, saying, "My daughter has just now died; but come, and place Your hand upon her, she will live." [19]And Jesus stood up and He and His disciples followed him. [20]But while they were going, a woman who had suffered from hemorrhages for twelve years came up behind [Him] and touched the border[f] of His cloak. [21]For she kept saying within herself, "If I can only touch His garment, I will be cured." [22]Then Jesus turned around and saw her, and said, "Be of good cheer, daughter! Your faith has made you well." And the woman was healed at that very moment.

[23]When Jesus reached the magistrate's house and saw the flute-players and the commotion of the crowd,[g] [24]He said, "Go away, for the little girl is not

---

[b]Literally, *sinners*.

[c]Literally, *those having it bad*.

[d]Cf. 1 Sam. 15:22; Hos. 6:6.

[e]Literally, *that which fills up*.

[f]Greek, *kraspedon*. This fringe or trimming was a tassel, made of twisted wool, which hung from each of the four corners of the square cloth which Jesus, like most Jews, wore as an outer garment. Cf. Num. 15:38-40; Deut. 22:12.

[g]The professional mourning, customary among Eastern peoples, had begun. Cf. Jer. 9:17.

dead, but is asleep." At that [remark] they began to laugh at Him. [25]But when the crowd had been put outside Jesus went in and took the little girl by the hand, and she stood up. [26]And the report about this [incident] spread through that whole countryside.

[27]As Jesus was passing along from there, He was followed by two blind men, who kept crying out, "Son of David, have pity on us!" [28]And when He entered the house, the blind men came to Him and Jesus asked them, "Do you believe that I am able to do this?" They said to Him, "Yes, Lord." [29]Then He touched their eyes and said, "According to your faith, so let it be done for you." [30]And their eyes were opened. Then Jesus sternly charged them, "Be careful not to let anyone know [about this]. [31]But they went forth and spread abroad His fame throughout that entire region.

[32]While they were going away, they brought to Him a demon-possessed man who was unable to speak. [33]But when the demon had been cast out, the speechless man began to talk.[h] The crowds marvelled and exclaimed, "Never has anything like this been seen in Israel!" [34]But the Pharisees kept saying, "He casts out demons in the power of the prince of demons."

[35]Jesus travelled through all the towns and villages, teaching in their synagogues, proclaiming the good news about the kingdom,[i] and healing every [kind of] disease and every [kind of] illness. [36]And as He looked at the multitudes, He was moved with deep compassion for them because they were bewildered and helpless, like sheep without a shepherd. [37]Then He said to His disciples, "The harvest is indeed abundant but the workers are few. [38]Therefore, ask the Lord of the harvest to thrust forth workmen into His harvest."

Chapter 10

Jesus called to Him His twelve disciples and gave them authority over unclean spirits,[a] to drive them out, and to heal every [kind of] disease and every [kind of] ailment. [2]These are the names of the twelve apostles: first, Simon who is called Peter, and Andrew his brother; James, the son of Zebedee, and John his brother; [3]Philip and Bartholomew; Thomas and Matthew the tax collector; James the son of Alphaeus, and Thaddaeus; [4]Simon the Cananaean,[b] and Judas Iscariot,[c] who later betrayed Him.

---

[h]Ingressive aorist.
[i]Objective genitive.

[a]Objective genitive.
[b]Or, the Zealot. Cf. Luke 6:15; Acts 1:13.
[c]Or, Judas, the man from Kerioth. Probably thus designated from his home town in southern Judah. Cf. Josh. 15:25. His father is named as Simon Iscariot (John 6:71).

⁵These twelve Jesus sent forth, after giving them the following instructions: "Do not go among the Gentiles and do not enter any town of the Samaritans. ⁶Go rather to the lost sheep of the house of Israel. ⁷And as you go, keep preaching, saying, 'The kingdom of heaven has drawn near!' ⁸Heal the sick, raise the dead, cleanse lepers, drive out demons. You received without charge; give without charge. ⁹Do not provide for yourselves gold or silver or copper coins in your belts. ¹⁰Take no provision-bag for your journey, no second tunic, nor [extra] sandals, nor [additional] staff.ᵈ For the worker deserves his support.

¹¹"Into whatever town or village you enter, find out who in it is a worthy person, and lodge at his houseᵉ until you leave [that place]. ¹²When you enter a house, wish it well. ¹³If indeed, the house is a worthy one, let your peace come upon it. If it is not a worthy one, let your peace return to you. ¹⁴And whoever does not receive you or listen to your message, when you depart from that house, or that town, shake off its dust from your feet. ¹⁵Truly I tell you, it will be more bearable for Sodom and Gomorrah in the day of judgment than for that town.

¹⁶"Remember, I, Myself, am sending you forth like sheep among wolves. So be as cautious as serpents and as blameless as doves. ¹⁷Always be on your guard against [ungodly] persons, for they will hand you over to councils, and flog you in their synagogues. ¹⁸On account of Me you will even be brought before governors and kings to bear witness to them and to the Gentiles. ¹⁹But when they hand you over, do not worry about how or what to say, for in that hour you will be given what you are to say. ²⁰Actually, you yourselves will not be the speakersᶠ but the Spirit of your Father will be speakingᶠ through you.

²¹"Brother will hand over brother to death, and [so will] a father [his] child. Even children will stand up against [their own] parents and cause them to be put to death. ²²You will be hated by all men on account of My name. But he who remains steadfast to the endᵍ will be saved.

²³"When they persecute you in oneʰ town, escape to another. For truly I tell you, by no means will you have gone through the towns of Israel until the Son of Man comes.ⁱ

²⁴"A disciple is not above his teacher, nor is a servant above his master. ²⁵It is sufficient for the disciple to be like his teacher, and the servant like his

---

ᵈCf. Mark 6:8.
ᵉLiterally, *and there remain*.
ᶠGreek futuristic present participle.
ᵍOr, until the final goal is reached.
ʰLiterally, *this*.
ⁱCf. Matt. 16:28; 24:34.

master. If[j] the head of the house has been called Beelzebul,[k] how much more the members of his household! [26]So do not let them terrify you, for there is nothing concealed that will not be uncovered, or hidden that will not be made known. [27]What I tell you in the darkness, declare in the light; and what you hear in private, proclaim from the housetops. [28]Stop being afraid of those who kill the body but cannot kill the soul; rather fear Him who is able to destroy both soul and body in Gehenna.[l] [29]Are not sparrows sold two for a pittance?[m] Yet not one of them falls to the ground without [the knowledge of] your Father. [30]And as for you, even the hairs of your head have all been counted. [31]So stop being afraid. You are more valuable than a multitude of sparrows.

[32]"Therefore, everyone who acknowledges Me before men, him will I, Myself, acknowledge before My Father who is in heaven. [33]But whoever denies Me before men, him will I Myself, deny before My Father who is in heaven.

[34]"Do not suppose for a moment[n] that I came to bring peace to the earth. I did not come to bring peace, but a sword. [35]As a matter of fact, I came to set a man at variance against his father, and a daughter against her mother, and a young wife against her mother-in-law. [36]Indeed, a man's foes [will be] members of his own household.[o] [37]Whoever loves father or mother more than Me is not worthy of Me; and whoever loves son or daughter more than Me is not worthy of Me. [38]And anyone who does not take his cross and follow after Me is not worthy of Me. [39]He who finds his. life will lose it, and he who loses his life for My sake will find it.

[40]"Whoever receives you receives Me, and whoever receives Me receives Him who sent Me. [41]He who receives a prophet in the name of a prophet[p] will receive a prophet's reward, and he who receives a righteous man in the name of a righteous man[q] will receive a righteous man's reward. [42]So whoever gives to one of these lowly ones even a cup of cool [water] in the name of a disciple,[r] truly I tell you that he will certainly not lose his reward."

---

[j]A condition assumed by the speaker as true. See note on Matt. 4:3.

[k]A term of vicious reproach, variously spelled. Among the Jews, the word became an appellation for Satan. Cf. Matt. 12:24-27.

[l]See note on 5:22.

[m]Greek, *assarion*. A small Roman copper coin worth about one-sixteenth of a denarius. In the present context it signifies a very meager and insignificant amount.

[n]Indicated by aorist subjunctive.

[o]Cf. Mic. 7:6. Matt. 10:21.

[p]That is, because he is a prophet.

[q]Or, because he is a righteous man.

[r]That is, by virtue of his character as a disciple.

Chapter 11

When Jesus had finished instructing His twelve disciples, He departed from that place in order to teach and preach in various localities.[a]

[2]Now when John in prison heard about the works performed by the Christ,[b] he sent [some] of his disciples [3]to ask Him, "Are You indeed the Coming One, or are we to look for another?" [4]In reply, Jesus said to them, "Go back and report to John what you hear and see: [5]blind men recover their sight, lame men walk, lepers are cleansed, the deaf hear, the dead are raised, and the good news is told to the poor.[c] [6]And blessed is whoever is not offended because of[d] Me."

[7]As [John's messengers][e] were departing, Jesus began to say to the crowds concerning John, "What did you go out into the wilderness to see? A reed being swayed by the wind? [8]Well, what did you go out to see? A man dressed in soft garments? Obviously those who wear soft garments live in the palaces of kings. [9]Then why did you go out? To see a prophet? Yes, I tell you, and much more than a prophet. [10]He is the one of whom it stands written, 'Behold I send My messenger ahead of You; he will prepare Your way before You.'[f] [11]Truly I tell you, among those born of women there has not appeared anyone greater than John the Baptizer; yet the person who is least in the kingdom of heaven is greater than he. [12]And from the days of John the Baptizer until now the kingdom of heaven is entered by force,[g] and forceful men press their way into it.[h] [13]For all the prophets and the Law gave their predictions until John. [14]And, if you are willing to receive it, he himself is the Elijah who was to come. [15]The one who has ears, let him listen!

[16]"To what shall I compare the present generation? It is like children sitting in the market places, calling to their playmates,[i] [17]'We have made wedding music[j] for you, but you did not dance. We sang the funeral dirge,[k] but you did not beat your breasts. [18]For John came neither eating nor drinking and people say, 'He is demon-possessed!' [19]The Son of Man came eating and drinking and they say, 'Look at this man! He is a glutton and a wine-drinker, a friend of tax-collectors and social outcasts!' But wisdom is vindicated by its consequences."

---

[a]Literally, *in their towns*. That is, cities in Galilee.

[b]Subjective genitive.

[c]Or, the poor are telling the good news.

[d]Causal use of preposition *en*.

[e]Cf. vs. 2.

[f]Mal. 3:1.

[g]Literally, *is treated by violence* (passive voice), or *makes its way by force* (middle voice).

[h]Or, seize it.

[i]Literally, *to the others*.

[j]Literally, *We played the flute*.

[k]Literally, *we mourned*. Cf. Luke 7:32.

[20]Then Jesus began to censure the cities in which most of His mighty acts had been performed, because they did not repent:[1] [21]"Woe to you, Chorazin! Woe to you, Bethsaida! For is the mighty works done among you had been performed in Tyre and Sidon, they would have repented long ago in sackcloth and ashes. [22]Nevertheless I tell you, it will be more bearable for Tyre and Sidon in the day of judgment than for you. [23]And you, Capernaum,[m] will you be exalted as high as heaven? You will be brought down to Hades![n] For if the mighty works done in you, had been performed in Sodom it would have remained until this day. [24]Furthermore, I tell you that it will be more bearable for the land of Sodom in the day of judgment than for you."

[25]At that time Jesus exclaimed, "I give acknowledgment to Thee, Father, Lord of heaven and earth, because Thou didst conceal these things from wise and cunning persons, and hast revealed them to babes. [26]Yes, Father, because to do so was well-pleasing in Thy sight.

[27]"All things have been handed over to Me by My Father, and no one really knows the Son except the Father, nor does anyone really know the Father except the Son and he to whom the Son chooses to reveal Him.

[28]"Come to Me, all you who are toiling and weary, and I, Myself, will give you rest. [29]Take My yoke upon you and learn from Me, because I am gentle and humble in heart, and you will find rest for your souls. [30]Indeed, My yoke is gentle and My load is light."

Chapter 12

At that time Jesus went through the grain fields on a Sabbath day. His disciples were hungry, so they began to pluck ears of grain[a] and eat them. [2]When the Pharisees noticed it, they said to Him, "Look, Your disciples are doing what it is not lawful to do on the Sabbath." [3]Jesus replied to them, "Have you not read what David did[b] when he and his followers were hungry—[4]how he entered the house of God, and he and his men ate[c] the

---

[1]See note on 3:8.

[m]Capernaum was highly responsible because it was so often favored by Jesus' presence and activity.

[n]*Hades,* equivalent to the Hebrew *Sheol,* means literally, "not seen." It is used of the unseen world, or realm of departed spirits (Luke 16:23; Acts 2:27, 31; Rev. 1:18; 20:13); of the forces of evil (Matt. 16:18); and in the present passage it denotes deep degradation.

[a]Cf. Deut. 23:25.

[b]Cf. 1 Sam. 21:4-6.

sacred bread,[d] which it was not lawful for him or those with him to eat, but only for the priests? [5]Or have you not read in the Law, how on the Sabbath days the priests in the Temple violate the Sabbath,[e] yet are guiltless? [6]But I tell you that something greater than the Temple is here. [7]And if you had known the meaning of the Scripture,[f] 'I desire mercy and not sacrifice'[g] you would not have condemned men who are without guilt. [8]For the Son of Man is Lord of the Sabbath.''

[9]Then He departed from that place and went into their synagogue. [10]A man with a withered hand was there. And some people questioned Him, "Is it lawful to heal on the Sabbath?" [11]He said to them, "What man among you, if he has one sheep and it falls into a pit on the Sabbath, will not take hold of it and lift it out? [12]How much more valuable, then, is a man than a sheep! So, it is lawful to do good on the Sabbath." [13]Then He said to the man, "Stretch out your hand!" He stretched it out, and it had become sound like the other. [14]But the Pharisees went out and made plans against Him, for the purpose of destroying Him.

[15]But Jesus, aware of [their intentions], withdrew from that place. Many people followed Him and He healed them all, [16]but He gave them strict orders not to make Him known. [17]Thus was fulfilled what was spoken through Isaiah the prophet, [18]"Behold My Servant whom I have chosen, My Beloved with whom My soul is well pleased.[h] I will put My Spirit upon Him, and He will proclaim justice to the nations. [19]He will not quarrel, nor cry aloud, nor will anyone hear His voice in the streets. [20]A crushed reed He will not break in pieces, and a smouldering lamp-wick He will not extinguish, until He makes justice victorious. [21]And in His Name[i] the nations will find hope."[j]

[22]Then a demon-possessed man who was blind and unable to speak was brought to Jesus; and He healed him, so that the man could talk and see. [23]All the crowds were astonished and kept saying, "This Man is not the Son of David, is He?" [24]But when the Pharisees heard it, they said, "This fellow drives out demons only through alliance with Beezebul,[k] the ruler of demons."

---

[c]Literally, *They ate.*

[d]Literally, *the loaves of the presentation.* Cf. Lev. 24:5-9.

[e]The priests themselves, by the labor involved in preparing the sacrifices commanded by the Law, technically violated the work restrictions of the Sabbath. Cf., e.g., Num. 28:9ff. This shows that ceremonial requirements are not absolute, but are transcended by a higher principle.

[f]Literally, *If you had known what it is.*

[g]Hos. 6:6.

[h]Timeless aorist. Cf. 3:17.

[i]That is, in the revelation of who and what He is.

[j]Cf. Isa. 42:1-4.

[k]See note on 10:25.

²⁵Knowing their thoughts Jesus said to them, "Every kingdom divided against itself is brought to ruin; and every city or house divided against itself will not stand. ²⁶So if Satan is driving out Satan, he must be divided against himself. Then how can his kingdom endure? ²⁷Furthermore, if I Myself expel demons by the agency of Beezebul, by whom do your sons expel them? Consequently, they themselves will be your judges. ²⁸But if I, Myself, drive out demons by the Spirit of God, then the kingdom of God has come upon you. ²⁹Or again, can anyone enter a strong man's house and seize his possessions unless he first binds the strong man? And then he can plunder his house.

³⁰"He who is not with Me is against Me, and he who does not gather with Me is scattering. ³¹Therefore I tell you, every sin and blasphemy may be forgiven men, but the blasphemy against the Spirit[l] will not be forgiven. ³²So whoever speaks a word against the Son of Man may be forgiven, but whoever speaks against the Holy Spirit will not be forgiven, either in the present age or in the [age] to come.

³³"Either make the tree good and its fruit good, or make the tree bad and its fruit bad; for a tree is known by its fruit. ³⁴You descendants of serpents, how can you say good things when you are wicked? For out of the fullness of the heart the mouth speaks. ³⁵A good man, from his good [inward] treasure, brings forth good things, but an evil man, out of his evil [inward] treasure brings forth evil things. ³⁶So I say to you that for every useless word men speak, they will give proper accounting concerning it on the day of judgment. ³⁷For each[m] of you by your words will be acquitted, or by your words you will be condemned."

³⁸Then some of the Law-experts[n] and Pharisees responded to Him, saying, "Teacher, we want to see a sign from You." ³⁹But He answered them, "A wicked and apostate generation is eager for a sign, but no sign will be given to it except the sign exemplified by the prophet Jonah.[o] ⁴⁰For just as Jonah was in the stomach of the sea-monster for three days and three nights,[p] so the Son of Man will be in the heart of the earth for three days and three nights. ⁴¹The people of Nineveh will stand up at the judgment together with the present generation and will condemn it, for they repented because of[q] the proclamation delivered by Jonah.[r] But look, something greater than Jonah is here! ⁴²The

---

[l]Objective genitive.
[m]Indicated by Greek singular pronoun and singular verb.
[n]Literally, scribes.
[o]Subjective genitive.
[p]Cf. Jonah 1:17 (Hebrew and Septuagint, 2:1).
[q]Causal *eis*. See note on 3:11.
[r]Subjective genitive.

Queen of the south[s] will rise up at the judgment together with the present generation and will condemn it, because she came from the ends of the earth to hear Solomon's wisdom. But look, something greater than Solomon is here!

[43]"When an unclean spirit goes out of a man, it wanders through waterless places in search of rest but finds none. [44]Then it says, 'I will return to my dwelling from which I came out.' So it returns and finds [the dwelling], swept, and set in order. [45]Then it goes and brings with it seven other spirits more wicked than itself, and they enter in and dwell there. So the last state[t] of that man is worse than the first. That is the way it will be with this present generation."

[46]While Jesus was still speaking to the crowds, behold, His mother and His brothers stood outside, desiring to talk with Him. [47]Someone told Him, "Look, Your mother and Your brothers are standing outside, wanting to talk with You." [48]But to the one who told Him [this] He replied, "Who is My mother, and who are My brothers?" [49]Then, pointing His hand toward His disciples, He said, "Look, these are My mother and My brothers! [50]For whoever does the will of My Heavenly Father, is My brother and sister and mother."

Chapter 13

On that day Jesus went out of the house and was sitting beside the lake. [2]So large were the crowds that gathered about that He stepped into a boat and sat [in it] while all the multitude stood along the shore. [3]Then He told them many things by means of parables. He said, "Listen, a sower went forth to sow. [4]As he was sowing, some [seed] fell beside the path-way; and the birds came and devoured them. [5]Some fell on rocky ground, where they did not have much soil. They sprang up quickly because there was no depth of earth; [6]but when the sun rose they were scorched and because they had no roots they were withered. [7]Some others fell among thorns, and the thorns grew up and choked them completely. [8]But other [seed] fell upon good soil and became productive—some [yielding] a hundred for one, some sixty, and some thirty. [9]The person who has ears, let him listen!"

[10]The disciples came to Him and asked, "Why do You speak to them in parables?" [11]He answered, "To you it has been granted to know the mysteries of the kingdom of heaven, but to others[a] it has not been granted. [12]Indeed, to the person who has, more will be given and he will be made to abound; but

---

[s]Cf. 2 Chron. 9:1-12.
[t]Literally, *the last things*.

[a]Literally, *but to those*.

whoever does not have, even what he has will be taken away from him. [13]The reason I speak to them in parables is because they look and yet do not see; they listen and yet do not perceive or understand. [14]Fulfilled in them is Isaiah's prophecy which says, 'You will surely hear but by no means understand; and you will surely look but by no means perceive. [15]For this people's heart has become insensitive, and their hearing has become dull, and they have closed their eyes. Otherwise, they might see with their eyes and hear with their ears, and understand and turn around, and allow Me to heal them.'[b] [16]But fortunate are your eyes because they see, and your ears because they hear. [17]Indeed, I tell you solemnly that many prophets and righteous men eagerly desired to see the things you are seeing, yet did not see them, and to hear what you are hearing, yet did not hear them.

[18]"So you listen to the [meaning of the] parable of the sower: [19]When anyone hears the message about the kingdom[c] but does not grasp its significance,[d] the evil one comes and snatches away what was sown in his heart. This is the seed sown[e] along the path-way. [20]The seed sown on the rocky ground refers to the man who hears the word and immediately receives it with joy; [21]yet he has no root in himself, so he continues only for a brief time. As soon as trial or persecution comes on account of the word, he is caused to stumble. [22]The seed sown among the thorns refers to the man who hears the word, but the anxieties of the present age and the delusion caused by wealth[f] choke off the word and it becomes unfruitful. [23]But the seed sown upon the good soil refers to the person who hears the word, grasps [its significance], and yields a return—producing in some instances a hundred for one, in some sixty, and in some thirty."

[24]He put before them another parable, saying, "The kingdom of heaven may be compared[g] to a man who sowed good seed in his field. [25]But while the workers were sleeping,[h] his enemy came and oversowed weeds among the wheat and went away. [26]When the blade sprouted and produced grain, then the weeds also appeared. [27]The servants of the house-owner came forward and said to him, 'Sir, did you not sow good seed in your field? Then why does it contain weeds?' [28]He replied to them, 'An enemy has done this.' The servants asked him, 'Do you want us to go and pull up [the weeds]?' [29]'No,' he said, 'for if you pull up the weeds you might uproot the wheat at the same time. [30]Let both grow together until the harvest. Then at harvest-time I will say to the reapers, 'Collect first the weeds and bind them in bundles to be burned; then gather the wheat into my barn.' "

---

[b]Cf. Isa. 6:9-10.
[c]Objective genitive.
[d]Literally, *does not put it together* or *does not take it in*.
[e]Literally, *the man who was seeded*.
[f]Subjective genitive.
[g]Proleptic use of Greek aorist.
[h]Literally, *while everyone was asleep*.

[31]He placed before them another parable: "The kingdom of heaven is like a grain of mustard seed which a man took and planted in his field. [32]It is indeed the smallest of all seeds, yet when it is full grown it is the largest of the shrubs and becomes a tree, so that the birds of the sky come and lodge in its branches."

[33]He spoke to them another parable: "The kingdom of heaven is like yeast which a woman took and mixed into three measures of flour until the whole [portion of dough] was leavened."

[34]All these things Jesus spoke in parables to the crowds. In fact, it was His practice not to speak anything to them without using a parable. [35]In this way was fulfilled what was spoken through the prophet, "I will open my mouth in parables; I will speak forth things kept hidden since the foundation of the world."[i]

[36]Then, having dismissed the crowds, Jesus went into the house. His disciples came to Him and said, "Explain fully to us[j] the parable about the weeds in the field." [37]He replied, "The sower of the good seed is the Son of Man. [38]The field is the world. The good seed refers to the sons of the kingdom. The weeds are the sons of evil.[k] [39]The enemy who sowed [the weeds] is the devil. The harvest-time is the consummation of the age, and the reapers are angels. [40]Just as the weeds are collected and burned in fire, so it will be at the completion of the age. [41]The Son of Man will send forth His angels, and they will gather out of His kingdom everything that causes sin and those who practice lawlessness, [42]and will cast them into the furnace characterized by fire,[l] where they will wail and grind their teeth.[m] [43]Then the righteous will shine like the sun in the kingdom of their Father. He who has ears, let him listen!

[44]"The kingdom of heaven is like a hidden treasure which a man found in a field. He hid [it again] and in his joy goes and sells everything he has and buys that field.

[45]"Again, the kingdom of heaven is like a merchant searching for excellent pearls. [46]When he found one pearl of very great value, he went forth, sold everything he had, and bought it.

[47]"Again, the kingdom of heaven is like a drag-net which was cast into the sea, and encloses all kinds of things. [48]When it was filled, men drew it ashore, sat down and collected the good things into containers but threw away the worthless objects [49]That is how it will be at the consummation of the age. The angels will appear and separate the wicked persons from among the righteous,

---

[i]Cf. Ps. 78:2.
[j]Or, make clear for us.
[k]Or, of the evil one.
[l]Descriptive genitive.
[m]Cf. Matt. 8:12.

[50]and throw the wicked into the furnace characterized by fire, where there will be wailing and grinding of teeth.

[51]"Have you understood all these things?" [Jesus asked]. They replied "Yes." [52]So He said to them, "Therefore every scholar[n] who has been instructed about the kingdom of heaven is like a house-owner who brings out of his storeroom things both new and old."

[53]When Jesus had finished these parables He moved on from that place. [54]And having come into His native town,[o] He was teaching the people in their synagogue in such a manner that they were astonished and they asked, "Where did He get this wisdom and these powers? [55]Is not this the builder's son? Is not His mother's name Mary, and are not His brothers James and Joseph and Simon and Judas? [56]And are not all His sisters here among us? Where, then, did He get all these things?" [57]So they were offended at[p] Him. But Jesus told them, "A prophet is not without honor except in his native town and among his own family." [58]And because of their unbelief He did not perform many powerful deeds there.

Chapter 14

At that time Herod the tetrarch[a] heard the report about Jesus[b] [2]and said to his attendants, "This is John the Baptizer. He has been raised from the dead, and that is why mighty powers are at work in him." [3]Herod had [earlier] arrested John, bound him and put him in prison on account of Herodias, the wife of his brother Philip. [4]For John had told him, "It is not lawful for you to have her."[c] [5]Herod wanted to kill John, but he was afraid of the people, because they regarded John as a prophet.

[6]However, during the celebration of Herod's birthday, the daughter of Herodias danced in the midst [of the guests] and Herod was so delighted [7]that he promised with an oath to give her whatever she might ask. [8]Having been urged by her mother, the girl said, "Give me here on a platter the head of John the Baptizer." [9]The king was grieved, yet because of his oaths and those reclining at dinner with him, he ordered [her request] to be granted. [10]So he sent and had John beheaded in the prison. [11]And his head was brought on a

---

[n]Literally, *scribe.*

[o]That is, Nazareth where He had been brought up. Cf. 2:23.

[p]Causal use of Greek preposition, *en.*

[a]That is, Herod Antipas, one of the sons of Herod the Great, and ruler 4 B.C. until A.D. 39 of Galilee and Perea, one fourth of the territory which had been controlled by his father.

[b]Objective genitive.

[c]Cf. Lev. 18:16; 20:21.

platter and given to the girl; and she took it to her mother. [12]John's disciples came forward and took away the body and buried it. Then they went and told Jesus.

[13]When Jesus heard [what had happened to John], He withdrew by boat to a solitary place by Himself. The crowds learned [where He had gone], and from the towns they followed Him on foot [along the edge of the lake]. [14]When Jesus came ashore and saw the vast crowd, He was moved with deep compassion for them and healed their sick.

[15]As evening approached, His disciples came to Him and said, "This is a desolate place, and the hour is already late. Dismiss the crowds in order that they may go into the villages and buy food for themselves." [16]Jesus replied, "They do not need to go away. You, yourselves, give them something to eat." [17]They said to Him, "We have nothing here except five cakes of bread and two fish." [18]He said, "Bring them here to Me." [19]He directed the crowds to sit down on the grass. Then He took the five cakes of bread and the two fish, looked up to heaven, gave thanks,[d] broke the cakes of bread and gave them to the disciples, and the disciples [distributed them] to the crowds. [20]They all ate and were satisfied; and from the excess, of the broken pieces, they took up twelve full wicker baskets. [21]Those who ate were about five thousand men, not counting women and children.

[22]Immediately afterward, Jesus compelled the disciples to get into the boat and go ahead of Him to the opposite shore, while He dismissed the crowds. [23]After sending away the crowds, He went up into the mountain by Himself to pray. And when evening came, He was there alone. [24]By that time the boat was already far out[e] from the land, being battered by the waves, for the wind was against them. [25]In the fourth watch of the night,[f] Jesus came toward them, walking on the lake. [26]When the disciples saw Him walking on the lake, they were terrified. "It is an apparition" they said, and they screamed with fear. [27]But at once Jesus spoke to them, saying, "Be of good courage, it is I. Stop being afraid!"

[28]Peter responded to Him, "Lord, if it is really You, order me to come to You on the water." [29]Jesus said, "Come!" Then Peter climbed down from the boat and began walking[g] on the water, making his way toward Jesus. [30]But when he felt [the force of] the wind,[h] he became frightened and began to sink. "Lord, save me!", he cried. [31]Instantly, Jesus stretched out His hand, caught hold of him and said to him, "Man of little faith! Why did you doubt?" [32]And after they had climbed up into the boat, the wind ceased. [33]Then the men in the boat knelt before Him and said, "You are indeed the Son of God!"

---

[d]Or, pronounced a blessing.

[e]Literally, *many stadia*. A stadion was about one-eighth of a Roman or English mile.

[f]Between 3:00 and 6:00 A.M.

[g]Ingressive aorist.

[h]Literally, *But looking at,* or *regarding, the wind.*

³⁴They made the crossing and reached the shore at Gennesaret. ³⁵And when the men of that district recognized Jesus, they sent into all the surrounding neighborhood, and brought to Him all those who were ill.ⁱ ³⁶And they kept begging Him to allow them to touch only the edgeʲ of his garment; and as many as touched [it] were completely healed.

Chapter 15

Then some Pharisees and Law-teachers from Jerusalem came to Jesus and asked, ²"Why do Your disciples transgress the tradition of the elders by not washing [ceremonially] their hands before they eat food?" ³Jesus answered them, "Why do you, yourselves, transgress the commandment of God for the sake of your tradition? ⁴For God has said, 'Honor your father and your mother,'ᵃ and 'He who curses his father or mother shall be put to death.'ᵇ ⁵But you say, 'Whoever says to his father or to his mother, "Whatever I might have owed for your supportᶜ [has been dedicated as a gift to God]" ⁶has no obligation whatsoever to his father or his mother.' So you have set aside the word of God by means of your tradition. ⁷You hypocrites! Isaiah prophesied correctly about you when he said, ⁸'This people honors Me with their lips, but their heart is far away from Me. ⁹They worship Me in vain, for the doctrines they teach [are only] precepts of men.' "ᵈ

¹⁰Then Jesus summoned the crowd and said to them, "Listen and understand: ¹¹It is not what goes into a person's mouth that defiles him, but it is what comes out of his mouth that defiles him."

¹²His disciples came forward and said to Him, "Do you know that the Pharisees were offended when they heard what you said?" ¹³He replied, "Every plant which My Heavenly Father has not planted will be uprooted. ¹⁴Let them alone. They are blind men leading blind men. And if a blind man leads a blind man, both will fall into a pit."

¹⁵Peter responded to Him, "Explain this parable to us." ¹⁶He replied, "Are you too, even yet, without perception? ¹⁷Do you not understand that whatever goes into the mouth passes through the stomach and is discharged into the drain? ¹⁸But the things which come out of the mouth issue from the heart, and those things defile a man. ¹⁹For out of the heart come forth evil thoughts, murders, adulteries, sexual sins, thefts, false witnessing, blasphemies. ²⁰These are the things that defile a person; but eating with hands [ceremonially] unwashed does not defile anyone."

ⁱLiterally, *having it bad.*
ʲSee note on Matt. 9:20.
ᵃExod. 20:12; Deut. 5:16.
ᵇExod. 21:17.
ᶜLiterally, *Whatever gift you might be owed by me.*
ᵈCf. Isa. 29:13.

²¹And Jesus left there and withdrew to the neighborhood of Tyre and Sidon. ²²And behold, a Canaanite woman from those borders came out and kept pleading, "Have pity on me, O Lord, Son of David! My daughter is badly demon-possessed." ²³But Jesus did not answer her a word. And His disciples approached and began to urge Him, saying, "Send her away, for she continues crying out behind us." ²⁴He replied, "I was sent only to the lost sheep of the house of Israel." ²⁵Nevertheless, the woman came and bowed down before Him and kept saying, "Lord, do help me, please!" ²⁶He answered, "It is not proper to take the children's bread and throw it to the little dogs."ᵉ ²⁷She replied, "That is true, Lord, yet even the little dogs partake of the crumbs which from time to time fallᶠ from their masters' table." ²⁸At that Jesus answered her, "O woman, great is your faith! Let your wish be granted." And her daughter was cured at that moment.

²⁹Jesus left that place and passed along the Sea of Galilee. Then He went up into the mountain and was sitting there. ³⁰And great crowds came to Him, bringing with them the lame, the crippled, the blind, those unable to speak, and many others. Eagerly they placed them at Jesus' feet and He healed them; ³¹so that the multitude marvelled when they saw speechless men talking, cripples made well, the lame walking around, and the blind seeing. And they praised the God of Israel.

³²Jesus called His disciples to Him and said, "I have deep concern for the multitude because they have remained with Me three days now and they have nothing to eat. I do not want to send them away hungry, for they may become exhausted on the road." ³³The disciples said to Him, "Where, in this remote region could we get enough bread to satisfy such a vast crowd?" ³⁴Jesus asked them, "How many cakes of bread do you have?" They answered, "Seven, and a few small fish." ³⁵He ordered the multitude to sit down on the ground. ³⁶And He took the seven cakes of bread and the fish, gave thanks, broke [them] and kept giving [portions] to the disciples, and the disciples [distributed them] to the multitudes. ³⁷And all [the people] ate and were satisfied; and from what was left over of the broken pieces, they took up seven full rope-baskets.ᵍ ³⁸Those who ate numbered four thousand men, not counting women and children.

³⁹Then, having sent away the crowds, Jesus entered into the boat and sailed to the borders of Magadan.

ᵉJesus here does not use the Greek word *kusin,* large dogs of the street (cf. 7:6; Luke 16:21; Phil. 3:2; 2 Pet. 2:22; Rev. 22:15), but He uses the dative plural of *kunarion,* the diminutive which means "little dog." The reference is to the house pets which are small enough to walk under the table and hence get the bits of food which fall to the floor.

ᶠLinear force of Greek present participle.

ᵍGreek, *sphuridas,* probably larger baskets than the *kophinous* of 14:20. Note the distinction in 16:9 *(kophinous)* and 16:10 *(sphuridas).* Cf. Mark 8:19, 20.

Chapter 16

The Pharisees and Sadducees approached and, to tempt Jesus, asked Him to show them a sign from heaven. [2]He answered them, "When evening has come, you say, '[It will be] fair weather, for the sky is red.' [3]And in the morning, 'Today [will be] stormy, for the sky is red and overcast.' You know how to interpret the appearance of the sky; can you not [discern] the signs of the times? [4]An evil and apostate generation is eager for a sign, but no sign will be given to it except the sign exemplified by Jonah."[a] And He left them and went away.

[5]When the disciples reached the other side [of the lake] they [discovered that they] had forgotten to bring any bread.[b] [6]Jesus said to them, "Be careful and keep on your guard against the yeast of the Pharisees and Sadducees." [7]And they began to reason[c] among themselves, saying, "[He said this because] we brought no bread." [8]But Jesus knew [their thoughts] and said, "Why this discussion among yourselves because you are without bread, You men of little faith? [9]Do you not yet understand? Can you not remember the five bread-cakes [distributed among] the five thousand and how many full wicker baskets you took up?"[d] [10]Or the seven bread-cakes [distributed among] the four thousand and how many full rope-baskets you took up?[e] [11]How can you fail to understand that I was not talking about [literal] bread when I told you to keep on guard against the yeast of the Pharisees and Sadducees." [12]Then they understood that He had not warned them against the yeast used in bread but against the doctrine taught by the Pharisees[f] and Sadducees.[f]

[13]When Jesus came into the neighborhood of Philip's Caesarea,[g] He began to question His disciples, saying, "Who do people say the Son of Man is?" [14]They replied, "Some say John the Baptizer; some, Elijah; and others, Jeremiah or [another] one of the prophets." [15]"But you," He said to them, "who do you say I am?" [16]Simon Peter replied, "Thou[h] art the Messiah, the Son of the living God!" [17]Jesus answered him, "How fortunate[i] you are, Simon Bar-Jonah[j] because human insight[k] did not reveal [this] to you but My

---

[a]Cf. Matt. 12:39-40.

[b]Cf. Mark 8:14.

[c]Inchoative imperfect.

[d]Cf. 14:20.

[e]Cf. 15:37.

[f]Subjective genitive.

[g]A city enlarged and beautified by Philip the Tetrarch, who named it in honor of Caesar Augustus. It was situated at the foot of Mount Hermon, and distinguished from Caesarea on the Mediterannean.

[h]Emphatic personal pronoun.

[i]See note on Matt. 5:3.

[j]An Aramaic expression meaning "son of Jonah" (or *John*).

[k]Literally, *flesh and blood.*

Father who is in heaven. [18]Furthermore, I tell you that you are Peter,[l] and upon this Rock I will build My church, and [the] gates of Hades[n] will not withstand it. [19]I will give you[o] the keys of the kingdom of heaven, and whatever you bind on the earth must already have been bound[p] in heaven, and whatever you loose on the earth must already have been loosed[p] in heaven." [20]Then He strictly charged the disciples not to tell anyone that He was the Messiah.[q]

[21]From that time Jesus began to make it clear to His disciples that it was necessary for Him to go to Jerusalem, and suffer many things from the elders and chief priests and Law-experts, and to be put to death, and raised up on the third day. [22]Then Peter took Him aside and began to reprimand Him, saying, "Mercy on You, Lord! This must never happen to You!" [23]But Jesus turned and said to Peter, "Get behind me, Adversary. You are a stumbling-block to Me;[r] because you are not thinking from the viewpoint[s] of God but from the viewpoint of men."

[24]Then Jesus said to His disciples, "If anyone wishes to come after Me, let him renounce himself and take up his cross and keep following Me. [25]Indeed, whoever wishes to save his life[t] will lose it; but whoever loses his life for My sake will find it.

[26]"Actually, what benefit would it be to a man if he were to gain the whole world, yet forfeit his soul? Or what can a man give that could buy back his soul? [27]The Son of Man is about to come in the glory of His Father accompanied by His angels, and then He will pay back every person according to each one's deeds. [28]I solemnly tell you that some who are standing here will certainly not taste of death until they have seen the Son of Man coming in His kingdom."[u]

------

[l]The Greek term is *petros,* common in *koine* literature for a detached rock or small stone.

[m]The Greek word is *petra,* which signifies a great boulder or mass of rock. Cf. Matt. 7:24f.; Mark 15:46; Luke 6:48; 8:6, 13. For metaphorical use of *petra* applied to Christ, the Foundation of the church, see Rom. 9:33; 1 Cor. 10:4; 1 Pet. 2:8.

[n]See note on 11:23.

[o]The Greek pronoun is singular, referring to Peter. In Matt. 18:18, the pronoun is plural, referring to the whole group of disciples.

[p]Rendering the Greek periphrastic future perfect passive participle.

[q]Or, Christ. See note on Matt. 1:1.

[r]Or, you are setting a trap for Me.

[s]Literally, *the things.*

[t]Or, soul.

[u]Jesus probably refers to His transfiguration, or to His death and resurrection. Cf. 17:1; 2 Pet. 1:16-19.

Chapter 17

Six days later, Jesus took with Him Peter and the brothers James and John and led them up into a high mountain by themselves. [2]There He was transfigured in their presence. His face shone like the sun, and His garments became white as the light. [3]Suddenly Moses and Elijah appeared to them, engaging in conversation with Jesus. [4]Then Peter said to Jesus, "Lord, how excellent it is for us to be here! If You wish, I will make here three shelters—one for You, one for Moses, and one for Elijah."

[5]While Peter was still speaking, suddenly a bright cloud enveloped them; and behold, out of the cloud came a voice, saying, "This is My Son, the Beloved, in whom I am[a] well pleased! Listen to Him!" [6]When the disciples heart it, they fell on their faces, because they were exceedingly terrified. [7]Then Jesus drew near and touched them. "Arise," He said, "and stop being afraid!" [8]When they raised their eyes, they saw no one at all except Jesus Himself.

[9]As they were coming down from the mountain Jesus ordered them, "Do not tell anyone about the vision until the Son of Man has risen from the dead." [10]The disciples asked Him, "Why then do the Law-teachers say that it is necessary for Elijah to come first?" [11]He replied, "Indeed, Elijah does come and will restore all things.[b] [12]As a matter of fact, Elijah has already come,[c] and they did not recognize him, but treated him as they pleased. In the same manner the Son of Man is about to suffer at their hands." [13]Then the disciples understood that He had spoken to them concerning John the Baptizer.

[14]When they returned to the crowd, a man approached, fell on his knees before Him, [15]and said, "Lord, have mercy on my son, for he is an epileptic[d] and is in a terrible condition.[e] Frequently, he falls into the fire and frequently, into the water. [16]I brought him to Your disciples but they were not able to cure him." [17]Jesus replied, "O faithless and perverted generation, how long shall I be among you? How long must I put up with you? Bring him here to Me!" [18]Then Jesus rebuked the demon and it came out of him; and the boy was cured from that moment.

[19]Afterward the disciples came to Jesus privately and asked, "Why could we not drive out [the demon]?" [20]He said to them, "Because you have so little faith. I tell you truly, if you had faith the size of a mustard seed, you

---

[a]Timeless aorist. Cf. 3:17.

[b]The reference is to John (note v. 13), whose preaching brought about a moral and spiritual restoration. Cf. Mal. 4:5-6.

[c]Cf. Luke 1:17.

[d]Or, a lunatic. Literally, *moon-struck*. See note on 4:24.

[e]Literally, *he has it bad.*

could say to this mountain, 'Move from here to there,' and it would move. In fact, nothing would be impossible for you. [21f]But this kind [of spirit] is driven out only by means of prayer and fasting."

[22]While Jesus [and His disciples] were traveling together in Galilee He said to them, "The Son of Man is about to be delivered into the hands of men, [23]and they will put Him to death, but on the third day He will be raised up." And [the disciples] were deeply grieved.

[24]After they reached Capernaum, the collectors of the double-drachma[g] came to Peter and said, "Your teacher pays the two-drachma tax, does He not?" [25]He replied, "Yes." When Peter came into the house, Jesus anticipated [what he was going to say] and asked him, "What is your opinion, Simon? From whom do earthly kings collect revenue or personal tax—from their sons or from other people?" [26]When Peter replied, "From other people," Jesuss said to him, "Then the sons are exempt. [27]But, to keep from giving them cause for offense, go to the lake and throw in a hook. Lift out the first fish you catch, open its mouth and [in it] you will find a stater.[h] Take that and pay them for Me and for you."

Chapter 18

At that time the disciples came to Jesus and asked, "Who is really greatest in the kingdom of heaven?" [2]He called forward a little child, and placed him in their midst [3]and said, "Truly I tell you, unless you experience a change [of attitude][a] and become like little children, you will never enter the kingdom of heaven. [4]Therefore, whoever makes himself lowly like this little child—that man is the greatest in the kingdom of heaven. [5]And whoever receives one such child in My Name receives Me. [6]It would be better for a person to have a large mill-stone[b] hung around his neck and to be drowned in the depth of the sea, than to cause to stumble one of these little ones who believe in Me.

[7]"Woe to the world on account of[c] its stumbling-blocks![d] Indeed, it is inevitable that occasions of stumbling occur, but woe to the man through

---

[f]The Nestle text, on the authority of a number of ancient manuscripts which omit v. 21, places it in the margin. But see Mark 9:29.

[g]The *didrachma,* or double-drachma, was a Greek silver coin equal to the Jewish half-shekel which every Jew above the age of twenty paid annually as a Temple tax. Cf. Exod. 30:13-16.

[h]The *stater* was a silver coin which had the value of four drachmas, hence was equivalent to the Temple tax for two persons.

[a]Literally, *unless you turn.*
[b]Literally, *a mill-stone turned by an ass.*
[c]Causal use of preposition, *apo.*
[d]Or, entrapments.

whom the entrapment comes! ⁸If your hand or your foot is a trap for you, cut it off and hurl it from you. It is better for you to enter into the life maimed or crippled than, with two hands or two feet, to be cast into the everlasting fire. ⁹And if your eye is a trap for you, pluck it out and hurl it from you. It is better for you to enter into the life with one eye, than to have two eyes and be thrown into the Gehenna characterized by fire.ᵉ

¹⁰"See to it that you never look down on one of these little ones; for I tell you that in heaven their angels continually behold My Heavenly Father's face.

¹²ᶠ"What do you think? If any man has a hundred sheep, and one of them goes astray, will he not leave the ninety-nine on the hills and go forth in search of the wandering one? ¹³And if he can find it, truly I say to you that he rejoices more over it than over the ninety-nine that did not go astray. ¹⁴Thus it is not the will of your Fatherᵍ in heaven that one of these little ones should ever be lost.

¹⁵"If your brother commits a sin,ʰ go and reprove him when you and he are alone. If he listens to you, you have won back your brother. ¹⁶But if he does not listen, take along with you one or two more [persons], in order that every statement may be confirmed by two or three witnesses.ⁱ ¹⁷If he refuses to listen to them, relate the matter to the church. And if he refuses to listen even to the church, treat him just as you would a pagan or a tax collector.

¹⁸"Truly I say to you, whatever things you bind on earth must already have been boundʲ in heaven, and whatever things you loose on earth must already have been loosedʲ in heaven.

¹⁹"Again I tell you truly, that if two of you agree on earth concerning any matter which they may ask, it will be granted to them by My Father who is in heaven. ²⁰For where two or three are gathered together in My Name, there I am in their midst."

²¹Then Peter approached and asked Him, "Lord, how often shall I forgive my brother if he sins against me? As many as seven times?" ²²Jesus answered him, "I tell you not as many as seven times, but as many as seventy times seven.ᵏ ²³That is why the kingdom of heaven may be compared to a certain

---

ᵉDescriptive genitive.

ᶠVerse 11 is placed in the margin of the Nestle text. But the thought is included in Luke 19:10.

ᵍLiterally, *it is not a thing willed before your Father*.

ʰSome manuscripts add, *eis se, against you*.

ⁱCf. Deut. 19:15.

ʲRendering the Greek periphrastic future perfect passive participle. Cf. 16:19. According to Rev. 3:7, the power of the keys is held by Christ himself. The disciples are commissioned to preach God's word, hence are to forbid or to permit those things for which they already have divine authority. Cf. Matt. 28:19-20.

ᵏOr, seventy-seven times. In other words, there is to be no limit to forgiveness.

king, who decided to settle accounts with his servants. [24]When he began the settlement, there was brought to him one debtor who owed sixty million denarii.[k] [25]But because[m] he did not have [the resources with which] to pay, his lord gave orders for him to be sold, along with his wife and his children and all his possessions, and payment to be made. [26]At that, the servant fell down and begged him, 'Be patient with me, please, and I will pay you everything!' [27]Moved with deep compassion, the lord of that servant released him and cancelled his debt.

[28]"But that servant went out and found one of his fellow-servants who owed him a hundred denarii.[n] He siezed him and began to choke[o] him. 'Pay back what you owe,' he said. [29]Therefore, his fellow-servant fell down and implored him, 'Be patient with me, please, and I will pay you!' [30]But he refused.[p] Instead, he went and threw him into prison until he should pay what he owed.

[31]"When the other servants saw what had happened, they were deeply grieved, and went and reported fully to their lord all that had taken place. [32]At once his lord summoned him. He said to him, 'You wicked servant. I forgave all that debt of yours because you begged me. [33]Should you not also have shown mercy to your fellow-servant, even as I on my part extended mercy to you?' [34]So his lord, stirred with wrath, handed him over to the torturers until he should pay everything he owed him. [35]That is the way My Heavenly Father will deal with you, if from your hearts each of you does not forgive his brother.''

Chapter 19

When Jesus finished these sayings, He departed from Galilee and went to the boundaries of Judaea on the other side of the Jordan. [2]Great crowds followed Him, and He healed them there.

[3]Some Pharisees came to Jesus, and tempted Him by asking, "Is it lawful for a man to divorce his wife for any cause whatever?" [4]He replied, "Have you not read that the Creator from the beginning made them male and female,

---

[l]Literally, *ten thousand talents*. One Attic talent was the equivalent of 6000 denarii, or about a thousand dollars.

[m]Causal participle.

[n]A denarius, equivalent to about 17c, was a day's pay for a common laborer. Cf. 20:2, 13. One hundred denarii (about $17.00) was exceedingly small, compared to the enormous amount (approximately $10,000,000) owed by the first debtor.

[o]Inchoative imperfect.

[p]Or, he was not willing.

[5]and said, 'For this reason a man shall leave his father and mother and be united to his wife, and the two shall be one flesh'?[a] [6]Thus they are no longer two but one flesh. Therefore, what God has yoked together, let no man separate."

[7]They asked Jesus, "Then why did Moses direct that [a husband] could divorce [his wife] by giving [her] a written statement of dismissal?"[b] [8]He answered them, "Owing to[c] your hardness of heart Moses permitted you to divorce your wives, but that was not God's original purpose.[d] [9]And I tell you, whoever divorces his wife for any reason except unchastity, and marries another, is guilty of adultery.

[10]The disciples said to Him, "If the ground for divorce is limited to sexual unchastity,[e] it is better not to marry!" [11]He replied, "Not all men can receive this precept [about marriage and divorce], but only those to whom it applies. [12]There are men for whom congenital defects make marriage impossible.[f] Others cannot marry because they have been emasculated by men. And there are those who decided to renounce sex[g] for the sake of the kingdom of heaven. Whoever is able to receive [this precept], let him do so."

[13]Then some little children were brought to Jesus, that He might put His hands on them and pray. The disciples reproved [the persons who brought] them. [14]But Jesus said, "Let the little children alone, and stop hindering them from coming to Me, for of such is the kingdom of heaven." [15]Then He placed His hands on them, and went away from that place.

[16]And, behold, a certain man came to Him and asked, "Teacher, what good thing shall I do in order that I may have eternal life?" [17]Jesus said to him, "Why are you questioning Me about what is good? There is but One who is good. If you wish to enter into life, keep the commandments." [18]"What sort [of commandments]?" he asked. Jesus replied, "These: 'You must not commit murder.' 'You must not commit adultery.' 'You must not steal.' 'You must not speak falsely about others.' [19]'Honor your father and your mother,' and 'Love your neighbor as [you love] yourself.' "[h]

[20]The young man said to Him, "I have observed all these things. What do I still lack?" [21]Jesus said to him, "If you want to be a man according to [the divine] standard,[i] go sell your possessions and give [the money] to the poor, and you will have treasure in heaven. Then come, and consistently follow

---

[a]Cf. Gen. 1:27; 2:24.

[b]Cf. Deut. 24:1.

[c]Causal use of preposition, *pros*.

[d]Literally, *but from the beginning it was not that way.*

[e]Literally, *if such is the situation between man and wife.*

[f]Literally, *there are eunuchs who were born thus.*

[g]Literally, *who made themselves eunuchs.*

[h]Cf. Exod. 20:12-16; Deut. 5:16-20; Lev. 19:18.

[i]Greek, *teleios:* "complete," "mature," or "perfect." Used of someone who has reached the goal, or met certain requirements.

Me." [22]But when the young man heard this statement,[j] he went away grieving, for he had great wealth.

[23]Then Jesus said to His disciples, "I tell you solemnly that it is difficult for a rich man to enter the kingdom of heaven. [24]Furthermore, I say to you, it is easier for a camel to go through the eye of a needle than for a wealthy person to enter the kingdom of God." [25]When the disciples heard this, they were utterly astonished. "Then who can be saved?" they asked. [26]Jesus looked straight at them and said, "With men this is impossible, but with God all things are possible."

[27]Then Peter spoke up and said to Him, "Look, we on our part have left everything and followed You. What's going to happen to us?"[k] [28]Jesus said to them, "Truly I assure you that in the new age,[l] when the Son of Man sits on the throne of His glory, you who have followed Me will yourselves sit on twelve thrones and judge the twelve tribes of Israel. [29]In fact, everyone who has given up houses or brothers or sisters or father or mother or children or lands for the sake of My Name will receive many times as much, and inherit eternal life. [30]But many [who are] first will be last, and [many who are] last [will be] first.

Chapter 20

"For the kingdom of heaven is like an estate-owner who went out early in the morning to hire men to work in his vineyard. [2]After agreeing with the workmen to pay them a denarius as a day's wage,[a] he sent them into his vineyard. [3]About nine o'clock[b] he went out and saw others standing idle in the market place. [4]He said to them, 'You also go [and work] in my vineyard, and I will pay you whatever is right.' [5]So they went. Again, he went out about noon, and also, about three o'clock,[c] and did likewise. [6]Finally, he went out late in the afternoon[d] and found others standing around, and he said to them, 'Why have you been standing here all day doing nothing?' [7]'Because no one has hired us,' they replied. He told them, 'You, too, go [and work] in the vineyard.'

---

[j]Literally, *when he heard that word.*
[k]Or, what then shall we get?
[l]Or, in the ultimate order of things. Cf. 2 Pet. 3:13; Rev. 3:21; 21:1-5.

[a]Literally, *on the basis of a denarius for the day.*
[b]Literally, *about the third hour.*
[c]Literally, *about the sixth and the ninth hour.*
[d]Or, about five o'clock. Literally, *about the eleventh* [hour].

⁸"When evening came,ᵉ the owner of the vineyard said to his administrator, 'Call the workmen and give them their pay, beginning with the last ones [who responded] and ending with the first ones.' ⁹When those came who [had begun working] late in the afternoon, each one received a denarius.ᶠ ¹⁰When those came who first [began working] they supposed they would receive more; but they, too, each received a denarius. ¹¹When they took it, they began to complainᵍ to the estate-owner. ¹²'These who came last have worked [only] one hour,' they said, 'yet you have made them equal to us who have endured the burden and heat of the [entire] day.' ¹³In reply he said to one of them, 'My friend, I am doing you no injustice. Did you not agree with me [to work] for a denarius? ¹⁴Take what is yours and go your way! I choose to give to the late-comerʰ the same amount that I give to you. ¹⁵Am I not free to do as I wish with my own property? Or are you enviousⁱ because I on my part am generous?' ¹⁶Thus the last ones will be first, and the first ones [will be] last."ʲ

¹⁷Jesus started for Jerusalem with His disciples. As they journeyed along the way, He took the Twelve aside and said to them, ¹⁸"Listen, we are going up to Jerusalem, and [there] the Son of Man will be betrayed to the chief priests and Law-teachers. They will condemn Him to death, ¹⁹and hand Him over to the Gentiles to be ridiculed and scourged and crucified. But on the third day, He will be raised up."

²⁰Then the mother of Zebedee's sons came to Jesus, accompanied by her sons, and bowed before Him to make a request of Him. ²¹He said to her, "What do you want?" She replied to Him, "Grant that these two sons of mine may sit, one at Your right and one at Your left, in Your kingdom." ²²Jesus answered and said, "You people do not realize what you are asking for yourselves. Are you able to drink the cup which I, Myself, am about to drink?" They replied, "We are able." ²³He told them, "You will, indeed, drink My cup, but a place at My right and at My left is not Mine to give, but is theirs for whom it has been prepared by My Father."

²⁴When the [other] ten [disciples] heard it, they were indignant at the two brothers. ²⁵But Jesus called [the entire group] to Him and said, "You know that the Gentile rulers dominate their subjects by outward might,ᵏ and their great men exercise tyrannyˡ over the people. ²⁶It is not to be like that among you. Instead, whoever wants to be great among you, let him be your servant, ²⁷and whoever wants to be first among you, let him be your slave—²⁸even as

---

ᵉCf. Deut. 24:15.

ᶠThat is, a full day's wage. Cf. vs. 2.

ᵍInchoative imperfect.

ʰLiterally, *to this last man.*

ⁱLiterally, *Or is your eye wicked?*

ʲCf. 19:30.

ᵏLiterally, *They lord it over them.*

ˡOr, authority.

the Son of Man came not to be served but to serve, and to give His life as a ransom in behalf of man.''[m]

[29]As they were leaving Jericho, a large crowd followed Him. [30]And two blind men who were sitting by the roadside, heard that Jesus was passing by, and they began to cry out, "Lord, Son of David, have mercy one us!" [31]The crowd rebuked them and tried to keep them quiet; but they cried out all the more, "Lord, Son of David, have mercy one us!" [32]Jesus stopped, and called them. "What do you want Me to do for you?" He asked. [33]They begged Him, "Lord, let our eyes be opened!" [34]Then Jesus, moved with deep compassion, touched their eyes, and instantly they received their sight. And they followed Him.

Chapter 21

When they drew near to Jerusalem and had reached Bethphage on the Mount of Olives, Jesus sent two disciples, [2]saying to them, "Go into the village opposite you, and immediately you will find a donkey having been tied,[a] and a colt with her. Untie [them] and bring [them] to Me. [3]If anyone questions what you are doing,[b] just say, 'The Lord needs them,' and he will send them at once." [4]Now this occurred to fulfill what was spoken through the prophet, [5]"Say to the daughter of Zion, "Look, your king is coming to you, gentle and seated upon a donkey, even[c] upon a colt, the foal of a beast of burden.' "[d]

[6]The disciples went and did just as Jesus had instructed them. [7]They brought the donkey and the colt, and placed their outer garments upon them, and He sat upon them.[e] [8]Most of the crowd spread their cloaks on the road, while others were cutting branches from the trees and spreading them on the road. [9]The throngs who went in front of Him and those who followed were shouting, "Hosanna[f] to the Son of David! Blessed is He who comes in the Name of the Lord! Hosanna in the highest!"

---

[m]Or, as a redemptive price, for all. The New Testament emphasizes the vicarious, costly, universal, and eternal character of Christ's atonement. Cf. Gal. 1:4; Col. 1:14; Heb. 9:11-28; 1 Pet. 1:18-21.

[a]Perfect passive participle. Cf. 16:19; 18:18.

[b]Literally, *says anything to you.*

[c]Ascensive use of Greek conjunction, *kai.*

[d]Cf. Zech. 9:9.

[e]That is, Jesus sat upon the garments, and rode the colt. Cf. Mark 11:7; Luke 19:35.

[f]Hosanna is transliterated from a Hebrew term which means *Grant deliverance!* or *Save us now!* In the present context it is apparently an expression of joy and triumph. The multitude seems to be invoking God's blessing upon Him whom they regard as the Messiah. Cf. Psa. 118:25-26.

[10]When He entered Jerusalem, the whole city was excited. People were asking, "Who is this?" [11]And the crowds kept saying, "This is the Prophet, Jesus from Nazareth in Galilee."

[12]Jesus entered into the Temple area and drove out all who were selling and buying there. He overturned the tables of the money-changers and the seats of those selling the doves, [13]and said to them, "It stands written, 'My house shall be called a house of prayer'[g] but you are making it a den of robbers."

[14]Then blind and lame people came to Him in the Temple precincts, and He healed them. [15]When the chief priests and the Law-teachers saw the marvelous things Jesus did, and [heard] the children shouting in the Temple courts, "God bless the Son of David!"[h] they became indignant.[i] [16]"Do you hear what these [children] are saying?" they asked Him. "Of course," Jesus replied. "And have you never read, 'Out of the mouths of babes and nursing infants Thou hast brought forth praise'?"[j] [17]Then He left them and went forth out of the city to Bethany, and spent the night there.

[18]Early the next morning as Jesus was returning to the city, He was hungry. [19]Noticing a fig tree by the roadside, He went over to it, but found on it nothing except leaves. So He said to it, "From now on you will never bear any more fruit." Instantly, the fig tree withered. [20]When the disciples saw it they exclaimed in amazement, "How did the fig tree wither so quickly?" [21]In reply Jesus said to them, "Truly I tell you, if you have faith, and do not waver, you will not only do what was done to the fig tree,[k] but even if you say to this mountain, 'Be lifted up and be hurled into the sea,' it will be done. [22]And everything for which you ask in prayer, if you keep believing,[l] you will receive."

[23]Jesus entered the Temple area and, while He was teaching, the chief priests and the elders of the people approached and asked Him, "By what sort of authority are You doing these things? And who gave You this authority?" [24]Jesus replied to them, "Let Me ask you one question and, if you give me the answer, then I will tell you by what sort of authority I am doing these things. [25]What was the origin of John's baptism? Was it from heaven,[m] or from men?" They discussed [the alternatives] among themselves [and concluded], "If we say 'From heaven,' He will ask us, 'Then why did you not believe him?' [26]But if we say, 'From men,' we have the people to fear, for they all regard John as a prophet." [27]So they said to Jesus, "We do not know." And He in turn[n] said to them, "Neither will I tell you by what sort of authority I am doing these things."

---

[g]Cf. Isa. 56:7; Jer. 7:11.
[h]Literally, *Hosanna to the Son of David.* See note on v. 9.
[i]Ingressive aorist.
[j]Cf. Ps. 8:2.
[k]Literally, *the thing of the fig tree.*
[l]Indicated by Greek conditional present participle.
[m]That is, from God.
[n]Literally, *And He himself.*

[28]"Now what is your opinion? A man had two sons. He went to the first, and said, 'My boy, go work today in the vineyard.' [29]He replied, 'I will, sir', but he did not go. [30]The [father] went to the second [son] and said the same thing. 'I will not go,' he replied; but afterward he was regretful and went. [31]Which of the two did the father's will?'' ''The second one, ''they replied. Jesus said to them, ''Truly I tell you, that tax-gatherers and prostitutes enter the kingdom of God ahead of you! [32]For John came to you in a way characterized by righteousness,[o] and you did not believe him; but the tax gatherers and prostitutes did believe him. And although[p] you saw [their response], you, yourselves, did not experience regret so as to believe him.

[33]"Listen to another parable: There was a certain estate-owner who planted a vineyard, built a fence around it, dug a winepress in it, and erected an observation-tower. Then he leased [the vineyard] to vine-growers and went abroad. [34]When harvest-time drew near, he sent his servants to the vine-growers to receive his [share of the] harvest. [35]But the vine-growers seized his servants, beat one, murdered another, and stoned a third. [36]Again, he sent other servants, more in number than the first ones, and they treated them the same way. [37]Finally, he sent his son to them. 'They will respect my son,' he thought. [38]But when the vine-growers saw the son, they said to each other, 'This is the heir. Come, let us kill him and take possession of his inheritance.' [39]So they seized him, threw him out of the vineyard, and killed him. [40]Now when the owner of the vineyard returns, what will he do to those vine-growers?'

[41]They replied, ''With vengeance,[q] he will put those wretches to death and will lease the vineyard to vine-growers of a different character[r]—men who will render to him [his share of] the harvests at the proper times.''

[42]Jesus asked them, ''Have you never read in the Scriptures, 'The stone which the builders rejected has become the keystone of the building; the Lord has done this, and it is marvelous in our eyes'?[s] [43]Therefore, I tell you that the kingdom of God will be taken away from you, and given to a people who will produce[t] the fruits required by it.[u] [44]Regarding this stone, any man who falls upon it will be broken to pieces; but he on whom it falls will be ground to dust.''

[45]After the chief priests and the Pharisees had listened to His parables, they knew that He was speaking about them. [46]Although they were eager to arrest Him, they were afraid of the crowds, because [the people] considered Him a prophet.

---

[o]Descriptive genitive.

[p]Concessive aorist participle.

[q]Literally, *badly.*

[r]Qualitative force of *hoitines,* Greek indefinite relative pronoun.

[s]Cf. Ps. 118:22-23.

[t]Futuristic present participle.

[u]Subjective genitive.

Chapter 22

Again Jesus addressed them in parables. He said, [2]"The kingdom of heaven may be compared to a certain king who planned wedding festivities for his son. [3]And he sent his servants to call those who had been invited to the festivities but they were not willing to come. [4]Next he sent other servants, saying, 'Tell those who have been invited: "Listen, I have prepared my banquet. My oxen and fattened cattle have been butchered, and everything is ready. Come to the festivities!"' [5]But they were not interested: one went off to his own farm, another to his place of business, [6]while the rest seized the king's[a] servants, insulted them, and murdered them. [7]At that the king was infuriated. He sent his soldiers and destroyed those murderers, and burned their city. [8]Then he said to his servants, 'Indeed, the wedding banquet is ready, but the ones invited were unfit. [9]Therefore, go to the crossing-places of the roads, and invite to the wedding festivities everyone you find.[b] [10]So the servants went forth into the thoroughfares and brought together all [the people] they found, both bad and good, and the banquet hall was filled with guests.

[11]"When the king came in to view the guests he saw there a man who was not wearing a wedding garment. [12]'Friend,' he said to him, 'how is it that you came in here without a wedding garment?' The man was speechless. [13]Then the king told the attendants, 'Bind his feet and hands and throw him out into the outside darkness, [where] there will be wailing and the grinding of teeth.' [14]For many are invited, but few are chosen."

[15]Then the Pharisees went and began a plot to ensnare Jesus in something He might say.[c] [16]They sent their disciples, accompanied by Herodians, to ask Him, "Teacher, we know You are honest and that You teach God's way in truth, and that You are not influenced by anyone's opinion,[d] because You seek no man's favor. [17]Now give us Your opinion. Is it lawful to pay tax to Caesar or not?" [18]Jesus, aware of their evil intention, replied, "You hypocrites, why are you putting me to the test? [19]Show Me the coin used to pay the tax." They handed Him a denarius.[e] [20]"Whose likeness and title are on it?" He asked them. [21]"Caesar's," they replied. Then He said to them, "Therefore, pay to Caesar the things that belong to Caesar, and to God the things that belong to God!" [22]When they heard this, they marvelled, and they left Him and went away.

---

[a]Literally, *his.*
[b]Literally, *as many as you find.*
[c]Literally, *in a word.*
[d]Literally, *it does not concern you about anyone.*
[e]A Roman silver coin. See note on 18:28.

²³That very day some Sadducees—those who say there is no resurrection—approached Jesus with the question, ²⁴"Teacher, Moses said, 'If a man dies without children, his brother shall marry the widow and raise up descendants for his brother.'ᶠ ²⁵Now there were among us seven brothers. The first married, but died childless, leaving his widow to his brother. ²⁶It happened the same way with the second [brother], and with the third, and with all the seven. ²⁷Last of all, the woman died. ²⁸Now at the resurrection to which of the seven will she be the wife? For they had all been married to her."ᵍ

²⁹Jesus answered them, "You are in error, because you do not know the Scriptures or the power of God. ³⁰For in the resurrection [state] people neither marry nor are given in marriage, but are like angels in heaven. ³¹But concerning the resurrection of the dead, have you not read what God spoke to you, saying, ³²'I am the God of Abraham, and the God of Isaac, and the God of Jacob'?ʰ He is not the God of dead [persons] but of living ones." ³³The crowds, after listening [to Him], were amazed at His doctrine.

³⁴When the Pharisees heard that Jesus had silencedⁱ the Sadducees, they gathered around Him.ʲ ³⁵And one of them, learned in the Law,ᵏ put Him to the test, asking, ³⁶"Teacher, which is the greatest commandment in the Law?' ³⁷Jesus answered him, " 'You must love the Lord your God with all your heart, and with all your soul, and with all your understanding.'ˡ ³⁸This is the greatest and first commandment. ³⁹The second is like it: 'You must love your fellow-man as yourself.'ᵐ ⁴⁰On these two commandments the entire Law and the Prophets are based."

⁴¹While the Pharisees were together Jesus asked them, ⁴²"What is your opinion about the Christ?ⁿ Whose Son is He?" They replied, "David's." ⁴³He asked them, "Then how is it that David, motivated by the Spirit, calls Him 'Lord', when he remarks, ⁴⁴'The Lord said to My Lord, "Sit at My right hand until I put Your enemies under Your feet" '?ᵒ ⁴⁵If David calls Him 'Lord', how can He be David's Son?" ⁴⁶No one was able to answer Him a word, nor from that day did anyone dare to question Him any further.

ᶠCf. Deut. 25:5-6.
ᵍLiterally, *For they all had her.*
ʰCf. Exod. 3:6, 15, 16; 4:5; 6:3.
ⁱLiterally, *muzzled.*
ʲLiterally, *they assembled together.*
ᵏThat is, an official interpreter of the Jewish written and oral Law.
ˡCf. Deut. 6:5.
ᵐCf. Lev. 19:18.
ⁿOr, the Messiah.
ᵒCf. Ps. 110:1.

Chapter 23

Then Jesus spoke to the crowds and to His disciples, [2]saying, "The Law-teachers and the Pharisees have assumed Moses' place of authority[a] [as expounders of the Scriptures]. [3]Therefore, do and keep observing everything they tell you. But do not follow their example; for they fail to practice what they teach.[b] [4]Furthermore, they tie together heavy burdens and put them upon [other] men's shoulders; yet they themselves are not willing to lift a finger to move them. [5]They perform all their deeds to be seen by men. Accordingly, they widen their phylacteries[c] and enlarge their tassels.[d] [6]They like the prominent place at banquets and the chief seats in the synagogues. [7][They like] to be greeted with respect in the market-places, and for people to call them 'Rabbi'.

[8]"But as for you, do not allow yourselves to be called "Rabbi', for ie one Teacher and all of you are brothers. [9]And do not call any man on the earth 'Father', for you have one Father—the Heavenly One. [10]Neither allow yourselves to be called 'Leaders', for you have one Leader—the Christ. [11]As a matter of fact, the [person who would be] greatest among you must be your servant. [12]Whoever exalts himself will be humbled, and whoever humbles himself will be exalted.

[13]"Woe to you, Law-teachers and Pharisees, hypocrites! You shut the kingdom of heaven in front of people—you, yourselves, are not entering, nor do you permit those to go in who are trying to enter.[e]

[14f]"Woe to you, Law-teachers and Pharisees, hypocrites! You devour the houses of widows, and for a pretense make long prayers. On account of this, you will receive more severe punishment.

[15]"Woe to you, Law-teachers and Pharisees, hypocrites! You travel over sea and land to make one proselyte, but when he becomes one, you make him twice as much a son of Gehenna[g] as you are.

[16]"Woe to you, blind guides! You say, 'If anyone takes an oath by the Sanctuary, it is not binding;[h] but if anyone takes an oath by the gold of the

---

[a]Literally, *they have sàt down in Moses' chair.*

[b]Literally, *for they say and do not.*

[c]Phylacteries were small parchment cases containing verses taken from the Pentateuch. One such case was worn on the forehead and one on the hand or arm by Jews, usually during prayer. Cf. Deut. 6:8; 11:18.

[d]See note on Matt. 9:20.

[e]Greek conative present participle.

[f]The Nestle text places v. 14 in the margin. However, the verse, in substance, is found in Mark 12:40 and Luke 20:47.

[g]See note on 5:22.

[h]Literally, *it is nothing.*

Sanctuary, he is bound [by his oath].' [17]You foolish and blind people! Which
is greater, the gold or the Sanctuary which has made the gold sacred? [18]Also
[you say], 'If any one takes an oath by the altar, it is not binding;[h] but if
anyone takes an oath by the offering upon it, he is bound [by his oath].'
[19]How blind you are! For which is greater, the offering or the altar which
makes the offering sacred? [20]Therefore, he who takes an oath by the altar
takes it by [the altar] and by everything upon it. [21]And he who takes an oath
by the Sanctuary takes it by [the Sanctuary] and by the One who dwells in it.
[22]And he who takes an oath by heaven takes it by the throne of God and by the
One who sits upon [the throne].

[23]"Woe to you, Law-teachers and Pharisees, hypocrites! You pay tithes[i] of
mint and dill and cummin,[j] but you have neglected the weightier matters of the
Law—justice and mercy and trustworthiness. These [more significant things]
you should have done without neglecting those others. [24]Blind guides! You
filter out a gnat, but gulp down a camel!

[25]"Woe to you, Law-teachers and Pharisees, hypocrites! You cleanse the
outside of the cup and the dish, but inside they are full of what you have taken
by robbery and greed.[k] [26]Blind Pharisee! Cleanse first the inside of the cup, in
order that the outside may become clean also.

[27]"Woe to you, Law-teachers and Pharisees, hypocrites! You are like
white-washed tombs which seem beautiful on the outside, but inside are full of
dead men's bones and all sorts of filth. [28]So outwardly you appear to men to
be righteous, but inwardly you are full of pretense and lawlessness.

[29]"Woe to you, Law-teachers and Pharisees, hypocrites! You build the
tombs of the prophets and decorate the monuments of the righteous. [30]And
you say, 'If we had lived in the days of our forefathers, we would not have
participated in [shedding] the blood of the prophets.' [31]By such language[l] you
are bearing witness against yourselves,[m] that you are the same in character[n] as
those who murdered the prophets. [32]You, yourselves, have filled up the
measure of [the guilt of] your forefathers.[o] [33]You serpents! Descendants of
vipers! How can you escape from the condemnation of Gehenna?

---

[i]Cf. Lev. 27:30; Deut. 14:22.

[j]Mint, dill (or anise) and cummin were aromatic herbs used to flavor foods and for
medicinal purposes.

[k]Literally, *full of the results of [your] plunder and self-indulgence.*

[l]Literally, *Thus.*

[m]Plural reflexive pronoun, here used as dative of disadvantage. See same idiom with
singular in 1 Cor. 4:4.

[n]Literally, *you are their descendants.*

[o]Or, You yourselves [go ahead and] complete what your forefathers began!

[34]"Listen! This is why I am sending to you prophets and learned men and able teachers.[p] Some of them you will kill—even crucify—and some you will scourge in your synagogues and persecute from city to city.[q] [35]And so upon you will come [retribution for] all the innocent blood poured out upon the earth, from the blood of righteous Abel to the blood of Zachariah, son of Barachiah, whom you put to death between the Sanctuary and the altar. [36]Solemnly, I tell you that [the culmination of] all these things will come upon the present generation.

[37]"O Jerusalem, Jerusalem, she who murders the prophets and stones the messengers sent to her! How often have I longed to gather your children together as a mother bird gathers her young ones under her wings, but you refused! [38]Look, your house is being abandoned to you! [39]Indeed, I tell you that from now on you will in no way see Me until you declare, 'Blessed is He who comes in the Name of the Lord!' "[r]

Chapter 24

Jesus left the Temple area, and as He was going away His disciples approached, to point out to Him the [grandeur] of the Temple buildings. [2]In reply He said to them, "You see all these things, do you not? Truly I tell you, by no means will there be left here one stone upon another—every one of them will be thrown down."

[3]While Jesus was sitting on the Mount of Olives, the disciples came to Him in private and said, "Tell us, when will these things happen, and what will be the sign of Your coming and of the consummation of the age?" [4]In reply Jesus said to them, "Make sure that no one leads you astray. [5]For many will come in My name, saying, 'I am the Messiah,' and they will mislead many. [6]You will hear of wars and threats of wars. Do not be alarmed. It is necessary [for such things] to happen, but the end is not yet. [7]Nation will rise up against nation, and kingdom against kingdom, and there will be famines and earthquakes in various places. [8]But all these things [are only] the beginning of birth-pangs.

[9]"Then men will hand you over to be tortured, and put to death, and you will be hated by all nations on account of My name. [10]At that time large

---

[p]Literally, *scribes*. Here in a good sense, i.e., expounders of the gospel. Cf. 13:52.
[q]Cf. 10:17; Acts 22:4; 26:11.
[r]Cf. Ps. 118:26.

numbers will be caused to stumble, and they will betray one another, and hate one another. [11]Many false prophets will appear and deceive many. [12]And on account of the increase of lawlessness, the love of the majority[a] will grow cold. [13]But whoever stands firm to the end will be saved. [14]This good news about the kingdom[b] will be preached throughout the entire inhabited earth, so that all peoples may hear it,[c] and then the end will come.

[15]"So when you see the detestable sacrilege, to which the prophet Daniel referred,[d] standing in the holy place—let the one who reads about it take notice—[16]then those in Judaea should flee to the mountains. [17]Anyone on the housetop should not come down to get the things that are in his house, [18]nor should any man in the field turn back to pick up his cloak. [19]How difficult it will be for pregnant women and for those who nurse infants in those days! [20]Pray that your departure may not be in winter, or on a Sabbath day. [21]For at that time there will be great distress, the like of which has not been since the world's beginning until now, and certainly will never occur again. [22]Actually, if those days were not shortened, no one at all could survive. But for the sake of [God's] chosen ones, those days will be cut short.

[23]"At that time, if anyone says to you, 'Look, here is the Messiah!' or 'There [He is]!' do not believe it. [24]For false Messiahs and pseudo-prophets will appear, and perform great signs and wonders so as to deceive, if possible, even the chosen ones. [25]Remember, I have warned you in advance. [26]So, if they say to you, 'Look, He is in the wilderness!' do not go out; or 'Look [He is] in some secluded place!' do not believe it. [27]For the coming of the Son of Man will be like lightening striking in the east and flashing across to the west. [28]Wherever the fallen body is, there will the eagles[e] be gathered.

[29]"Now immediately after the distress of those days the sun will be darkened, and the moon will not give its light. The stars will fall from the sky, and the forces of the heavens will be shaken.[f] [30]Then the sign of the Son of Man will appear in the sky, and all the peoples of the earth will beat their breasts [in despair] when they see the Son of Man coming on the clouds of the sky, with power and great glory. [31]And He will send forth His angels with a mighty trumpet-blast, and they will gather together His chosen ones from the four winds—from one end of the heavens to the other.[g]

---

[a]Literally, *the love of the many.*

[b]Objective genitive.

[c]Literally, *for a witness to all the nations.*

[d]Cf. Dan. 9:27; 11:31; 12:11; Mark 13:14; Luke 21:20.

[e]Or, vultures.

[f]Cf. Luke 21:25-26; 2 Pet. 3:10-12; Rev. 6:13.

[g]Literally, *from [the] extremities of [the] heavens unto [the] extremities of them.*

³²"Learn a lesson from the fig tree: As soon as its branch becomes tender and puts forth its leaves, you know summer is near. ³³So also, when you see all these things, know that He[h] is near—at the very door. ³⁴Truly I tell you, this generation[i] will certainly not pass away until all these things take place. ³⁵Sky and earth will pass away, but My words will never pass away.

³⁶"But concerning that day and hour, no one knows—not even the angels in heaven, nor the Son,[j] but only the Father. ³⁷Just as it was in the days of Noah,[k] so it will be when the Son of Man comes. ³⁸For in those days before the flood, people were eating and drinking, marrying and giving in marriage, until the very day Noah entered the ark. ³⁹They did not realize [the danger] until the deluge came and swept them all away. It will be like that at the coming of the Son of Man. ⁴⁰At that time, two men will be in the field—one will be taken, and one will be left. ⁴¹Two women will be grinding with a millstone—one will be taken, and one will be left.

⁴²"Therefore keep alert, because you do not know what day your Lord is coming. ⁴³But remember this: If the housemaster had known what time the thief was coming, he would have remained awake and not permitted his house to be broken open. ⁴⁴Therefore you yourselves keep ready, because at an hour when you do not expect Him, [l]the Son of Man is coming.

⁴⁵"Who then is the faithful and sensible servant whom the lord has put in charge of his household, to give to them their food at the proper time? ⁴⁶Fortunate is that servant who is found doing this when his lord comes. ⁴⁷Truly I tell you, he will put him in charge of all his possessions. ⁴⁸But if that servant is wicked and says to himself,[m] 'My lord delays [his coming]', ⁴⁹and begins to beat his fellow-servants, and eats and drinks with drunkards, ⁵⁰the lord of that servant will come on a day when he does not expect [him] and at an hour which he does not know. ⁵¹His lord will scourge him severely,[n] and assign him a place with the hypocrites, where there will be wailing and grinding of teeth."

---

[h]Or, it.

[i]The Greek word *genea*, rendered "generation," may refer to the people living at a given period, hence to Jesus' contemporaries. But *genea* can also mean "family," "nation," "race," or "kind."

[j]The Greek phrase, *oude ho huios, nor the Son*, is not found in some manuscripts.

[k]Cf. Gen. 6:9-13.

[l]Literally, *in which hour you think not.*

[m]Literally, *But if that wicked servant says in his heart.*

[n]Literally, *he will cut him in two.*

Chapter 25

''Then the kingdom of heaven will be like ten bridesmaids who each took a torch[a] and went forth to meet the bridegroom. [2]Five of them were foolish and five [were] sensible. [3]The foolish ones took their torches but did not take along [sufficient reserves of] oil. [4]But the sensible ones took containers of oil along with their torches. [5]While the bridegroom delayed [his coming], they all became drowsy,[b] and fell asleep.

[6]''In the middle of the night there was a cry, 'Look, the bridegroom! Come forth to meet him!' [7]Then all those bridesmaids arose and lit their torches. [8]The foolish ones said to the sensible ones, 'Give us some of your oil, for our torches are going out.' [9]But the sensible ones replied, 'No! There may not be enough for us and for you. You had better go to the dealers and buy for yourselves.' [10]While they were going away to buy, the bridegroom came. Those who were ready went in with him to the wedding festivities, and the door was shut. [11]Afterward, the other bridesmaids appeared. 'Lord, Lord,' they begged, 'open [the door] for us!' [12]But he replied, 'Truly I tell you, I do not know you!' [13]Therefore, keep alert, for you do not know the day or the hour.

[14]''It is like a man who, before going on a journey, summoned his personal servants and put his money in their charge. [15]To one he have five talents,[c] to another two, and to another one—to each in accordance with his own ability. Then he took his departure. [16]Immediately, the man who had received the five talents went and traded with them, and gained five more. [17]In like manner, he [who had received] the two [talents] gained two more. [18]But the man who had received the one [talent] went and dug a hole in the ground and buried his master's money.

[19]''After a long time, the master of those servants returned and settled accounts with them. [20]The man who had received the five talents came forward bringing five additional talents, and said, 'Master you entrusted to me five talents. Look, I have gained five more talents!' [21]His master said to him, 'Well done, good and trustworthy servant. You have been faithful over a few things; I will put you in charge of many things. Come and share your master's joy.' [22]The man [who had received] the two talents came forward and said, 'Master, you entrusted to me two talents. Look, I have gained two more talents.' [23]His master said to him, 'Well done, good and trustworthy servant. You have been faithful over a few things; I will place you in charge of many things. Come and share your master's joy.'

------

[a]Literally, *taking the torches of themselves*.

[b]Or, began to nod. Ingressive aorist.

[c]A talent was the equivalent of about one thousand dollars. See note on 18:25.

²⁴"Then the man who had received the one talent came forward and said, 'Master, I knew you are a strict man. You reap where you did not sow and you gather where you did not scatter. ²⁵And I was afraid and went and buried your money in the gound. Look, I am returning it to you.'^d ²⁶But his master answered him, 'You evil and lazy servant! So you knew that I reap where I have not sown and gather where I have not scattered? ²⁷Then you ought to have invested my money with the bankers, and at my return I could have received back my capital^e with interest. ²⁸Therefore, take away the talent from him and give it to the man who has the ten talents. ²⁹For to everyone who has, more will be given; and he will have abundance. But from the man who has nothing, even what he has will be taken from him. ³⁰And throw the useless servant out into the outside darkness, where there will be wailing and grinding of teeth!'

³¹"When the Son of Man comes in His glory, and all the angels with Him, then He will sit on the throne of His glory, ³²And in front of Him will be gathered all the nations. And He will separate the people one from another, just as a shepherd separates the sheep from the goats. ³³He will place the sheep on His right, but the goats on the left.

³⁴"Then the King will say to those on His right, 'Come, you who have the blessing of My Father, inherit the kingdom prepared for you since the foundation of the world. ³⁵For I was hungry, and you have Me food; I was thirsty, and you gave Me drink; I was a stranger, and you received Me with hospitality; ³⁶naked, and you clothed Me; I was ill, and you cared for Me; I was in prison, and you came to Me.'

³⁷"Then the righteous will answer Him, 'Lord, when did we see You hungry and feed You; or thirsty and give You drink? ³⁸When did we see You a stranger and receive You with hospitality; or naked and clothe You? ³⁹When did we see You ill or in prison and come to You?' ⁴⁰The King will answer them, 'Truly I tell you, in so far as you did it to one of these brothers of mine—[even] to the least [of them]—you did it to Me.'

⁴¹"Then He will say to those on the left, 'Depart from Me, you accursed ones, into the eternal fire prepared for the devil and his angels. ⁴²For I was hungry, and you gave Me nothing to eat; I was thirsty, and you gave Me nothing to drink; ⁴³I was a stranger, and you did not show Me hospitality; naked, and you did not clothe Me; ill and in prison, and you did not come to help Me'. ⁴⁴Then they too will answer, 'Lord, when did we see You hungry, or thirsty, or a stranger, or naked, or ill, or in prison, and did not minister to You?' ⁴⁵Then He will answer them, saying, 'Solemnly I tell you, in so far as you did not do it to one of the least of these, you did not do it to Me.' ⁴⁶And these will go away into everlasting punishment, but the righteous into everlasting life.''

---

^dLiterally, *here is what is yours.*
^eLiterally, *what was mine.*

Chapter 26

When Jesus had finished all these discourses, He said to his disciples, [2]"You know that after two days the Passover [festival] begins, and the Son of Man will be handed over[a] to be crucified."

[3]Then the chief priests and the elders of the people gathered in the palace of the high priest, whose name was Caiphas, [4]and made plans to seize Jesus by deception and have Him put to death. [5]But they said, "Not during the festival, for it might cause a riot among the people."

[6]While Jesus was at Bethany, in the house of Simon who had been a leper,[b] [7]there came to Him a woman bringing an alabaster jar of very expensive perfume, which she began to pour[c] on His head as He was reclining at table. [8]When the disciples saw this, they were indignant. "Why this waste?" they asked. [9]"This [perfume] could have been sold for a large sum and [the money] given to the poor." [10]But Jesus was aware [of their comments] and said to them, "Why are you troubling the woman? She has done an excellent thing for Me. [11]You will always have the poor with you, but you will not always have Me. [12]Actually, when she poured this perfume upon My body, she did it in preparation for My entombment. [13]Truly I tell you, wherever this gospel is proclaimed in the whole world, what this woman has done will be told, also, as a memorial of her."

[14]Then one of the Twelve—the man called Judas Iscariot—went to the chief priests [15]and said, "What are you willing to give me if I, myself, hand Jesus over to you?" They laid before him[d] thirty silver pieces.[e] [16]And from that time Judas began seeking[f] an opportunity to betray Him.

[17]On the first [day] of the [Festival of] Unleavened Bread, the disciples came to Jesus and asked, "Where do You want us to make preparations for You to eat the Passover meal?"[g] [18]He said, "Go into the city to a certain man and tell him, 'The Teacher says, "My time is near. At your house,[h] I am going to observe the Passover with My disciples." ' " [19]So the disciples did as Jesus directed them, and prepared the Passover supper.

[20]When evening came, Jesus was reclining at table with the twelve disciples. [21]As they were eating He said, "Truly I tell you, one of you is about to betray Me." [22]They were deeply grieved and started asking Him one after another,[i] "Surely it is not I, is it Lord?" [23]He answered, "One who has

---

[a]Futuristic present passive indicative.

[b]Literally, *Simon the leper*.

[c]Ingressive aorist.

[d]Or, they weighed out for him.

[e]Cf. Zech. 11:12. Thirty shekels of silver was the price of a slave. Exod. 21:32.

[f]Inchoative imperfect.

[g]Cf. Exod. 12:3ff.

[h]Literally, *With you*.

[i]Literally, *each one*.

dipped his hand with Mine in the dish, he it is who will betray Me. [24]The Son of Man is going away just as it stands written concerning Him, but woe to the person through whom the Son of Man is betrayed! It would have been better for that individual if he had never been born!" [25]Then Judas, the one who was betraying Him, spoke up and said, "Surely it is not I, is it, Rabbi?" Jesus replied to him, "You, yourself, have said it."[j]

[26]While they were eating, Jesus took bread, blessed and broke it, and gave it to the disciples. "Take this and eat it," He said, "it is My body." [27]Then he took a cup, and offered thanks, and He gave it to them. "All of you drink from it," He said, [28]"for this is My blood—the covenant [blood][k]—to be poured out[l] in behalf of many for the forgiveness of sins. [29]But I tell you, from now on, I will not again drink from this fruit of the vine until that day when I drink it new with you in My Father's kingdom."

[30]After they had sung a hymn,[m] they went out to the Mount of Olives. [31]Jesus then told them, "Tonight, all of you will be caused to stumble on account of[n] Me. For it stands written, 'I will strike the shepherd and the sheep of the flock will be scattered.'[o] [32]But after I have risen, I will go before you into Galilee."

[33]Peter responded to Him, "Even if all others are caused to stumble on account[n] of You, I, myself, will never at any time be caused to stumble."

[34]Jesus said to him, "Solemnly I tell you, during this night, before the rooster crows, you are going to disown Me three times." [35]Peter declared to Him, "Even if I must die with You, I certainly will not by any means[p] disown You!" And all the disciples expressed the same confidence.[q]

[36]Then Jesus went with the disciples to a place called Gethsemane, and said to them, "Sit here, while I go over there and pray." [37]He took with Him Peter and the two sons of Zebedee. And deep sorrow came over Him, and He was greatly distressed. [38]Then He said to them, "My soul is overwhelmed with grief, even to the point of death. Stay here and keep watching with Me." [39]Then going a little farther, He fell on His face and prayed.[r] "My Father," he said, "if it is possible, let this cup pass away from Me. Nevertheless, let Thy will be done, not Mine."

---

[j]The Greek idiom expresses an affirmative answer.

[k]That is, the blood which ratifies the new covenant. Cf. Heb. 7:22; 9:11ff; 10:19, 29; 12:24; 13:20.

[l]Greek prophetic present participle.

[m]The Passover meal was usually concluded by singing from the Hallel (the praise Psalms), probably from the Hallel proper (Pss. 113-118).

[n]Causal use of Greek preposition, *en*.

[o]Cf. Zech. 13:7.

[p]A strong assertion, indicated by the Greek double negative, *ou me*.

[q]Literally, *spoke likewise*.

[r]Cf. Heb. 5:7.

[40]When He came back to the disciples He found them sleeping, and He said to Peter, "So you men were not able to watch with Me for one hour? [41]Remain alert and keep praying, so that you may not fail when you are tested.[s] The spirit indeed is eager, but the bodily nature is weak."

[42]Again, a second time, He withdrew and prayed. "My Father," He said, "if it is not possible for this [cup] to depart [from Me] unless I drink it, let Thy will be done." [43]He came again and found them sleeping, for their eyes had become heavy. [44]Again, He left them and withdrew and prayed a third [time], repeating the same words. [45]Then He came to the disciples and said to them, "Are you still sleeping and taking your rest?[t] Wake! The hour has arrived when the Son of Man is being betrayed into the hands of evil men. [46]Get up! Let us go! See, he who betrays me is close at hand!"

[47]Even while He was speaking, Judas, one of the Twelve, came, accompanied by a large crowd. They were sent by the chief priests and elders of the people, [and were armed] with swords and clubs. [48]Now, Jesus' betrayer had arranged to give them a signal. He had said, "The man whom I greet with a kiss, He is the one. Seize Him." [49]So at once he went to Jesus and said, "Greetings, Rabbi!" and kissed Him fervently. [50]Jesus said to him, "Fellow, what a thing for you to do!"[u] Then they came forward, and arrested Jesus, and held Him.

[51]Quickly, one of the men who was with Jesus reached for his sword, drew it, and struck at the high priest's servant, and cut off his ear. [52]"Put your sword back in its place," Jesus told him, "for all who take up the sword will perish by means of the sword. [53]Do you suppose that I cannot call upon My Father who would at once place at my disposal more than twelve legions of angels? [54]But then how could the Scriptures, [which say] it must happen this way, be fulfilled?"

[55]At that moment Jesus said to the crowds, "Did you come forth with swords and clubs to take Me as you would a robber? Day after day I sat in the Temple precincts teaching, yet you never arrested Me. [56]But all this has taken place in order that the writings of the prophets might be fulfilled." Then all the disciples deserted Him and fled.

[57]The officers who had arrested Jesus led Him away to Caiaphas the high priest, at whose residence[v] the Law-teachers and the elders had assembled. [58]Now Peter followed Him at a distance until [he reached] the courtyard of the high priest, and he went inside and sat down with the attendants to see the outcome.

---

[s]Or, may not enter into temptation.

[t]The context indicates that this statement is a question, although here it is not thus indicated by Nestle. But see Mark 14:37 and Luke 22:46.

[u]Literally, *you are here for this!*

[v]Literally, *where*.

59Meanwhile, the chief priests and the entire Sanhedrin were seeking false testimony against Jesus, so that they could bring about His death. 60But they did not find [any evidence against Him] although many false witnesses came forward. 61Finally, two came forward [who] stated, "This Man said, 'I am able to destroy God's Sanctuary, and to rebuild it in three days.' "

62Then the high priest stood up and asked Jesus, "Have You no answer? What [about the charge] these men are bringing against You?" 63But Jesus remained silent. Then the high priest said to Him, "I charge You under oath before the living God, to tell us whether You are the Messiah, the Son of God!" 64Jesus replied, "You, yourself, have said it.w Furthermore I tell you, soon you will see the Son of Man sitting at the right hand of the Almighty and coming on the clouds of heaven."

65At that the high priest tore his outer robes and said, "He has uttered blasphemy! What further need have we of witnesses? Now you have heard His blasphemy. 66What is your verdict?" And they answered, "He deserves death!" 67Then they spit in His face and struck Him with their fists. Others slapped Him with their open hands, 68and said, "Demonstrate your prophetic power, You Messiah! [Tell us], who struck You?"

69While all this was going on Peter was outside [the high priest's judgment hall] sitting in the courtyard. And a certain servant girlx came over to him. "You also were with Jesus the Galilean!" she said. 70But Peter denied it in front of them all. "I do not know what you are talking about," he declared. 71Then as he went over toward the gateway, another [servant-girl] saw him and she said to the people who were there, "This fellow was with Jesus the Nazarene!" 72And again he denied it, [asserting] with an oath, "I do not know the man!"

73A little later the bystanders came up and said to Peter, "You certainly are [one] of them, for even your accent gives you away."y 74Then he began to cursez and to declare by solemn oath, "I do not know the man!" At that moment a rooster began crowing.a 75Then Peter remembered Jesus' prediction, "Before the rooster crows, you will disown Me three times."b And he went outside, and wept bitterly.

---

wSame expression as in v. 25, where see note.
xCf. John 18:16-17.
yPeter, who was from Galilee, had a different accent than the Judeans.
zThat is, to wish himself accursed if what he says is not the truth. Cf. 1 Kings. 19:2.
aIngressive aorist.
bCf. Matt. 26:34.

Chapter 27

When early morning came, all the chief priests and the elders of the people took action against Jesus to bring about His death. ²So they bound Him, then led [Him] away and handed [Him] over to Pilate, the governor.ᵃ

³When Judas, who had betrayed Him, saw that Jesus was condemned [to die], he was seized with remorseᵇ [for what he had done]. So he returned the thirty silver pieces to the chief priests and elders. ⁴"I have sinned by betraying an innocent man,"ᶜ he said. But they replied, "What is it to us? That is your responsibility!"ᵈ ⁵Then Judas hurled down the silver pieces toward the Sanctuary, and went out and hanged himself.

⁶The chief priests picked up the silver pieces and said, "It is not lawful to put this money into the [Temple] treasury, since it is [the] price of blood." ⁷So after discussing the matter, they used the money to buy the potter's field as a burial place for strangers. ⁸This is why that piece of ground is called the "Field of Blood"ᵉ until the present day. ⁹Then was fulfilled the saying [spoken] through the prophet Jeremiah,ᶠ "And they took the thirty silver pieces, the price of him who had been valued, on whom the sons of Israel had set a price, ¹⁰and used them to buy the potter's field, just as the Lord directed me."

¹¹Then Jesus was brought before the governor, and the governor questioned Him. "Are you really the King of the Jews?"ᵍ Jesus replied, "You are correct."ʰ ¹²However, while charges were being brought against Him by the

---

ᵃThe Jewish council condemned Jesus to die, but only the representative of imperial Rome could have a man put to death. So the Sanhedrin turned Jesus over to the governor. Pilate's official place of residence was at Caesarea. But the procurator thought it expedient to be in Jerusalem during feast times to prevent the strong nationalistic sentiments of the Jews from breaking out in riots.

ᵇJudas experienced regret (indicated by the aorist passive participle of *metamelomai*, "to be sorry afterward") because of the consequences of his deed; but he did not repent (metanoeo) of his sin. The latter verb means *to think differently* and involves a change of heart and life. Cf. Matt. 3:2, 8 (cognate noun); 4:17; 11:20, 21; 12:41; Acts 2:38; 3:19, 17:30.

ᶜLiterally, innocent blood. Cf. Deut. 27:25.

ᵈLiterally, *You yourself will see [to that]*.

ᵉCf. Acts 1:19.

ᶠMatthew here seems to group together the thought of passages derived from both Jeremiah and Zechariah, and to attribute the source to Jeremiah, the best known of the two prophets. Cf. Jer. 32:7-9; Zech. 11:12-13.

ᵍCf. Luke 23:2.

ʰLiterally, *You yourself are saying it*. Thus an affirmative answer is expressed. Here the present tense is used, as in Mark 15:2; Luke 23:3; John 18:37. In Matt. 26:25, 64, we find the same idiom with the aorist, *You yourself have said so*. *See note on Matt. 26:25*.

chief priests and elders Jesus made no reply. [13]Pilate said to Him, "Do You not hear how many accusations they are making against You?" [14]But Jesus gave him no answer—not even one word—so that the governor was very much astonished.

[15]Now at the [Passover] festival season it was customary for the governor to liberate a prisoner—one whom they chose. [16]At that time they were holding a notorious prisoner called Barabbas. [17]So when [the crowd] had assembled, Pilate asked them, "Whom do you want me to release for you—Barabbas, or Jesus who is called Christ?" [18]For he knew that because of their envy the leaders[i] had delivered Jesus over [to be sentenced to death].

[19]While he was sitting on the judgment seat his wife sent him a message, saying, "Have nothing to do with that innocent man, for I have been greatly disturbed this very day because of a dream I had about Him." [20]However, the chief priests and the elders persuaded the crowds to ask for the [release of] Barabbas and for the execution of Jesus. [21]The governor [again] asked them, "Which of the two do you want me to release for you?" They replied, "Barabbas!" [22]Pilate said to them, "Then what shall I do with Jesus, who is called Christ?" They all said, "Let Him be crucified!"[j] [23]Pilate said, "Why? What wrong has He done?" But all the more they kept on crying out, "Let Him be crucified!"

[24]When Pilate saw that he was gaining nothing, but that[k] riot was imminent, he took water and washed his hands[l] in front of the crowd, and said, "I am innocent of the blood of this man. It is your responsibility." [25]And all the people answered, "Let His blood be on us and on our children!" [26]Then Pilate released Barabbas to them, but he had Jesus scourged and handed Him over to be crucified.

[27]Then the governor's soldiers took Jesus into the Praetorium[m] and gathered the entire detachment[n] [of troops] around Him. [28]They stripped Him and put a scarlet cloak around Him. [29]Out of thorns they plaited a crown and placed it on His head. They put a cane in His right hand, and knelt in front of Him in mockery, saying, "Hail, king of the Jews!" [30]Then they spit upon Him, and they took the cane and kept striking Him on the head. [31]When they finished ridiculing Him, they removed from Him the cloak [of mockery] and put on Him His [own] garments, and led Him away to crucify Him.

[32]On their way out [of the city] they found a certain Cyrenian named Simon, whom they compelled to carry Jesus' cross. [33]And when they reached

---

[i]Literally, *they*.

[j]Crucifixion was the Roman method of execution.

[k]Cf. Ps. 26:6; 73:13.

[l]Perhaps the Governor's palace, or, in the present context, the soldiers' quarters.

[m]Greek, *speiran*, "cohort" or "battalion," which usually numbered between 500 and 600 men.

[n]*Golgatha* is an Aramaic term. Our word *Calvary* is from the Latin equivalent.

a place called Golgotha,[o] which means "Place of a Skull," [34]they offered Him some wine mixed with a bitter drug,[p] which He tasted but refused to drink.

[35]After they had crucified Him, they divided His garments among themselves by casting lots.[q] [36]Then they sat down and kept guard over Him there. [37]Above His head they placed a written statement of the accusation against Him: "THIS IS JESUS, THE KING OF THE JEWS."

[38]At the same time two bandits were crucified along with Him, one on His right, and one on His left.[r] [39]The people who passed by kept insulting Him, shaking their heads [40]as they said, "You who could destroy the Sanctuary and rebuild it within three days, save Yourself! If You are God's Son, then come down from the cross!" [41]In like manner the chief priests, along with the Law-teachers and elders, kept mocking Him and saying, [42]"He saved others, but He is not able to save Himself! He is the king of Israel, Let Him now come down from the cross and we will believe on Him! [43]He has trusted in God! Let God[s] deliver Him now if He cares for Him, for He said, 'I am God's Son.' " [44]Even the bandits also, who had been crucified with Him, ridiculed Him in the same way.

[45]Now from the sixth hour until the ninth hour[t] there was darkness over all the land. [46]And about the ninth hour Jesus cried out with a loud voice, saying, "Elei, Elei,[u] lema sabachthanei?", which means, "My God, My God, why hast Thou forsaken Me?"

[47]Some of the bystanders who heard, said, "This man is calling for Elijah." [48]And immediately one of them ran and took a sponge which he soaked with sour wine,[v] attached it to a cane and offered it to Him to drink. [49]But the rest said, "Wait, Let us see if Elijah comes to deliver Him!"

[50]Then Jesus gave another loud outcry and yielded up His spirit. [51]And suddenly, the curtain[w] of the Sanctuary was torn in two from top to bottom.[x] The earth was shaken, and the huge rocks[y] were split. [52]The tombs were opened, and the bodies of many holy people[z] who had died were raised. [53]They came out of the graves and, after His rising, went into the holy city and appeared to many.

---

[o]A compound which would have some stupefying effect. Cf. Psa. 69:21.

[p]Cf. Ps. 22:18.

[q]Cf. Isa. 53:12.

[r]Literally, *Him*.

[s]That is, from noon until three o'clock.

[t]Cf. Ps. 22:1. Matthew gives *Elei, Elei* (Hebrew). In Mark 15:34, it is *Eloi, Eloi* (Aramaic). Both Matthew and Mark have *lama sabachthanei* (Aramaic), "Why hast Thou forsaken Me?"

[u]Vinegar, or cheap wine, was often mixed with bitter herbs and given to condemned criminals in order to dull their senses and lessen their agony.

[v]The inner veil which hung between the Holy Place and the Holy of Holies. Cf. Exod. 26:31-33; Heb. 9:3, 7-8; 10:19-20.

[w]Literally, *from above to below*.

[x]Greek, plural of *petra*. See note on 16:18.

[y]Apparently saints who had been buried in the vicinity of Calvary.

[z]Literally, *and those with him*.

[54]When the centurion and his men[a] [who were] keeping watch over Jesus saw the earthquake and the [other] things happening, they were seized with terror and exclaimed, "Surely this Man was God's Son!"

[55]Now many women were there, observing from a distance. They had followed Jesus from Galilee [and had been] in the habit of ministering[b] to His needs. [56]Among them were Mary of Magdala, and Mary the mother of James and Joses, and the mother of Zebedee's sons.

[57]When evening approached, there came a wealthy man from Arimathaea. His name was Joseph[c] and he, himself, had also become a disciple of Jesus. [58]This man went to Pilate and made a request for the body of Jesus. Then Pilate gave orders [that it] be given [to him]. [59]So Joseph took the body, wrapped it in clean linen cloth, [60]and placed it in his own new tomb which he had cut out of the cliff-side.[d] Then he rolled a large stone against the entrance of the tomb, and went away. [61]But Mary of Magdala and the other Mary were there, sitting across from the grave.

[62]The next day, the one after the Day of Preparation,[e] the chief priests and the Pharisees went together to Pilate, [63]and said, "Sir, we recall that while that impostor was yet alive He said, 'After three days I will rise again.' [64]So will you give orders that the grave be guarded securely until the third day, to prevent His disciples from coming and stealing the body and telling the people, 'He was raised from the dead,' and the last deception would be worse than the first." [65]Pilate said to them, "Take a [military] guard. Go, make [the tomb] as secure as you know how." [66]So they went and made the tomb secure, attaching a seal to the stone and setting a guard [of Roman soldiers to watch it].

Chapter 28

But after the Sabbath, at the coming of dawn on the first day of the week,[a] Mary Magdalene and the other Mary came to take a look at the bomb. [2]To their amazement,[b] a violent earthquake occurred, for an angel of the Lord descended from heaven, came to the stone and rolled it back and was sitting upon it. [3]His appearance was like lightning, and his garment was as white as snow. [4]The guards were so fearful of him that they trembled and became like dead men.

---

[a]Greek nominative plural feminine present participle.
[b]Cf. Mark 15:43; Luke 23:50; John 19:38.
[c]Greek, *petra*.
[d]The Day of Preparation (Friday) was the day before the Sabbath (Saturday).

[a]Literally, *on the first* [*day*] *with reference to the Sabbath. That is, the first day after the Sabbath*.
[b]Or, Suddenly.

[5]The angel said to the women, "You[c] stop being afraid! Indeed, I know that you are looking for Jesus who was crucified. [6]He is not here, for He was raised just as He said. Come, see the place where He was lying. [7]Then go quickly and say to His disciples, 'He has been raised from the dead, and now He is going on ahead of you into Galilee; there you will see Him.' This is my message for you."[d]

[8]With awe and great joy the women[e]left the tomb quickly and ran to tell His disciples. [9]As they went,[f] Jesus met them and said, "Greetings!"[g] And the women drew near and took hold of His feet and worshipped Him. [10]Then Jesus said to them, "Stop being afraid! Go tell My brothers to go into Galilee.[h] There they will see Me."

[11]While they were on their way, behold, some of the guards came into the city and reported to the chief priests all that had happened. [12]After meeting with the elders and discussing the matter, they gave a large bribe[i] to the soldiers, [13]and told them, "You are to say, 'His disciples came by night and stole Him while we were asleep.' [14]And if the governor hears of this, we will convince [him] and make sure you have nothing to worry about. [15]So the guards[j] took the money and did as they were instructed. And that story has been spread by the Jews until this very day.

[16]The eleven disciples went to Galilee, to the mountain where Jesus had directed them. [17]And when they saw Him, they worshipped [Him], although some hesitated to believe. [18]Then Jesus came nearer and spoke to them. "All authority in heaven and on earth has been given to Me." [19]"Therefore, go make disciples of all the nations, baptizing them into the name[k] of the Father and of the Son and of the Holy Spirit, [20]teaching them to observe all things I have commanded you. And remember, I Myself am with you all the days until the consummation of the age."

---

[c]Emphatic by use of personal pronoun *humeis*, in addition to subject expressed in the verb.

[d]Literally, *Remember, I have told you*.

[e]Indicated by the Greek nominative plural aorist feminine participle.

[f]Or, Suddenly.

[g]The Greek, *Chairete*, a term of salutation, may also be translated by such English expressions as *"Rejoice!"* *"Hello!"* or *"Good morning!"*

[h]Cf. 26:32.

[i]Literally, *a considerable amount of silver*.

[j]Literally, *they*.

[k]*Into the name* denotes possession or ownership. Hence, Christian baptism symbolizes dedication of the believer's life to the service of God.

Mark

Chapter 1

The beginning of the good news[a] about Jesus Christ the Son of God. [2]Just as it stands written in Isaiah the prophet,[b] "Behold, I send My messenger before Thy face; he will prepare Thy way. [3]The voice of one calling in the wilderness, 'Prepare the way of the Lord. Make straight His paths.' " [4]John the Baptizer appeared in the wilderness, proclaiming a baptism characterized by repentence[c] based upon the forgiveness of sins. [5]The entire Judean populace and all the inhabitants of Jerusalem were going out to him, and were being baptized by him in the Jordan River, making full confession[d] of their sins.

[6]John wore clothing made of camel's hair, and he had a leather belt around his waist. His food was locusts[e] and wild honey. [7]In his proclamation, he said, "The One stronger than I is coming after me. I am not worthy to bend down and untie His sandal straps. [8]I indeed have baptized you with water, but He Himself will baptize you with the Holy Spirit."

[9]In those days[f] Jesus came from Nazareth of Galilee, and was baptized by John in the Jordan. [10]Instantly, as Jesus was coming up out of the water, He

---

[a]The Greek term *euangelion,* commonly rendered *gospel* (from the Anglo-Saxon *godspell,* meaning "good story" or "glad tidings" is used in the New Testament of the good news of salvation through Jesus Christ.

[b]Some manuscripts read, *in the prophets.* Cf. Isa. 40:3; Mal. 3:1.

[c]Descriptive genitive.

[d]Or, making public confession. Literally, "confessing out."

[e]Cf. Lev. 11:21-22.

[f]Cf. Luke 3:23.

saw the sky being rent and the Spirit, like a dove, coming down upon Him. [11]And out of heaven came a voice, "Thou art My Son, the Beloved; in Thee I am well pleased."[g]

[12]And immediately, the Spirit drove Him forth into the wilderness. [13]And He remained in the desolate region forty days, while being tempted by Satan. He was among the wild beasts, but the angels ministered to Him.

[14]Now after John had been put in prison, Jesus came into Galilee preaching the good news from God.[h] [15]"The time is fulfilled," He said, "and the kingdom of God has drawn near. Repent,[i] and believe in the good news."

[16]As Jesus went walking along by the Lake of Galilee, He saw Simon, and Andrew the brother of Simon[j] throwing their circular casting-net into the lake, for they were fishermen. [17]Jesus said to them, "Come after Me, and I will make you to become fishers of men." [18]And right then, they left the nets and followed Him.

[19]He went on a little farther, and saw James the son of Zebedee, and John his brother. They too, were in their boat, repairing the nets.[k] [20]At once Jesus called them, and they left their father Zebedee in the boat with the hired men and went forth after Him.

[21]They went into Capernaum, and immediately, on the Sabbath day He entered the synagogue and began to teach.[l] [22]The people were amazed at His doctrine, for He was teaching them as one having authority[m] and not like the Law-experts.

[23]Now at that time, there was in their synagogue a man with an unclean spirit, who cried out, [24]"Why are You interfering with us,[n] Jesus You Nazarene? Have You come to destroy us? I know You, who You are—the Holy One of God!" [25]But Jesus rebuked him: "Be silent,[o] and come out of him!" [26]The unclean spirit, after throwing the man into a convulsion and shrieking loudly, came out of him. [27]The people were all so amazed that they kept asking one another, "What is this? A new kind of teaching! With authority He commands even the unclean spirits, and they obey Him!" [28]And reports about Him spread quickly everywhere, into the whole surrounding region of Galilee.

---

[g]Timeless aorist. See same idiom in Matt. 3:17; Luke 3:22.

[h]Subjective genitive.

[i]Present imperative of *metanoeo*, "to think differently." This verb indicates a change of mind and direction. Cf. 6:12; Matt. 11:20, 21; 12:41.

[j]Cf. John 1:40-42.

[k]Or, getting the nets ready [for the next cast]. Cf. Matt. 4:21.

[l]Inchoative imperfect.

[m]The authority *(exousia)* inherent in His own person and character.

[n]Or, What have we in common with You?

[o]Literally, "Be muzzled."

[29]Immediately, they left the synagogue and, accompanied by James and John, entered the house of Simon and Andrew. [30]Now, Simon's mother-in-law was lying ill with a fever, and at once, they told Jesus about her. [31]He went to her, took hold of her hand, and raised her up. The fever left her, and she began to serve[p] them.

[32]When evening came, after the sun had set,[q] they began bringing to Him all who were ill,[r] and those who were demon-possessed. [33]The entire city was gathered together at the door [of Peter's house].[s] [34]And Jesus healed many who were ill[r] with various diseases, and He drove out many demons. But He would not permit the demons to speak, because they knew who He was.

[35]Early in the morning, while it was still dark,[t] Jesus rose up and left the house[u] and departed to a secluded place, and there He was praying. [36]And Simon and his companions tracked Him down. [37]When they found Him, they told Him, "Everyone is looking for You!" [38]But Jesus replied, "Let us go elsewhere, into the nearby country-towns, in order that I may preach in them also,[v] for that is why I came." [39]So He went through all Galilee, preaching in their synagogues and driving out the demons.

[40]A leper came to Jesus, fell on his knees, and begged Him, saying, "If You are willing, You can make me clean." [41]Moved with deep compassion, Jesus extended His hand, and touched him. "I am willing," He said to him, "Be cleansed!" [42]Instantly, the leprosy went away from the man, and he was cured. [43]Then Jesus hurried him away with the stern admonition, [44]"Make sure that you say nothing [about this] to anyone; but go, show yourself to the priest [that he may examine you and pronounce you clean]. Then offer, concerning your cleansing, the things Moses commanded for the certification of a cure."[w] [45]But the man went out and began to talk about the incident publicly,[x] and to spread the word far and wide, so that Jesus could no longer enter a town openly, but remained outside in desolate places. Yet people kept coming to Him from every direction.

---

[p]Inchoative imperfect.

[q]After the Sabbath ended at sunset, travel restrictions did not apply, so the people started carrying their sick to Jesus.

[r]Literally, "having it bad."

[s]Cf. 1:29.

[t]Literally, "very much in the night."

[u]Literally, "and went out."

[v]Literally, "there."

[w]Literally, "for a witness to them." Cf. Lev. 14:2-32.

[x]Literally, "to proclaim many things."

Chapter 2

Some days later, Jesus returned to Capernaum, and it was reported that He was at home.[a] [2]And many people were gathered together so that there was no longer any room, not even in front of the door. And He kept speaking the word to them.

[3]Then some came, bringing to Him a paralytic, carried by four men. [4]But not being able to bring [the paralytic] to Jesus on account of the crowd, they uncovered the roof [over the place] where He was; and when they had dug an opening through it, they lowered the mat on which the paralyzed man was lying.

[5]When Jesus saw their faith, He said to the paralytic, "Son, your sins are forgiven." [6]There were some Law-experts sitting there, and they questioned in their hearts, [7]"Why does this man talk like that? He blasphemes! Who can forgive sins but God alone?"

[8]Immediately Jesus, in His spirit,[b] knew what they were thinking. "Why are you questioning these things in your hearts?" He asked them. [9]"Which is easier, to say to the paralytic, 'Your sins are forgiven,' or to say, 'Arise and take up your mat and walk'? [10]But in order that you may be convinced that the Son of Man has authority upon the earth to forgive sins"—He said to the paralyzed man, [11]"I say to you, Arise, take up your mat, and go home." [12]The man arose, took up his mat at once, and went out in view of everyone, so that they were all astonished. The gave praise to God, and exclaimed, "We have never seen anything like this!"

[13]Again, Jesus went out beside the lake and all the crowd kept coming to Him, and He continued teaching them. [14]As He was going along, He saw Levi,[c] the son of Alpheus, sitting at the tax-office. "Follow Me," He said to him. And he arose and followed Him.

[15]Later[d] Jesus was at dinner at Levi's house,[e] and a large number of tax collectors and outcasts were reclining at table with Jesus and His disciples, for there were many of these, and they were beginning to follow[f] Him. [16]But when the Law-experts of the Pharisees saw that He was eating in company with the outcasts and tax-collectors, they asked His disciples, "Why does He eat with tax-collectors and outcasts?" [17]Jesus heard [their remark], and replied, "People who are strong do not need a physician, but those who are ill.[g] I did not come to call righteous persons, but sinners."

---

[a]Literally, "in the house." Probably the home of Peter. Cf. 1:29.
[b]Or, by His Spirit.
[c]Levi was also known as Matthew. See note on Matt. 9:10.
[d]Literally, "And it came to pass."
[e]Literally, "in his house."
[f]Inchoative imperfect.
[g]Literally, "those having it bad."

[18]Now it was customary[n] for the disciples of John [the Baptizer] and the Pharisees to fast. Some people came and asked Jesus, "Why do John's disciples and the disciples of the Pharisees practice fasting, but Your disciples do not practice fasting?"

[19]Jesus answered, "The wedding guests cannot fast while the bridegroom is with them, can they? As long as they have the bridegroom with them, they are not able to fast. [20]But the time will come when the bridegroom will be taken from them, and then, in that day, they will fast. [21]No one sews a patch of new cloth[i] on an old garment. If he does, the patch pulls away from it—the new from the old—and the tear becomes worse. [22]Neither does anyone pour new wine into old wineskins. If he does, the wine will burst the containers, and both the wine and the wineskins are lost. But new wine [is poured] into new wineskins."

[23]One Sabbath day Jesus was going through the grain fields. As His disciples walked along, they began to pluck the heads of grain.[j] [24]The Pharisees said to Him, "Look, why are they doing that which is not lawful on the Sabbath?"[k] [25]He replied, "Have you never read what David did when he was in need, and he and his followers were hungry? [26]How he went into the house of God during the time of Abiathar[l] the high priest, and took for food the loaves of the presentation,[m] which only the priests were permitted to eat, and he even shared them with the men who were with him?" [27]And Jesus went on to say to them, "The Sabbath came about for the benefit of man, and not man for the benefit of the Sabbath. [28]So the Son of Man is Lord even of the Sabbath."

Chapter 3

Again Jesus went into a synagogue. And there was a man present whose hand was withered. [2]And they kept watching Jesus closely to see if He would heal the man on the Sabbath, so that they might make an accusation against Him. [3]Jesus said to the man with the withered hand, "Stand up and come forward."[a] [4]Then He asked them, "Is it lawful on the Sabbath to do good or to do harm, to save life or to kill?" But they remained silent. [5]Having looked

---

[h]Indicated by the Greek periphrastic imperfect.

[i]Or, unshrunken cloth.

[j]Cf. Deut. 23:25.

[k]Cf. Exod. 34:21.

[l]Or, Abiathar [who later became] the high priest. Cf. 1 Sam. 21:1-6; 22:20; 23:6.

[m]Cf. Exod. 25:30; Lev. 24:5-9, Heb. 9:2.

[a]Literally, "Stand up in the midst."

around at them with anger, being grieved because of[b] their hardness of heart, He said to the man, "Stretch out your hand!" He stretched it out, and his hand was completely restored. [6]At once the Pharisees went out and began plotting[c] with the Herodians against Him to destroy Him.

[7]But Jesus, in company with His disciples, withdrew to the lake-side, and throngs of people from Galilee followed. [8]Also, from Judaea, and from Jerusalem, and from Idumea, and beyond the Jordan, and around Tyre and Sidon, a great multitude, because they kept hearing[d] about the things He was doing, came to Him. [9]So He told His disciples to keep a small boat in constant readiness for Him, on account of the crowd, to prevent them from crushing Him. [10]For He healed so many that all who were tormented by diseases kept pressing upon Him in order to touch Him.[11]And whenever the unclean spirits saw Him, they fell down before Him, crying out, "You[e] are the Son of God!" [12]But He kept warning them sternly not to make Him known.

[13]Jesus went up on the mountain,[f] and summoned the men whom He especially wanted, and they came to Him. [14]He appointed twelve to be with Him continually, so that He might send them forth to preach [15]and give them authority to drive out demons. [16]He designated these[g] twelve: Simon, to whom He gave the additional name, Peter; [17]and James, the son of Zebedee and John, the brother of James—to them He gave the additional name Boanerges, that is, Sons of Thunder; [18]and Andrew and Philip and Bartholomew and Matthew and Thomas and James the son of Alphaeus, and Thaddeus and Simon the Cananaean[h] [19]and Judas Iscariot,[i] the man who betrayed Him.

[20]Then Jesus returned home. And again such a large crowd gathered that [Jesus and His disciples] did not even get a chance to eat. [21]When His relatives heard [of what was happening] they went to take charge of Him; for they said,[j] "He is out of His mind." [22]But the Law-experts who came down from Jerusalem said, "He is possessed by Beelzebul,"[k] and, "He drives out demons because He is allied with the ruler of the demons." [23]So Jesus called them to Him and answered them in parables, "How can Satan drive out Satan?" He asked. [24]"If a kingdom is divided against itself, that kingdom cannot stand. [25]And if a household is divided against itself, that household will not be able to endure. [26]So if Satan has revolted against himself and been divided, he cannot survive, but his defeat is certain. [27]No one is able to enter a strong man's house and devastate his furnishings, unless he first binds the strong man; and then he will plunder his house.

---

[b]Causal use of Greek preposition, *epi*.

[c]Inchoative imperfect.

[d]Causal present participle.

[e]Emphatic pronoun.

[f]Cf. Luke 6:12.

[g]Anaphoric use of the Greek article. Cf. vs. 14, for previous reference to the Twelve.

[h]Or, Simon the Zealot. Cf. Acts 1:13; Luke 6:15.

[i]See note on Matt. 10:4.

[j]Or, for people were saying.

[k]See note on Matt. 10:25.

[28]"Solemnly I tell you, that all the sinful acts the sons of men [commit] and all the blasphemies they speak are pardonable, with one exception—[29]whoever blasphemes against the Holy Spirit will never be forgiven, but is held fast by an eternal sin."[1] [30][He made this statement] because they were saying, "He has an unclean spirit."

[31]Then Jesus' mother and His brothers arrived.[m] They stood outside, and sent [someone] to call Him. [32]A crowd was sitting around Jesus and they told Him, "Listen, Your mother and Your brothers and Your sisters[n] are outside, asking for You." [3]He answered, "Who are My mother and My brothers?" [34]Then He looked around at those sitting in a circle about Him, and said, "Look!" [These are] My mother and My brothers! [35]Whoever does the will of God, that person is My brother and sister and mother."

Chapter 4

Again Jesus began to teach by the lake-side. And a very large crowd gathered about Him, so He stepped into a boat and sat [in it] on the lake while all the people were along the shore at the water's edge.[a] [2]He taught them many things by means of parables, and in His doctrine said to them, [3]"Listen! Behold, a sower went out to sow. [4]And as he scattered the seed, some fell by the side of the path, and the birds came and devoured it. [5]Some fell on rocky ground where it did not have much soil; immediately it sprang up because it had no depth of earth. [6]But when the sun rose, it [the plant] was scorched; and because it had not root it withered. [7]Other seed fell among thorn-bushes, and the thorns came forth and choked it, so it produced no fruit.[8]But some seed fell into excellent soil and yielded a harvest that came up and increased and produced up to thirty and up to sixty and even to a hundred [times as much as was planted]." [9]And Jesus went on to say "Who has ears to hear, let him listen."

[10]When Jesus was alone, those around Him, along with the Twelve, began to ask Him about the parables. [11]He told them, "To you has been disclosed the mystery[b] of God's kingdom, but to outsiders everything is expressed in parables, [12]in order that they may look and look, but not see, and hear and hear, but not understand, lest they turn and be forgiven."[c]

---

[1]Or, is guilty of an eternal sin.

[m]Cf. vs. 21.

[n]Jesus' brothers and sisters (cf. Mark 6:3; Matt. 13:55-56) may have been children of Joseph by a previous marriage, or children of Mary born after Jesus.

[a]Literally, "facing the lake."

[b]Secret, or hidden truth.

[c]Cf. Isa. 6:9-10.

¹³And He said to them, "Do you not understand this parable? Then how can you grasp the meaning of all the parables? ¹⁴The sower sows the word. ¹⁵The seed by the side of the path refers to persons[d] in whom the word is sown, but when they hear it, immediately Satan comes, and takes away the word which has been sown in them. ¹⁶The seed sown upon the rocky ground refers to persons who, as soon as they hear the word, receive it with joy. ¹⁷But it takes no root in them[e]—they are short-lived. When, on account of the word, trouble or persecution comes they quickly fall away.[f] ¹⁸The seed sown among the thorns refers to persons who hear the word, ¹⁹but the anxieties of the present age, the deceitfulness of wealth, and the eager pursuit of other things, enter in and choke the word, so that it produces no fruit. ²⁰But the seed sown upon the excellent soil refers to those who hear the word, and welcome it, and bear fruit up to thirty, and up to sixty, and even to a hundred [times as much as was planted]."

²¹Also He said to them, "A lamp is not brought in to be placed under a grain-measure or under a bed, is it? It is to be set upon the lampstand, is it not? ²²Actually, nothing is hidden except to be manifested, and nothing is concealed but to be brought into the open. ²³If anyone has ears to hear, let him listen."

²⁴He went on to say to them, "Consider carefully what you hear. With what measure you measure it will be measured to you, and more will be added to you. ²⁵For the man who has, to him more will be given; and he who has not, even what he has will be taken from him."

²⁶And He said, "The kingdom of God is like a man who scatters seed upon the ground; ²⁷and he sleeps by night and rises by day, while the seed sprouts and grows, he, himself, knows not how. ²⁸The land, spontaneously of itself, produces crops, first the stalk, then the ear, then the full grain in the ear. ²⁹And whenever the crop is ready immediately the sickle is put in, for the harvest-time has come."

³⁰He went on to ask, "To what may we compare the kingdom of God, or by what figure may we illustrate it? ³¹It is like a grain of mustard seed, which, when sown in the ground, is smaller than any seed on the earth. ³²Yet, when it is planted it grows up and becomes the largest of all the garden-herbs. It puts forth great branches, so that the birds of the sky can lodge under its shade."

³³So by means of many such parables, He continued speaking to them the word, to the extent that they were able to receive it. ³⁴Without a parable He did not make it a practice to speak to them, but privately it was His custom to make everything plain to His own disciples.

---

[d]Literally, "these are."
[e]Literally, "they have no root in themselves."
[f]Literally, "are offended, or caused to stumble."

[35]That day, when evening came, He said to them, "Let us cross over to the other side."[g] [36]So they left the crowd and took Him, just as He was, in the boat; and other boats accompanied Him. [37]A fierce windstorm struck, and the waves began pouring into the boat, so that it soon began to fill. [38]Now Jesus was in the back part of the boat, sleeping on the steerman's cushion. So they woke Him and said to Him, "Master, we are sinking! Don't You care?"[h] [39]And He stood up, rebuked the wind and said to the sea, "Silence! Be muzzled and remain subdued!"[i] And the wind ceased raging and there was a great calm. [40]And He said to them, "Why are you so timid? How is it that you have no[j] faith?" [41]They were exceedingly terrified, and said to one another, "Just who is this man, that even the wind and the sea obey Him?"

Chapter 5

They came to the other side of the lake to the country of the Gerasenes. [2]And as soon as Jesus stepped from the boat, there came toward Him, out of the tombs, a man under the control of an unclean spirit. [3]The man had his dwelling among the tombs, and no one was able any more to bind him, not even with a chain. [4]Often, he had been bound with shackles and chains, but he had torn apart the chains and crushed the shackles into fragments. No one was strong enough to subdue him.[a] [5]Always by night and day, among the tombs and the mountains, he was continually crying out and slashing himself with stones.

[6]When he saw Jesus from a distance, he ran and fell down before Him, [7]and cried out with a loud voice, "Why are You interfering with me,[b] Jesus, Son of the Most High God? I implore You, in God's name, not to torment me." [8]For Jesus had said to him, "You unclean spirit, come out of the man!" [9]"What is your name?" Jesus asked him. He answered, "My name is Legion, for we are many." [10]Then, he continued begging Jesus not to send them out of that vicinity.

[11]Now on the mountain-side, there was a large herd of swine feeding. [12]The unclean spirits begged Him, "Send us among the swine, so that we may enter into them." [13]He gave them permission, and the unclean spirits came out and entered into the swine, and the herd—about two thousand in number—rushed madly down the precipice and were drowned in the lake.

---

[g]Or, to the region beyond. Cf. 1:38.

[h]The Greek negative particle *ou* indicates that an affirmative answer is expected.

[i]Indicated by Greek perfect passive imperative.

[j]Some manuscripts insert *oupo*, negative adverb of time, so that Jesus' question is, Have you *not yet* faith?

[a]Cf. Acts 19:16.

[b]Cf. Matt. 8:29.

[14]The men who had been tending [the swine] fled and reported [these things] in the city and in the countryside, and the people came to see what had happened. [15]As they approached Jesus and saw the demoniac—the man who had been possessed by the legion—sitting down, clothed and in his right mind, they were afraid. [16]Those who had observed it, told the people what had happened to the demoniac and about the swine. [17]Then the people began to implore Jesus to go away from their borders.

[18]As Jesus was entering the boat, the man who had been demon-possessed requested that he be allowed to go with Him. [19]However, Jesus did not permit him [to do so], but told him, "Go home to your own people, and tell them what things the Lord has done for you and has shown pity to you." [20]So the man departed and began to proclaim in the Decapolis[c] what things the Lord had done for him. And everyone was amazed.

[21]When Jesus had crossed again by boat to the other side, a large crowd gathered around Him as He stood on the lakeshore. [22]Then, one of the synagogue-rulers, whose name was Jairus, approached and when he saw Jesus he knelt at His feet [23]and earnestly appealed to Him. "My little daughter is about to die,"[d] he said. "Please come and lay Your hands upon her, so that she may be healed and live." [24]Jesus went with him, and a large crowd followed Him and they kept pressing upon Him.

[25]And there was a woman who for twelve years had been distressed with hemorrhages.[e] [26]She had suffered much from [the treatments given by] many physicians, and had spent everything she had, yet was not helped in any way but rather had grown worse. [27]When she heard about Jesus,[f] she came up behind Him in the crowd and touched His garment. [28]For she kept saying, "If only I can touch even His garments, I shall be healed." [29]Instantly, the source of her bleeding was stopped and she felt in her body that she was cured from the affliction.

[30]Jesus, immediately knowing within Himself that power had gone out from Him, turned around in the crowd and asked, "Who touched My garments?" [31]The disciples said to Him, "You see the crowd pressing against You, yet you ask, 'Who touched Me?'" [32]But He continued looking around to see her who had done this. [33]Then the woman, frightened and trembling because she knew what had happened to her, came and fell down before Him and told Him the whole truth. [34]He said to her, "Daughter, your faith has made you well. Go in peace, and remain free[g] from your affliction."

[35]While Jesus was still speaking, messengers came from [the home of] the synagogue-ruler. "Your daughter has died," they said. "Why trouble the

---

[c]Or, throughout the Ten Cities. These were a group of towns located southeast of the Sea of Galilee, and populated mostly by Gentiles.

[d]Literally, "has it at the last," i.e., she is at the point of death.

[e]Cf. Lev. 15:25-27.

[f]Literally, "the things concerning Jesus."

[g]Literally, "continue being whole."

Teacher any further?'' [36]But Jesus overhearing[h] their remark, said to the synagogue-ruler, ''Stop being fearful! Just keep believing!''

[37]Jesus did not permit anyone to accompany Him except Peter and James and John, the brother of James. [38]When they reached the house of the synagogue-ruler, He saw a tumult, with people weeping and mourning loudly. [39]He went in and said to them, ''Why are you making this commotion and weeping? The child is not dead—she is asleep.'' [40]They laughed at Him. But after Jesus had put them all out, He took along the child's father and mother and those with Him, and went in where the child was. [41]He took hold of her hand and said to her, ''Talitha, koum!'' which means, ''Little girl, I say to you, get up!'' [42]Immediately, the little girl stood up and began walking around, for she was twelve years of age. And at that[i] they were utterly astonished. [43]Jesus gave them strict orders not to let anyone know about this. And He told them to give her something to eat.

Chapter 6

Then Jesus went forth from there and came to His native place;[a] and His disciples went with Him. [2]And when the Sabbath came He began to teach in the Synagogue. And the large congregation,[b] as they listened, were astonished. ''Where did this man get these things?'' they asked. ''And what kind of wisdom has been given to Him? And what about the powerful deeds He is doing?[c] [3]Is He not the builder, Mary's son, and a brother of James and Joses and Jude and Simon? And do not His sisters live here among us?'' So they were stumbling because of Him.

[4]But Jesus told them, ''A prophet is not without honor except in his native place, and among his relatives, and in his own home.'' [5]And He was not able to do any mighty deed there, except lay His hands upon a few sick persons and cure them. [6]And He was amazed at their unbelief.

So He went around from village to village teaching. [7]Then He summoned the Twelve, and began to send them forth two by two, giving them authority over the unclean spirits. [8]He ordered them to take nothing for the journey except a staff—no food, no provision-bag, no money[d] in their belts. [9]They

---

[h]Or, disregarding.
[i]Or, Instantly.

[a]Or home-town. Jesus grew up in Nazareth. Cf. 1:9, 24; Luke 4:16.
[b]Literally, ''the many.''
[c]Literally, ''occurring through His hands?''
[d]Literally, ''No copper coins.''

were to wear sandals, and not to clothe themselves with two tunics.[e] [10]And He went on to tell them, "Wherever you enter into a house, abide there[f] until you depart from that vicinity. [11]And whatever place will not receive you or hear you, as you are going away from there shake off the dust from under your feet as a testimony against them."

[12]So they went forth, and preached that people should repent. [13]They drove out many demons, and anointed with oil[g] many sick persons and cured them.

[14]In the meantime, King Herod[h] heard [about these things] for the name of Jesus had become well known. People were saying, "John, the Baptizer has been raised from the dead, and that is why mighty powers are at work in Him." [15]But others remarked, "He is Elijah." Still others were saying, "He is a prophet like one of the prophets [of old]." [16]But when Herod heard [these remarks] he declared, "John, whom I, myself, did behead, has been raised [from the dead]!" [17]For Herod, himself, had sent and arrested John and put him in prison[i] on account of Herodias, his brother Philip's wife whom he had married. [18]For John had told Herod, "It is not lawful for you to have your brother's wife."[j]

[19]So Herodias maintained a grudge against John[k] and was determined to kill him, but she could not, [20]because Herod was afraid of John, knowing him [to be] an upright and holy man, so he protected him. When he heard John at length, he was greatly disturbed yet he listened to him with much interest.[l]

[21]An opportunity[m] came [for Herodias] when Herod, during his birthday festivities, gave a banquet for his nobles, the military commanders, and the leading men of Galilee, [22]at which Herodias' daughter herself came in and danced. Her performance so pleased Herod and those reclining with him at table that the king said to the girl, "Ask me whatever you wish and I will give it to you." [23]And he made an oath to her, "Anything you ask I will give you, up to half of my kingdom!" [24]She went out and said to her mother, "What shall I ask?" The mother replied, "The head of John the Baptizer." [25]Without delay she returned quickly to the king and made the request, saying, "I want you to give me, at once upon a platter, the head of John the Baptizer."

[26]The king was deeply grieved, yet on account of his oaths and of his dinner guests, he did not have the will to reject her request. [27]So at once, the king sent an executioner with orders to bring John's head. [28]And the executioner went and beheaded John in the prison. Then he brought the head on a platter

[e]Some persons of wealth wore an inner and an outer tunic. The apostles were instructed to dress simply and trust God to supply their needs. Cf. Matt 10:9-10.
[f]Cf. Luke 10:7.
[g]Cf. James 5:14.
[h]Herod Antipas. See note on Matt. 14:1.
[i]Cf. 1:14.
[j]Cf. Lev. 18:16, 18; 20:21.
[k]Literally, "she had it in for him."
[l]Or, gladly.
[m]Literally, "a convenient day."

and delivered it to the girl, and the girl gave it to her mother. [29]When John's disciples heard [of his execution], they came and took his body and placed it in a tomb.

[30]The apostles gathered together Jesus and reported to Him everything they had done and taught. [31]Then He said to them, ''You yourselves come privately to a solitary place and rest a little.'' For so many people were coming and going, that they had no opportunity even to eat. [32]So they started in the boat for a secluded place to be alone. [33]But many people saw them leaving, and recognized them, and from all the towns they hurried together on foot [around the lake] and got there ahead of them. [34]So when Jesus stepped ashore He saw a large crowd, and He was moved with deep compassion for them because they were like sheep without a shepherd; and He began to teach them many things.

[35]When the hour grew late,[n] His disciples came to Him and said, ''This is a desert place, and the hour has grown late. [36]Dismiss the people in order that they may go into the neighboring farms and villages, and buy themselves something to eat.'' [37]But He said to them, ''You yourselves give them something to eat.'' They replied, ''Are we to go and spend two hundred denarii[o] for bread to feed them?'' [38]''How many bread-cakes have you?'' He asked. ''Go and see.'' When they found out, they said, ''Five, and two fish.''

[39]Jesus directed them all to be seated in companies on the green grass. [40]So they sat down in groups of hundreds and fifties in [an arrangement that looked like] flower-beds.[p] [41]Then Jesus took the five bread-cakes and the two fish and, looking up toward heaven, He gave thanks and broke the bread-cakes and kept giving portions to the disciples to distribute to the people. He also divided the two fish among all. [42]They all ate and were fully satisfied. [43]And from the broken pieces [of the bread-cakes] and from the fish they took up twelve full wicker-baskets. [44]Those who ate the food numbered five thousand men.

[45]Immediately, Jesus compelled His disciples to get into the boat and go on ahead to the other side toward Bethsaida, while He dismissed the crowd. [46]After He had told them farewell, He went away into the hills to pray.

[47]When evening came, the boat was in the middle of the lake while He was alone on the land. [48]He saw the disciples struggling at the oars, for the wind was against them. About the fourth watch[q] of the night Jesus came toward them, walking on the lake. He intended to come along beside them.[r] [49]But when they saw Him walking on the lake, they thought it was an apparition,

---

[n]Literally, ''And already much time of day had passed.''

[o]See note on Matt. 18:28.

[p]It was a beautiful sight—the people, dressed in garments of various colors, sitting on the green grass with the setting sun casting its rays across them.

[q]See note on Matt. 14:25.

[r]Or, He was on the point of going by them.

and they screamed aloud, [50]for they all saw Him and were terrified. But at once He spoke to them, and said, "Be of good cheer! It is I! Stop being afraid!" [51]Then He climbed up into the boat beside them, and the wind ceased. The disciples were exceedingly astonished, [52]for they had not grasped the significance of [the incident concerning] the bread-cakes, but their heart remained insensitive.

[53]And having made the crossing, they came ashore at Genesharet and anchored there. [54]When they stepped out of the boat, people recognized Jesus immediately, [55]and they ran around the entire countryside and began to bring on stretchers those who were ill,[s] to wherever they heard He was. [56]And wherever He went—into villages or cities or hamlets—they placed the sick in the open places and begged Him to let them touch even the border[t] of His garment. And as many as touched Him were healed.

Chapter 7

The Pharisees and certain of the Law-experts who had come from Jerusalem gathered around Jesus. [2]They saw some of His disciples eating food with defiled hands,[a] that is [with hands ceremonially] unwashed. [3]For the Pharisees and all the Jews do not eat without [a ritual] washing of their hands up to the wrists[b] maintaining the tradition handed down by the elders.[c] [4]And [when they return] from the market-place,[d] they will not eat without [first] sprinkling themselves. There are also many other things which they have received and hold fast, [such as special] washings of cups and pitchers and bronze vessels.

[5]So the Pharisees and the Law-experts asked Jesus, "Why are Your disciples not conducting themselves according to the custom handed down by the elders,[e] but eat food with defiled hands?" [6]And He said to them, "Truly did Isaiah prophecy concerning you hypocrites, as it stands written, 'This people honors Me with their lips, but their heart keeps far away from Me. [7]And in vain do they worship Me, because they teach[f] doctrines [which are] precepts of men.'[g] [8]You have left God's commandment and are clinging to human tradition."

---

[s]Literally, "those having it bad."
[t]Or, tassel. See note on Matt. 9:20.
[a]Literally, "common hands."
[b]Or, over clenched fingers. That is, rubbing the fist of one hand in the palm of the other.
[c]Subjective genitive.
[d]Or, a public gathering.
[e]Subjective genitive.
[f]Greek causal present participle.
[g]Cf. Isa. 29:13.

[9]He went on to say to them, "You cleverly set aside God's commandment in order to keep your tradition! [10]For Moses said, 'Honor your father and your mother,'[h] and 'Anyone who curses his father or mother shall be put to death.'[i] [11]But you say 'If a man says to his father or his mother, "Anything of mine that might have been of help to you is Korban" ' "—that is, a gift [vowed to God][j]—[12]"you no longer permit him to do anything for his father or mother. [13]In that way you nullify God's word in favor of[k] your tradition which you have handed down. And you practice many similar things."

[14]Then Jesus called the crowd to Him again and said to them, "Listen to Me, all of you, and understand. [15]Nothing that enters a man from the outside can defile him, but the things proceeding out of man are the things that defile him."

[17][l]When Jesus went indoors away from the crowd, His disciples questioned Him about the illustration [He had used]. [18]"Are you also without discernment?" He asked them. "Do you not understand that nothing entering a person from the outside can defile him? [19]For it does not go into his heart, but into his stomach and is discharged into the drain, making all foods clean?"[m] [20]And He continued, "That which comes from within a person is what defiles him. [21]For from within, out of men's hearts, come forth evil designs: fornications, thefts, murders, [22]adulteries, greed, iniquities, deceit, sensuality, an evil eye, blasphemy, arrogance, foolishness. [23]All these wicked things come from within, and defile a person."

[24]Then Jesus left that place and went into the borders of Tyre. He entered a house, and did not want anyone to know it; but He was not able to escape notice. [25]Immediately a woman, whose little daughter was possessed by an unclean spirit, heard about Him and came and threw herself at His feet. [26]The woman was a Gentile,[n] by birth a Phoenician who lived in Syria. She kept begging Jesus to drive the demon out of her daughter. [27]He said to her, "First let the children be filled; for it is not proper to take the children's bread and throw it to the little dogs."[o] [28]But she answered and said to Him, "Yes, Lord; but even the little dogs under the table habitually eat from the crumbs dropped

---

[h]Cf. Exod. 20:12; Deut. 5:16.

[i]Exod. 21:17; Lev. 20:9.

[j]See note on Matt. 15:5.

[k]Or, by means of.

[l]Verse 16, *If anyone has ears to hear, let him listen,* is listed by the Nestle text as a variant reading.

[m]Indicated by *katharizon, making clean,* nominative singular masculine present active participle, which connects the thought with the words of Jesus beginning in v. 18.

[n]Literally, "a Greek." Here the term is used in a general sense of a person who was non-Jewish.

[o]The Greek word is the dative plural of *kunarion,* a diminutive, hence the reference is to the *small puppies* that were household pets. See note on Matt. 15:26. For the wild dogs of the streets there is a different word, *kuon.* The plural of the latter word is used as a term of reproach. Cf. Matt. 7:6; Phil. 3:2; Rev. 22:15.

by the children."[p] [29]Then He said to her, "Because of that answer, go [home]. The demon has gone out of your daughter." [30]The woman went away to her house and found the little child lying on the couch and the demon gone.

[31]When Jesus returned from the borders of Tyre, He went by way of Sidon to the Sea of Galilee, passing through the neighborhood of Decapolis.[q] [32]Some people brought to Him a deaf man who had a speech impediment, and they asked Him to place His hand upon him. [33]Jesus took him aside from the crowd by himself, and put His fingers into the man's ears. He spit and touched his tongue. [34]Then He looked up to heaven and groaned, and said to him, "Ephphatha!" which means, "Be opened!" [35]The man's ears were opened, and immediately his tongue was loosed from its impediment, and he began to speak plainly.

[36]Jesus charged the people expressly not to tell anyone. But the more He ordered them [not to make it known], the more widely they kept proclaiming it. [37]Their astonishment knew no bounds. "He has done all things well!" they exclaimed. "He makes even the deaf to hear and the speechless to speak!"

Chapter 8

In those days, when there was again a large crowd and they had nothing to eat, Jesus summoned the disciples and said to them, [2]"I have deep concern for the crowd because they have been with Me for three days now and they have nothing to eat. [3]If I send them home hungry they will become exhausted on the way. Besides, some of them have travelled a great distance."

[4]His disciples replied, "Where could anyone secure food enough for these people here in this desert region?" [5]Jesus asked them, "How many bread-cakes do you have?" "Seven," they replied. [6]Then He directed the multitude to sit down on the ground. And He took the seven bread-cakes and, after giving thanks, He broke them and kept giving them to His disciples for distribution; and they distributed them to the crowd. [7]Also, they had a few small fish. These He blessed and directed that these, too, be distributed. [8]So the people ate and were satisfied, and they took up seven rope-baskets[a] full of the broken portions that were left over. [9]Now there were about four thousand men [who had eaten]. Jesus then dismissed the people. [10]And immediately, He entered into the boat with His disciples and went to the bordees of Dalmanutha.

---

[p]Subjective genitive.

[q]Or, the Ten Towns. See note on 5:20.

[a]Accusative plural of *spuris*, or *sphuris*. See note on Matt. 15:37. Cf. Acts 9:25.

[11]And the Pharisees came forth and began to argue with Him, asking Him for a sign from heaven, testing Him. [12]He groaned deeply in His spirit, and said, "Why is this generation seeking a sign? Truly I tell you, no sign will be given to this generation." [13]Then He left them, embarked again, and went away to the other side.

[14]The disciples had forgotten to take along food, and they had nothing with them in the boat except one loaf. [15]And Jesus cautioned them, saying, "Look, beware of the yeast of the Pharisees and the yeast of Herod." [16]And they kept reasoning with one another [whether He had spoken like He did] because they had no bread. [17]Jesus, aware [of their discussion], said to them, "Why are you reasoning about having no bread? Do you not yet realize or understand? Is your heart in a state of hardness? [18]You have eyes, can you not see? And you have ears, can you not hear? And do you not remember [19]when I broke the five bread-cakes for the five thousand, how many wicker-baskets full of broken portions you took up?" They said to Him, "Twelve." [20]"When [I broke] the seven [bread-cakes] for the four thousand, how many full rope-baskets of broken portions did you gather?" They replied, "Seven." [21]And He said to them, "Do you not yet understand?"

[22]And they come to Bethsaida.[b] There the people brought to Jesus a blind man, and begged Him to touch him. [23]He took hold of the blind man's hand, and led him outside the village. Then He put saliva on the man's eyes and placed His hands on him and asked him, "Do you see anything?" [24]He looked up and said, "I can see people but they look like trees walking about." [25]Then again Jesus put His hands upon the man's eyes, and he saw clearly and was restored and could see everything plainly, even from a distance. [26]And Jesus sent him home, saying, "Do not even go into the town."

[27]Then Jesus and His disciples went forth to the villages near Caesarea Philippi. On the way He began to question His disciples and said to them, "Who do people say that I am?" [28]They told Him, some say, "John the Baptizer;" but others say, "Elijah;" and others, "One of the prophets." [29]And He went on to question them, "But you—who do you say I am?" And Peter answered and said to Him, "Thou[c] art the Christ!" [30]And He gave them strict orders not to tell anyone about Him.

[31]Then Jesus began to teach them that it was necessary for the Son of Man to suffer many things, to be rejected by the elders and the chief priests and the Law-teachers, and be killed, and after three days rise again. [32]And He made this statement openly. Then Peter took Him aside and began to reprove Him. [33]But Jesus turned around and, looking at His disciples, reproved Peter. "Get

---

[b]This is Bethsaida Julius, located on the eastern side of the Sea of Galilee.
[c]Emphatic.

behind me, Adversary,"[d] He said, "because you do not have in mind the things of God but the things of man." [34]Then Jesus summoned the crowd, along with His disciples, and said to them, "If anyone wishes to come after Me, let him renounce himself and take up his cross, and keep on following Me. [35]For whoever wishes to save his life will lose it, and whoever loses his life for my sake and the sake of the good news will save it. [36]What does it profit a man to gain the whole world and forfeit his soul? [37]For what can a man give in exchange for his soul?

[38]"Indeed, whoever is ashamed of Me and My words in this adulterous and sinful generation, of him will the Son of Man also be ashamed when He comes in the glory of His Father with the holy angels."

Chapter 9

And He went on to say to them, "Truly I tell you, there are some of the people standing here who will not by any means taste of death until they see the kingdom of God has come with power."

[2]Six days later, Jesus took Peter and James and John and brought them up into a high mountain alone by themselves. And He was transfigured in their presence. [3]His garments became dazzling, exceedingly white, such as no bleacher on the earth could whiten them. [4]And there appeared to them Elijah with Moses, and they were talking with Jesus.

[5]Then Peter said to Jesus, "Rabbi, it is good for us to be here! So let us make three pavilions—one for You, one for Moses, and one for Elijah." [6]For he did not know how to react[a] [to the vision], for they were terrified.

[7]Then a cloud overshadowed them, and out of the cloud came a voice, "This is My beloved Son. Listen to Him!" [8]Then suddenly, when they looked around, they no longer saw anyone with them but Jesus only. [9]As they were coming down from the mountain, He charged them expressly not to relate to anyone what they had seen until after the Son of Man had risen from the dead. [10]And they got hold of the saying about the [Son of Man] rising from the dead, and discussed among themselves what it might mean.

[11]And they went on to question Him, saying, "Why do the Law-teachers say that Elijah must first come?" [12]And He said to them, "Elijah, indeed, does come first, and puts all things in order.[b] Yet why does it stand written concerning the Son of Man that He must suffer many things and be treated

---

[d]Or, [agent of] Satan.
[e]Cf. 9:32; Luke 18:34.

[a]Literally, "what to answer."
[b]Cf. Mal. 3:5-6; Matt. 11:13-14; 17:10-13.

with contempt? [13]However, I tell you that as a matter of fact Elijah has come, and they did to him whatever they wished, just as it stands written concerning him.''

[14]When they returned to the [other nine] disciples they saw a large crowd around them, and Law-teachers arguing with them. [15]As soon as the crowd saw Him, they were greatly amazed, and they ran forward and began welcoming Him. [16]He asked the Law-teachers[e] what they were discussing with the disciples.[d] [17]And one of the crowd answered Him, ''Teacher, I have brought my son to You. He is under the control of a dumb spirit, [18]and whenever it seizes him, it throws him down, and he foams at the mouth and grinds his teeth; and he is wasting away.[e] I asked Your disciples to cast it out, but they could not.''

[19]Jesus answered them, ''O unbelieving generation, how long shall I be with you? How long shall I bear with you? Bring him to Me!'' [20]And they brought him to Jesus. And when the spirit saw Jesus, immediately it threw the boy into convulsions so that he fell to the ground and rolled about, foaming at the mouth. [21]Jesus asked his father, ''How long has this been happening to him?'' And he replied, ''From childhood. [22]Often it has tried to destroy him by throwing him into fire and into water. But, if You are able to do anything, please have compassion on us and help us!''

[23]Jesus said to him, ''Regarding your statement,[e] 'If You are able'—all things are possible to the person who believes!'' [24]At once, the boy's father cried out [with tears[f]] and exclaimed, ''I do believe! Please help my lack of faith!'' [25]Now when Jesus saw that a crowd came running together, He rebuked the unclean spirit, saying to it, ''Speechless and deaf spirit, I command you: Go forth out of him and never enter him again!'' [26]After shrieking and throwing him into many violent fits, it went out. And [the boy] lay there like a corpse,[g] so that most of the people said, ''He is dead!'' [27]But Jesus took hold of his hand, and lifted him, and he stood up.

[28]After Jesus had gone indoors, His disciples asked Him privately, ''Why were we, ourselves, not able to cast it out? [29]And He told them, ''This kind of thing can be driven out by nothing except prayer.''

[30]They went forth from that place and passed along through Galilee. But He did not want anyone to know [about His presence] [31]for He continued teaching His disciples and kept saying to them, ''The Son of Man is being delivered into the hands of men, and they will kill Him, but three days after He has been put to death, He will rise up.'' [32]However, they did not understand what He meant, and they were afraid to question Him.

[33]They reached Capernaum, and after He was in the house He asked them, ''What were you discussing on the road?'' [34]They were silent, for on the way

[e]Literally, ''them.''
[d]Or, becomes rigid, or exhausted.
[e]Indicated by the Greek article.
[f]Added by a number of manuscripts.
[g]Literally, ''became like one dead.''

they had argued with one another about who was greatest. [35]So He sat down, summoned the Twelve and said to them, "If anyone wants to be first, he must be last of all and servant of all." [36]Then He took a little child, and placed it in their midst. And He put His arms around it, and said to them, [37]"Whoever receives one of such little children in My name receives Me. And whoever receives Me receives not Me but Him who sent Me."

[38]John said to Him, "Teacher, we saw someone who does not follow us expelling demons in Your name, and we tried to stop[h] him because he was not following us." [39]But Jesus said, "Cease trying to stop him; for no one who performs a mighty work in My name can at the same time speak evil about Me. [40]Anyone who is not against us is for us. [41]For whoever gives you a cup of water to drink in [My] name—because you belong to Christ—truly I say to you, that he will certainly not lose his reward. [42]And whoever causes to stumble one of these little ones who believe [in Me] it would be better for him if a great mill-stone[i] had been placed around his neck and he had been thrown into the sea.

[43]"If your hand is about to entrap you, cut it off! It is better to enter into life maimed than, having two hands, to go away into hell,[j] into the fire that is never put out. [45][k]And if your foot starts to entrap you, cut it off! It is better for you to enter into the life maimed than, having two feet, to be cast into hell. [47]And if your eye starts to entrap you, pluck it out! It is better for you, with one eye, to enter into the kingdom of God than, having two eyes, to be cast into hell, [48]where 'their worm does not die and the fire is not extinguished.'[l]

[49]"Indeed, everyone will be salted with fire. [50]Salt is good, but if the salt becomes tasteless, how can you restore its quality as salt? Have salt in yourselves, and maintain peace with one another."

Chapter 10

Jesus left that place and went into the borders of Judaea and of Peraea.[a] And again, crowds gathered about Him, and again, as His custom was, He began teaching them.

---

[h]Greek conative imperfect.

[i]Literally, "a mill-stone for a donkey," i.e., turned by a donkey in grinding grain. Such a stone was much heavier than one used in a hand-mill.

[j]Greek, *Gehenna*. See note on Matt. 5:22.

[k]Vv. 44 and 46, which lack strong manuscript evidence, are omitted by the Nestle text. However, the content of these two verses is preserved in v. 48, which is well attested

[l]Cf. Isa. 66:24.

[a]Literally, "and beyond the Jordan."

[2]Some Pharisees approached and tried to entrap Him by asking, "Is it lawful for a husband to divorce his wife?"[b] [3]And He answered them, "What did Moses command you?" [4]And they replied, "Moses permitted [a man] to write a dismissal certificate and to divorce [his wife]."[c] [5]Jesus said to them, "Owing to your hardheartedness Moses granted that concession for you. [6]But from the beginning of creation God made them male and female.[d] [7]This is why a man will leave his father and his mother [and be joined to his wife[e]] [8]and the two shall be one flesh.[f] Thus they are no longer two but one flesh. [9]Therefore, what God has yoked together, let no man separate."

[10]In the house, the disciples again asked Jesus about this. [11]And He said to them, "Whoever divorces his wife and marries another woman is guilty of adultery against her. [12]And if she[g] divorces her husband and marries another man, she is guilty of adultery."

[13]People kept bringing little children to Him in order that He might touch them, but the disciples censured [those who brought] them. [14]But when Jesus noticed it, He was displeased. "Permit the little children to come to Me," He said. "Stop hindering them! For of such ones is the kingdom of God. [15]Truly I say to you, whoever does not receive the kingdom of God like a little child, will by no means enter into it." [16]And He took [the children] in His arms and continued blessing them and placing His hands upon them.

[17]As Jesus was resuming His journey, a man ran up and knelt before Him and asked, "Good teacher, what must I do that I may gain life eternal?" [18]And Jesus said to him, "Why do you call Me good? No one is good except One—God, Himself. [19]You know the commandments: 'Do not murder. Do not commit adultery. Do not steal. Do not bear false witness. Do not cheat. Honor your father and mother.' "[h]

[20]"Teacher," he replied, "all these things I have observed since my youth." [21]Jesus, with deep affection, looked searchingly at the man and said to him, "You lack one thing. Go sell all you have and give to the poor people, and you will have treasure in heaven. Then come, follow Me from now on."[i] [22]But at that saying the man became downcast, and he went away grieving, for he had many possessions.

[23]Then Jesus looked around and said to His disciples, "How difficult it is for those who have riches to enter into the kingdom of God!" [24]The disciples were amazed at His words. So Jesus again said to them, "Children, how

---

[b]Cf. Matt. 19:3.

[c]Cf. Deut. 24:1.

[d]Cf. Gen. 1:27.

[e]Listed as a variant by the Nestle text.

[f]Cf. Gen. 2:24.

[g]Unlike the Mosaic legislation, Greek and Roman law permitted a wife to divorce her husband.

[h]Cf. Exod. 20:12-17; Deut. 5:16-20.

[i]Linear force of Greek present imperative.

difficult it is to enter into the kingdom of God! ²⁵It is easier for a camel to go through the eye of the needle than for a rich man to enter into the kingdom of God!''

²⁶They were exceedingly astonished, and said to themselves, ''Then who can be saved?'' ²⁷Jesus looked searchingly at them, and answered, ''With men it is impossible, but not with God; for all things are possible with God.''

²⁸Peter began to say to Him, ''Look, we on our part have left everything and have continued following You!'' ²⁹Jesus said, ''Truly I say to you, there is no one who gave up home or brothers or sisters or mother or father or children or fields for Me and for the good news, ³⁰who will not receive now, in this age a hundred times as many homes and brothers and sisters and mothers and children and fields, along with persecutions, and in the coming age life eternal. ³¹But many [who are now] first will be last, and the last [will be] first.''

³²Now they were on the road going up to Jerusalem, and Jesus was walking in front of them. They were amazed, and those that followed were afraid. So again, He took the Twelve aside and began to tell them what was about to happen to Him. ³³He said, ''Listen, we are going up to Jerusalem, and the Son of Man will be betrayed to the chief priests and the Law-teachers, and they will condemn Him to die and hand Him over to the Gentiles, ³⁴who will mock Him and spit upon Him and scourge Him and kill Him. But after three days He will rise.''

³⁵Then James and John, the sons of Zebedee, approached Jesus and said to Him, ''Teacher, we want You to do for us whatever we ask.'' ³⁶He said to them, ''What do you want Me to do for you?'' ³⁷They replied, ''Grant that we may sit, one at Your right and one at Your left, in Your glory.'' ³⁸''You do not realize what you are asking,'' Jesus told them. ''Are you able to drink the cup that I, Myself, am drinking, or to be baptized with the baptism which I, Myself, and undergoing?'' ³⁹And they replied to Him, ''We are able!'' But Jesus told them, ''The cup which I, Myself, drink you shall drink, and the baptism with which I, Myself, am immersed you shall undergo. ⁴⁰But as to sitting at My right or at My left—that is not Mine to give; it belongs to those for whom it has been prepared.''

⁴¹When the Ten heard [about this] they became indignant at James and John. ⁴²But Jesus called them together and said to them, ''You know that those regarded as ruling the Gentiles, exercise dominion over them, and their great men govern by force.^j ⁴³But it is not like that among you. Whoever wishes to become great among you must be your servant; ⁴⁴and whoever wishes to be first among you must be a slave of all. ⁴⁵For even the Son of Man did not come to be served but to serve and to give His life to bring about the release of many.''^k

---

^jLiterally, ''wield authority over them.''
^kOr, as a ransom in behalf of many.

[46]They entered into Jericho. And as He was going out from Jericho with His disciples and a considerable crowd, Bartimaeus (the son of Timaeus) a blind beggar, was sitting by the side of the road. [47]When he heard that it was Jesus the Nazarene, he began to cry out, saying, "Jesus, Son of David, have pity on me!" [48]And many kept admonishing him to be silent, but he continued crying out all the more, "Son of David, have pity on me!" [49]Then Jesus stopped and said, "Call him." They called the blind man, and told him, "Be of good courage! Get up! He is calling you!" [50]The man threw aside his outer garment, jumped up, and came to Jesus. [51]Jesus said to him, "What do you want Me to do for you?" And the blind man said to Him, "Rabboni,[1] let me see again!" [52]Then Jesus said to him, "Go, your faith has cured you permanently."[m] And immediately, he recovered his sight, and began to follow Jesus along the road.

Chapter 11

When they drew near to Jerusalem, in the vicinity of Bethphage and Bethany, at the Mount of Olives, Jesus sent two of His disciples, [2]saying to them, "Go into the village which is ahead of you, and as soon as you enter it, you will find tied there a colt on which no man has ever sat. Untie [the colt] and bring it. [3]If anyone asks you, 'Why are you doing this?' say, 'The Lord needs it, and without delay He will send it back here.' "

[4]So they went and found a colt tied outside at a door-way which faced the open street,[a] and they started to untie it. [5]Some of the bystanders asked them, "What are you doing, loosing the colt?" [6]They answered just as Jesus had told them, and the men let them take it.[b] [7]Then they led the colt to Jesus, and threw their cloaks across its back, and He sat on it. [8]Many persons spread their outer garments on the road, while others cut leafy branches out of the fields [and scattered them in the way]. [9]And the people who went in front [of Him] and those who followed kept shouting, "Hosanna![c] Blessed is He who comes in the Name of the Lord! [10]Blessed be the coming kingdom of our father David! Hosanna in the highest [heavens]!"

[11]Jesus entered Jerusalem [and went] into the Temple area, where He looked around at everything. But since the hour was already late, He went out to Bethany, accompanied by the Twelve.

---

[1]An Aramaic word meaning *my Teacher* or *my Lord*. A stronger form than Rabbi. Cf. John 20:16.

[m]Indicated by perfect tense of Greek verb.

[a]The Greek term, *amphodon,* literally "a road around" [something], may mean a curved street, a street corner, possibly a crossing of ways, or simply a street.

[b]Literally, "they let them go."

[c]See note on Matt. 21:9.

¹²The next morning, as they were leaving Bethany, Jesus felt hungry. ¹³In the distance He saw a fig tree on which were leaves, so He went [over to see] if He could find any fruit on it. When He reached it, He found nothing except leaves, because it was not the season for figs. ¹⁴He said to it, "May no one ever again eat fruit from you!" And His disciples were listening [to what He said].

¹⁵When they reached Jerusalem, Jesus entered the Temple precincts, and began to drive out those who were selling and those who were buying in the forecourt[d] of the Temple. He overturned the tables of the money-changers and the counters of those who were selling doves. ¹⁶In fact, He would not permit anyone to carry any sort of object through the Temple. ¹⁷Then He proceeded to teach them and said, "Does it not stand written, 'My house shall be called a house of prayer for all the nations'? But you, yourselves, have turned it into a den of robbers."[c]

¹⁸When the chief priests and the Law-teachers heard [about what He had done] they began to seek a way to destroy Him. They were afraid of Him, for all the crowd was fascinated by [the manner and content of] His teaching. ¹⁹When evening came, Jesus and His disciples, as was their practice[g] went outside the city.

²⁰As they passed along the next morning, they noticed that the fig tree was withered from its roots. ²¹Then Peter, remembering, remarked to Him, "Master, look! The fig tree You denounced has withered away!" ²²Jesus answered, "Have faith in God.[h] ²³Truly I tell you, that whoever says to this mountain, 'Be lifted up and be hurled into the sea,' and does not doubt in his heart but believes that what he says is happening, it will be done for him.[i]

²⁴"Therefore I tell you, all things for which you go on praying and asking, keep believing that they have been granted,[j] and they will be yours. ²⁵And whenever you stand praying, if you have anything against anyone forgive him, so that your Heavenly Father also may forgive you your misdeeds."

²⁷ᵏThey came back to Jerusalem and, while Jesus was walking in the Temple precincts, the chief priests and the law-teachers and the elders approached ²⁸and asked Him, "By what kind of authority are You doing these things? Or who gave You this authority, so that you do them?" ²⁹Jesus replied, "I will ask you one question. Answer me, and I will tell you by what kind of authority I am doing these things. ³⁰The baptism proclaimed by John—was it of heaven or of men? Answer me!"

---

[d]That is, the Court of the Gentiles.

[c]Cf. Isa. 56:7; Jer. 7:11.

[f]Literally, "they."

[g]Iterative force of Greek imperfect tense.

[h]Objective genitive.

[i]Literally, "it will be to him."

[j]Literally, "that you have received [them]."

[k]Verse 26 does not appear in many of the most reliable manuscripts, hence is omitted by the Nestle text. But the thought of verse 26 is found in Matt. 6:14; 18:35. Cf. Luke 6:37.

[31]They began reasoning among themselves: "If we say, 'From heaven,' He will ask, 'Then why did you not believe him?' [32]But if we say, 'From men?' " they were afraid of the crowd, for all held that John was truly a prophet. [33]So they replied to Jesus, "We do not know." Then Jesus said to them, "Neither will I, Myself, tell you by what kind of authority I am doing these things."

Chapter 12

And He began to speak[a] to them by means of parables: "A man planted a vineyard, and put a wall around it, and dug a juice-trough for the winepress, and built a tower. Then he leased it to tenants and went on a journey. [2]In due time he sent a servant to the tenants to receive from them some of the products of the vineyard. [3]But they seized the servant, beat him, and sent him away empty-handed. [4]Again, he sent to them another servant, and him they beat over the head, and treated shamefully. [5]The vineyard-owner[b] sent yet another [messenger] and that one they killed. [He sent] many others, some of whom they beat, and murdered the rest. [6]He had one [messenger] left, a beloved son. Last of all, he sent him to them, thinking, 'They will respect my son.' [7]But those tenants said to each other, 'This is the heir. Come, let us kill him, and the estate will be ours.' [8]So they seized him and killed him, and cast his body outside the vineyard. [9]Now what will the vineyard-owner do? He will come and will destroy the tenants, and he will lease the vineyard to others. [10]Have you never read this Scripture: 'The stone which the builders rejected has become the chief stone of the corner. [11]This is the Lord's doing, and it is marvelous in our eyes'?''[c]

[12]His listeners realized He had spoken the parable against them, and they wanted to seize Him. However, they were afraid of the crowd; so they left Him alone and went away.

[13]Later they sent to Jesus some of the Pharisees and Herodians to entrap Him in His speech. [14]These came and said to Him, "Teacher, we know that You are a truthful man, influenced by no one's opinion; for You do not show any favoritism but in truth You teach the way of God. Is it lawful to pay personal tax to Caesar or not? Should we pay it or should we not pay it?" [15]Knowing their hypocrisy, Jesus said to them, "Why are you testing Me? Bring Me a silver coin[d] and let Me look at it." [16]They brought one and He asked them, Whose likeness and title are these?'' "Caesar's," they told Him. [17]Then Jesus said to them, "Pay, in full, to Caesar what belongs to Caesar,

---

[a]Cf. 4:2.
[b]Literally, "he."
[c]Cf. Ps. 118:22-23.
[d]Literally, "a denarius." See note on Matt. 18:28.

and to God what belongs to God." And they were greatly amazed at Him.

[18]Some Sadducees—people who claim there is no resurrection—came to Jesus and questioned Him. [19]"Teacher," they said; "Moses instructed us that if a man's brother dies and leaves a wife but no child, his brother should take the [widow as his] wife and raise up offspring in the name of his brother.[e] [20]Now there were seven brothers. The first took a wife but died, leaving no children. [21]The second took her, and he died without leaving children. Then the third did likewise. [22]Thus the seven [one after another married her[f] and] did not leave children. Last of all, the woman also died. [23]In the resurrection, when they rise again, whose wife will she be? For all seven had her as a wife."

[24]Jesus said to them, "Are you not deceiving yourselves because you know neither the Scriptures nor the power of God? [25]When people rise from the dead, they neither marry nor are given in marriage, but are like angels in heaven. [26]But concerning the dead, that they are raised up, have you not read in the Book of Moses, in the passage about the bush, how God spoke to him, saying, 'I am the God of Abraham and the God of Isaac and the God of Jacob'[g] [27]He is not the God of dead persons but of living ones. You are deceiving yourselves greatly."

[28]One of the Law-teachers, who had heard the discussion and realized that Jesus had answered them well, approached and asked Him, "Which is the most important of all the commandments?" [29]Jesus replied, "The most important is: 'Hear, O Israel, The Lord our God is one Lord, [30]and you must love the Lord your God with all your heart, and with all your soul, and with all your mind, and with all your strength.'[h] [31]The second is this: 'You must love your neighbor as yourself.'[i] There is no other commandment greater than these."

[32]The Law-teacher said to Him, "An excellent answer, Teacher! You are correct in saying, 'He is One, and there is no other than He;[j] [33]and to love Him with all the heart, and with all the understanding and with all the strength, and to love one's neighbor as oneself is more [significant] than all the whole burnt-offerings and sacrifices." [34]Jesus, observing how sensibly he had answered, said to him, "You are not far from the kingdom of God." After that, no one dared to question Him any more.

[35]While He was teaching in the Temple precincts, Jesus said, "What do the Law-teachers mean by saying that the Messiah[k] is David's son? [36]David himself, motivated by the Holy Spirit, declared, 'The Lord said to My Lord: Sit at My right hand until I put Your enemies under Your feet.'[l] [37]David

---

[e]Cf. Deut. 25:5-10.
[f]Cf. Luke 20:31.
[g]Cf. Exod. 3:2, 6.
[h]Cf. Deut. 6:4-5.
[i]Cf. Lev. 19:18.
[j]Cf. Deut. 4:35.
[k]Or, the Christ.
[l]Cf. Ps. 110:1.

himself calls Him 'Lord', so how can He be David's son?'' And the large crowd kept listening to Jesus with delight.

[38]In His discourse Jesus said, ''Keep on your guard against the Law-teachers who like to walk about in long robes and to receive expressions of respect in the market places, [39]and [to occupy the] chief seats in the synagogues, and the places of prominence at banquets. [40]They rob widows of their homes, and for a pretense go on saying long prayers. These will receive greater condemnation.''

[41]Jesus sat down opposite the Temple treasury,[m] and observed how the people were putting money into the receptacles. Many rich persons were tossing in large amounts. [42]But one poor widow came and threw in two mites,[n] worth only a fraction of a cent. [43]Jesus summoned His disciples and said to them, ''Truly I tell you, this poor widow has put in more than all [the others] who contributed to the Temple treasury. [44]For they all gave out of their abundance; but this woman, out of her poverty, gave everything she had—her entire livelihood.''

Chapter 13

As Jesus was leaving the Temple area, one of His disciples said to Him, ''Teacher, look at the huge stones and the magnificent buildings!'' [2]Jesus said to him, ''Do you see these great structures? Not a stone will be left upon another—absolutely[a] every one will be thrown down.''

[3]As Jesus was sitting on the Mount of Olives opposite the Temple, Peter and James and John and Andrew questioned Him privately [4]''Tell us when these things will take place'' they said, ''and what [will be] the sign when all these things are about to be accomplished.''

[5]Then Jesus began to tell them, ''Watch, so that no one leads you astray. [6]Many will come in My name,[b] saying 'I am [He]' and they will deceive many. [7]And when you hear [the noise of] battles and reports of wars, do not be alarmed. It is necessary [for such things] to happen, but the end is not yet. [8]For nation will rise against nation and kingdom against kingdom. There will

---

[m]This treasury, located in that part of the Temple area known as the Court of the Women, consisted of thirteen brazen, funnel-shaped receptacles in which were placed various monetary offerings and the Temple tax.

[n]Literally, ''two lepta, equal to a quadrans.'' The leptos was the smallest copper coin in use. Two of them had the value of a Roman quadrans, equivalent to about two-fifths of a cent in our money.

[a]The Greek double negative, *ou me,* is used twice in this sentence, making the statement strongly emphatic.

[b]That is, false Messiahs will claim the title and authority which belong only to Jesus Christ.

be earthquakes in various places, and there will be famines. These things [are the] beginning of birth-pains.

⁹"But you yourselves keep on the alert. You will be delivered over to councils, and in synagogues you will be beaten. You will stand before rulers and kings on account of Me, to bear witness before them ¹⁰And [before the end comes] the gospel must first be proclaimed to all the nations.

¹¹"So whenever you are seized and delivered up, do not worry beforehand as to what you should say. But say whatever is given you in that hour, for it will not be you speaking—it will be the Holy Spirit.

¹²"Brother will betray brother to death, and a father his child. Children will rise up against parents and cause them to be put to death. ¹³You will be hated by everyone because of My name. But he that perseveresᶜ to the end will be saved.

¹⁴"When you see the detestable thing that brings desolationᵈ standing where heᶜ ought not—may the one reading take note—then let those in Judaea flee to the hills. ¹⁵Whoever is on the roof, let him not come down or go inside to take anything out of his house. ¹⁶And whoever is in the field, let him not return to the things behind [—not even] to pick up his cloak. ¹⁷And woe to the pregnant women and to those who nurse infants in those days. ¹⁸Pray that it may not happen in winter. ¹⁹For those will be days of distress, the like of which has not occurred since the beginning of God's creation until now, and never again will occur. ²⁰And if the Lord had not shortened the [number of those] days, not a person would be saved. But for the sake of the elect, whom God has chosen for Himself,ᶠ He has cut shortᵍ the days.

²¹"At that time, if anyone tells you, 'See, here is the Christ!' 'Look, [He is] there!' do not believe it. ²²For false Christs and pseudo-prophets will appear, and they will perform signs and wonders for the purpose of deceiving the chosen ones, if that were possible. ²³But you on your part keep alert. I have told you all things beforehand.

²⁴"But in those days, after that distress, the sun will be darkened and the moon will not give its light. ²⁵The stars will be falling out of the sky, and the

---

ᶜLiterally, "he that did endure." The Greek aorist participle is proleptic, stating a future event as if it were already a fact.

ᵈSee note on Matt. 24:15.

ᵉThe Greek perfect participle, *hestekota, standing,* is masculine which personifies that which causes desolation. In the parallel passage (Matt. 24:15) the perfect participle, *hestos, standing,* is neuter, designating the detestable thing as a force or power. Luke 21:20 identifies the agents of desolation as camps of soldiers, probably a reference to the devastation of the Temple by the Roman armies which destroyed the city of Jerusalem in A.D. 70.

ᶠSelected, not in the sense of predetermined favoritism but on the basis of moral fitness. God's elect, or chosen ones, are the persons who have responded affirmatively to the divine invitation extended to all. Cf. John 3:16; Rom. 1:16; 9:6-8; Gal. 3:29; 2 Pet. 3:9.

ᵍProleptic Greek aorist indicative.

powers in the heavens will be shaken. [26]Then the Son of Man will be seen coming in [the] clouds with great power and glory.[h] [27]And then He will send the angels and gather together His chosen ones from the four winds, from the extremity of the earth to the extremity of heaven.

[28]"Now from the fig tree learn a lesson: As soon as[i] its branch becomes tender and it puts forth leaves, you know that the summer is near. [29]In like manner, when you see these things happening, you will know that it[j] is near, at the doors. [30]Truly I tell you, that this generation[k] will certainly not pass away until all these things take place. [31]The sky and the earth will pass away, but My words will not pass away. [32]But concerning that day or the hour, no one knows—not even the angels in heaven, nor the Son, but only the Father. [33]Stay alert! Keep awake! For you do not know when the time is. [34]It is like a man traveling abroad: he departed from his house, after giving authority to his servants—to each his own responsibility—and commanding the doorkeeper to watch. [35]So keep awake, for you do not know when the Master of the house is coming—whether in the evening, or at midnight, or at cock-crowing, or in the morning. [36]Be careful so that he does not come suddenly and find you sleeping. [37]Moreover, what I say to you, I say to everyone, Keep awake!"

Chapter 14

It was now two days before the Passover and the Festival of Unleavened Bread. And the chief priests and the Law-teachers were looking for an opportunity to seize Jesus by cunning and bring about His death. [2]"It must not be during the festival," they said, "or there may be a riot among the people."

[3]Jesus was at Bethany, in the house of Simon the leper.[a] As He reclined at table, there came a woman with an alabaster vase containing expensive perfume of genuine nard. She broke off the [neck of the] alabaster vase and poured [the perfume] down on Jesus' head. [4]Some [of those present] were indignant [and said] to one another "Why has this perfume been wasted? [5]It could have been sold for more than three hundred denarii[b] and [the money] given to the poor." And they began to express their resentment against her.

[6]But Jesus said, "Leave her alone. Why are you troubling her? She has done a beautiful thing to Me. [7]As a matter of fact, you will always have the poor with you, and whenever you desire you can do well to them; but you will not always have Me. [8]She has done what she could. She has anointed My

---

[h]Cf. Acts 1:9, 11.
[i]Literally, "When already."
[j]Or, He.
[k]See note on Matt. 24:34.

[a]Doubtless so called because Jesus had healed him of leprosy.
[b]About $51.00. See note on Matt. 18:28.

body beforehand for its entombment. [9]Truly I say to you, wherever the gospel is proclaimed in the entire world, what this woman did will, also, be told in memory of her.''

[10]Then Judas Iscariot,[c] one of the Twelve, went away to the chief priests in order that he might [discuss plans to] deliver Jesus to them. [11]When they heard [what he said] they were glad and promised[d] to pay him money. So Judas began looking for an opportunity to betray Him.

[12]On the first day [of the festival] of Unleavened Bread, when it was customary to sacrifice the Passover lamb, Jesus' disciples said to Him, ''Where do You want us to go and make preparations for You to eat the Passover supper?'' [13]He commissioned two of His disciples and said to them, ''Go into the city, and a man carrying a jar of water will meet you. Follow him, [14]and into whatever house he enters, say to the owner, 'The Teacher asks, ''Where is My guestroom where I may eat the Passover supper with My disciples?' '' [15]And he will show you a large upper room spread with furnishings in readiness. There make preparations for us.''

[16]So the disciples departed and went into the city and found [everything] just as Jesus had told them; and they made ready the Passover. [17]When evening came He arrived with the Twelve. [18]And as they were reclining at [the] table eating, Jesus said, ''Truly I tell you that one of you will betray Me—one who is eating with Me.'' [19]They began to grieve and to ask Him one by one, ''Surely it is not I, is it?''[e] [20]He said to them, ''It is one of the Twelve—one who is dipping [bread] into the dish with Me. [21]Certainly the Son of Man will go, just as it stands written concerning Him, but woe to that man by whom the Son of Man is being betrayed! Better for that man if he had never been born.''

[22]While they were eating, Jesus took bread and after blessing it He broke it and gave it to them, ''Take it,'' He said, ''this is My body.'' [23]Then He took a cup and, after offering thanks, He gave it to them, and they all drank from it. [24]And He said to them, ''This is My blood of the covenant—the [blood] which is being poured out on behalf of many.[f] [25]Truly I say to you, that certainly I will drink no more from the fruit of the vine until that day when I drink it new in the kingdom of God.''

[26]And after singing a hymn,[g] they went out to the Mount of Olives. [27]And Jesus said to them, ''You will all be caused to stumble because it stands written, 'I will strike the shepherd, and the sheep will be scattered.'[h] [28]But after I am raised up, I will go ahead of you into Galilee.''

---

[i]The Greek double negative expresses a strongly emphatic assertion.

[j]Interpreting the Aramaic, *Abba, Father,* as a metonym for *God.* See same idiom in Rom. 8:15; Gal. 4:6.

[k]In the light of vv. 37 and 42, this statement of Jesus seems to be a question. See note on Matt. 26:45.

[l]Or, Enough of that! Literally, ''It is enough!''

[m]Literally, ''he.''

²⁹Peter said to Him, "Even if everyone [else] stumbles, I will not!" ³⁰And Jesus answered him, "Truly I tell you that today—in this very night, before a cock crows twice—you yourself will deny Me three times." ³¹But Peter kept insisting emphatically, "If it becomes necessary for me to die with You, I will certainly not[i] deny you!" And they all spoke in like manner.

³²And they came to a place called Gethsemane, and Jesus said to His disciples, "Sit here while I pray." ³³And He took along with Him Peter and James and John, and He began to show indications of astonishment and anxiety! ³⁴"My soul is deeply grieved to the point of death," He said to them. "Remain here and keep alert!" ³⁵And having gone forward a little, He fell upon the ground and began praying that, if [it were] possible, the hour might pass from Him. ³⁶And He went on to say, "O God,[j] My Father, all things are possible for Thee. Take this cup away from Me. Yet, not what I will, but what you will."

³⁷He came back and found them sleeping, and He said to Peter, "Simon, are you asleep? Did you not have strength to say awake one hour? ³⁸Keep watching and keep praying, so that you may not fall into temptation. One's spirit indeed is eager but human nature is weak."

³⁹A second time He went away and prayed, saying the same words. ⁴⁰And coming back again, He found them alseep; for their eyes were heavy and they did not know what to say to Him. ⁴¹The third time He came and said to them, "Are you still sleeping and resting?[k] You have slept long enough![l] The hour has come. Behold, the Son of Man is being betrayed into the hands of sinners. ⁴²Get up! Let us go [to meet them]. Look, the one betraying Me has drawn near!"

⁴³And immediately, while He was still speaking, Judas, one of the Twelve, arrived, and with him a crowd with swords and clubs, who were from the chief priests and the Law-teachers and the elders. ⁴⁴Now the one betraying Him had given them a signal. "The man I shall kiss," he had said, "is the One. Arrest Him and take Him away securely." ⁴⁵So when the traitor[m] came, he at once approached Jesus and said, "Rabbi," and kissed Him. ⁴⁶And the men seized Jesus and took Him in charge.

⁴⁷But a certain one of those standing by drew his sword, and struck the high priest's servant and cut off his ear. ⁴⁸But Jesus said to them, "Did you come out with swords and clubs to seize Me as you would a bandit? ⁴⁹Day after day

---

ᶜJudas, man of Kerioth. See note on Matt. 10:4.

ᵈOr gave orders. Cf. Matt. 26:15.

ᵉThe Greek interrogative particle, *meti*, expects a negative answer.

ᶠSee note on Matt. 20:18.

ᵍProbably a portion of the Hallel. See note on Matt. 26:30.

ʰCf. Zech. 13:7.

I was face to face with you in the Temple precincts, and you did not arrest Me. However, [this is taking place] so that the Scriptures may be fulfilled.[n]

[50]And all [the disciples] forsook Him and fled. [51]A certain young man, with only a linen cloth[o] wrapped around his bare body, did try to follow[p] Him. [52]The Temple police[q] started to seize the young man, and he left the linen cloth [in their hands] and fled naked.

[53]They led Jesus away to the high priest. And all the chief priests and the elders and the Law-teachers assembled. [54]Peter had followed Jesus from a distance into the courtyard of the high priest, and was sitting with the Temple police, warming himself before the light of the fire.

[55]Meanwhile, the high priests and the entire Sanhedrin were seeking evidence against Jesus, as a basis for passing the death sentence upon Him, but they could not find any. [56]Although many were bearing false witness against Him, their statements did not agree. [57]Finally, some men stood up and testified falsely against Jesus, saying, [58]"We actually heard Him say, 'I, Myself, will destroy this Sanctuary made with hands, and in three days I will build another made without hands.' " [59]Yet even on that point their testimony did not agree.

[60]Then the high priest stood up in the midst, and questioned Jesus. "Do You make no answer?" he asked. "What [is it which] these men are charging against You?" [61]But Jesus remained silent and did not answer at all.[r] The high priest questioned Him further. "Are You[s] the Christ the Son of the Blessed One?" he asked. [62]"I am," Jesus replied, "and you will see the Son of Man sitting at the right hand of Power[t] and coming with the clouds of heaven." [63]At that, the high priest tore his garments. "Why do we need any more witnesses?" he exclaimed. [64]"You heard the blasphemy. What is your verdict?" They all condemned Jesus, declaring that He should be put to death. [65]And some began to spit at Him and to cover His face and to strike Him with their fists and to say to Him, "Prophesy!"[u] Even the Temple police, as they took charge of Him, hit Him in the face.

[66]While Peter was in the courtyard below, one of the high priests's servant-girls came along [67]and noticed him warming himself. She took a careful look at him and said, "You too, were in company with the Nazarene,

---

[n]Cf. Isa. 53:4 ff.

[o]A tunic or shirt. In this instance, perhaps a sheet.

[p]Greek conative imperfect.

[q]Literally, "They."

[r]Cf. Isa. 53:7.

[s]Emphatic.

[t]That is, vindicated and exalted by the Almighty God.

[u]The Greek infinitive, *anathematizein, to anathematize,* means to call down divine judgment upon oneself if one is not telling the truth.

Jesus!'' [68]But Peter denied it. "I do not know or understand what you are talking about," he replied. And he went outside into the entrance-way. [69]There the servant-girl saw him, and furthermore, she began telling the bystanders, "This fellow is one of them!" [70]But Peter again denied it. In a little while the bystanders said to Peter, "You certainly are one of them, for unquestionably you are a Galilean!" [71]Peter began to invoke curses [on himself][v] and to swear, "I do not know this man you are talking about!" [72]At that moment, for the second time, a rooster crowed. Then Peter remembered that Jesus had told him, "Before a rooster crows twice, you will deny Me three times."[w] And when he thought about it, he began to weep.

Chapter 15

And very early in the morning, the chief priests with the elders and Law-teachers—the whole Sanhedren—formulated their charge [to present to the governor].[a] Then they bound Jesus, and led Him away and handed Him over to Pilate.[b]

[2]Pilate asked Him, "Are you[c] the king of the Jews?" And Jesus replied, "You have spoken correctly."[d] [3]Then the chief priests made many accusations against Him. [4]Pilate questioned Him again. "Have You no reply to make?" he asked. "Look at how many charges they are presenting against You!" [5]But Jesus made no further reply whatever, so that Pilate wondered.

[6]Now during the Festival, it was customary to release a prisoner whom the people requested. [7]There was a man named Barabbas, who had been imprisoned with some insurgents who in their insurrection had committed murder. [8]The crowd went up [to Pilate's judgment seat] and began to ask that he do for them what was customary. [9]Pilate answered, "Do you want me to release to you the King of the Jews?" [10]For he was aware that the chief priests had handed Jesus over on account of envy. [11]However, the chief priests stirred up the crowd to ask for the release of Barabbas, instead. [12]Pilate asked them again, "Then what shall I do with the Man you call the King of the Jews?" [13]And they cried out, "Crucify Him!" [14]Pilate said to them, "Why? What wrong has He done?" They only cried out more loudly, "Crucify Him!"

---

[v]Cf. v. 30.

[a]Only the Roman procurator had the judicial authority to carry out the death penalty. See note on Matt. 27:2.

[b]Pontius Pilate was procurator of Judea, A.D. 26-36.

[c]The Greek pronoun is emphatic, and in this context probably an expression of scorn.

[d]See note on Matt. 27:11.

[15]So Pilate, willing to satisfy the crowd, released Barabbas for them; and after scourging Jesus, delivered Him to be crucified. [16]Then the soldiers led Jesus into the courtyard, which is the Praetorium, and called together the entire detachment of troops.[e] [17]They dressed Jesus in a purple robe, and twisted some thorns into a crown and put it on Him. [18]Then they began saluting Him [with the words], "Hail, King of the Jews!" [19]They kept striking His head with a stick, and spitting on Him, and bending their knees in [pretended] reverence to Him. [20]When they had finished mocking Him, they took off the purple robe and dressed Him in His own clothes, and led Him forth to crucify Him.

[21]A certain man, Simon a Cyrenian, the father of Alexander and Rufus,[f] was coming in from the country and, as he was passing by, [the executioners] compelled him to carry the cross.

[22]They brought Jesus to the site called Golgotha which, being interpreted, means Place of a Skull. [23]They tried to give[g] Him wine mixed with myrrh, but He refused it.[h] [24]Then they crucified Him and divided His clothes among them, casting lots [to determine] what each [soldier] should take.

[25]It was the third hour[i] when they crucified Him. [26]And the inscription, stating the accusation against Him, was written above Him: THE KING OF THE JEWS.

[27]They crucified two robbers with Him, one on His right and one on His left. [29][j]And the people who passed by kept blaspheming Him, shaking their heads and saying, "Ha! You who [talked about] destroying the Sanctuary and rebuilding it in three days![k] [30]Save Yourself by coming down from the cross!" [31]In the same way the chief priests, together with the Law-teachers, made fun of Him among themselves, and kept saying, "He saved others, but He cannot save Himself! [32]Let the Christ, the King of Israel now come down from the cross, so that we may see and believe!" Even the men who were crucified with Him were reviling Him.

[33]At midday,[l] darkness came over the whole land until the ninth hour. [34]And at the ninth hour[m] Jesus cried out in a loud voice, *"Eloi, Eloi, lama*

---

[e]See notes on Matt. 27:27.

[f]Cf. Rom. 16:13.

[g]Greek conative imperfect.

[h]According to Matt. 27:34, Jesus tasted the drugged wine but did not drink it. He did not receive any narcotic drug, but with complete consciousness He endured the agony of the cross and, with perfect self-surrender to the will of God, He met death in full possession of all His faculties.

[i]That is, nine o'clock in the morning, Jewish time.

[j]Because v. 28 is not found in the oldest extant manuscripts, it is placed in the margin of the Nestle text. But see Luke 22:37. Cf. Isa. 53:58.

[k]Cf. Mark 14:58.

[l]Literally, "And the sixth hour having come."

[m]Jesus had now been hanging on the cross six hours.

sabachthanei?"[n] which, being interpreted, means "My God, My God, for what purpose has Thou forsaken Me?"[o] [35]Some of the bystanders heard Him and commented, "Listen, He is calling Elijah!" [36]And someone ran and soaked a sponge in sour wine, fastened it to a reed and gave Him a drink,[p] saying, "Wait, let us see if Elijah comes to take Him down."

[37]But Jesus gave a loud cry and gave up His life[q] [38]Then the veil of the Sanctuary was torn in two from top to bottom.[r] [39]When the centurion who stood facing Jesus saw how He died, he said, "This Man was certainly God's Son!"

[40]Now there were also women watching from a distance. Among them were Mary the Magdalene, and Mary the mother of the younger James and of Joses, and Salome. [41]These women used to follow Jesus and minister to Him when He was in Galilee. Also [observing were] many other women who had come up with Him to Jerusalem.

[42]Now it was already late afternoon on Preparation Day, that is, the day before the Sabbath. [43]Joseph of Arimathaea, an honorable councillor,[s] who also himself was waiting for the kingdom of God, arrived and went boldly to Pilate and requested the body of Jesus. [44]Now Pilate was surprised to hear that Jesus had died so soon.[t] He summoned the centurion and asked him how long He had been dead. [45]And having been assured by the centurion [that Jesus was dead] Pilate released the corpse to Joseph, [46]who purchased fine linen cloth, took down the body and wrapped it in the linen.[u] Then he placed the body in a tomb which had been cut out of massive rock,[v] and rolled a stone against the entrance of the tomb. [47]And Mary the Magdalene and Mary the [mother] of Joses were watching where the body was placed.

---

[n]A transliteration from Aramaic, the provincial language of Palestine.

[o]Cf. Ps. 22:1.

[p]See note on Matt. 27:48. Jesus took the sour wine, or vinegar, which was the ordinary drink of laborers and soldiers (cf. John 19:29-30), but not the stupefying wine (Mark 15:23).

[q]Literally, "He breathed out [*His spirit*]."

[r]Cf. Heb. 9:3, 7-9; 9:24-28; 10:19-22.

[s]That is, Joseph was an influential member of the High Council (the Sanhedrin) in Jerusalem.

[t]Sometimes crucified persons lived several days before dying.

[u]Cf. John 11:44.

[v]Genitive singular of *petra*. See note on Matt. 16:18.

Chapter 16

When the Sabbath had passed, Mary the Magdalene, Mary the [mother] of James, and Salome bought aromatic oils in order that they might go and anoint the body of Jesus.[a] [2]And very early in the morning on the first day following the Sabbath[b] they reached the tomb just after sunrise. [3]They were saying to each other, "Who will roll away for us the stone from the entrance of the tomb?" [4]But when they looked up, they saw that the stone—although it was a very large one—had already been rolled back.

[5]And having entered the tomb, they saw a young man sitting at the right, dressed in white apparel, and they were struck with astonishment. [6]But he said to them, "Stop being astonished. You are looking for Jesus the Nazarene, the One who has been crucified. He has been raised. He is not here. Look, that is the place where they laid Him! [7]Now go, say to His disciples and to Peter, 'He is going before you into Galilee. You will see Him there, just as He told you.' "[c]

[8]They went out and fled from the tomb, for trembling and bewilderment were gripping them. They said nothing to anyone [along the way], because they were frightened.

[9][d]After He arose early on the first day of the week,[e] He appeared first to Mary the Magdalene, from whom He had expelled seven demons. [10]She went and reported it to those who had been with Him, while they were mourning and weeping. [11]When they heard He was alive and had been seen by her, they did not believe it.

[12]After these things He appeared in a different form to two of them while they were walking along on their way into the country. [13]They also went and told the rest; but neither did they believe them.

---

[a]Literally, "and anoint Him."

[b]Same idiom as in Matt. 28:1, where see note.

[c]Cf. 14:28.

[d]In the extant Greek manuscripts, there are several different endings for Mark's Gospel, although all agree as far as 16:8. Our earliest uncials, Sinaiticus and Vaticanus (fourth century texts) end with vs. 8. But the uncials Alexandrinus (fifth century), Ephraemi Rescriptus (fifth century), and Bezae (sixth century), contains vv. 9-20. Most other uncial and cursive manuscripts along with the Versions and Patristic writers, support the inclusion of the longer ending.

[e]Literally, "on the first [day] with reference to the Sabbath," i.e., the day following the Sabbath.

[14] Later, He appeared to the Eleven as they reclined at a meal, and He reproved [them on account of] their unbelief and hardness of heart, because they had not believed the ones who had seen Him after He had been raised.[f]

[15] Also He told them,[g] "Go into all the world and preach the good news to the whole creation. [16] He who believes and is baptized will be saved, but he who does not believe will be condemned. [17] Moreover, these signs will follow the believers: in My Name they will drive out demons;[h] they will speak in new languages;[i] [18] they will take up serpents;[j] and if they drink anything deadly, it will by no means harm them; they will lay hands on sick persons and they will get well.[k]

[19] So the Lord Jesus, after He had spoken to them, was taken up into heaven, and He sat down at the right of God. [20] And the disciples[l] went forth and preached everywhere, the Lord working with them and confirming the word by the signs which kept accompanying it.

---

[f] The Greek perfect passive participle, *egegermenon*, "having been raised," emphasizes the fact that Jesus was resurrected and lives permanently in the dimension of existence that transcends time and space. Cf. the perfect passive indicative in 1 Cor. 15:4.

[g] Cf. Mark 14:28; 16:7; Matt. 28:10.

[h] Cf. Mark 3:15; 6:13; Luke 10:17; Acts 8:7.

[i] Speech of various peoples in the Gentile world. Cf. Acts 2:1-11; Rev. 5:9; 7:9; 10:11; 11:9; 13:7; 14:6; 17:15.

[j] Cf. Acts 28:3-5.

[k] Cf. Luke 9:1; Acts 28:8-9; James 5:14-15.

[l] Literally, "those men, or "those persons."

Luke

Chapter 1

Since many have taken in hand to draw up a detailed account of the events which have been fully established among us, [2]just as they who from the first were eyewitnesses and ministers of the word related them to us, [3]it seemed expedient for me also, inasmuch as I have traced carefully all [these] matters from the start, to write an orderly account for you, most excellent Theophilus,[a] [4]so that you may be certain about the reliability of the declarations concerning which you have been informed.

[5]In the days of Herod,[b] king of Judea, there lived a certain priest named Zacharias, who belonged to the priest-section of Abijah.[c] His wife, whose name was Elizabeth, was [also] a descendant of Aaron. [6]And they were both righteous before God, walking blamelessly in all the commandments and ordinances of the Lord. [7]But they were childless, because Elizabeth was barren, and both were far advanced in age.

---

[a]The title *kratiste, noblest,* or *most illustrious,* or *most excellent,* by which Luke addresses Theophilus, is applied to high Roman officials. See Acts 23:26; 24:3; 26:25.

[b]Called by later historians, Herod the Great. He was an Edomite, and ruled Judaea from 37 B.C. until his death in 4 B.C.

[c]The priests were divided into twenty-four courses or main divisions of service, according to the arrangement followed since the time of David. Cf. 1 Chron. 24:3-19; 2 Chron. 8:14. Twice a year each division or section conducted the daily worship of the sanctuary in regular rotation for a week at a time, the divisions being changed every Sabbath day.

⁸One day when it was the responsibility of Zacharias' priest-group to officiate before God, and he was performing his duty, ⁹he was chosen by lot,ᵈ according to the custom of the priesthood, to enter the Sanctuary of the Lord and burn the incense.ᵉ ¹⁰The whole crowd of people were praying outside at the hour of the incense-burning. ¹¹Then there appeared to him an angel of the Lord, standing at the right side of the altar on which the incense was burned. ¹²Having seen this, Zacharias was troubled, and fear fell upon him. ¹³But the angel said to him, "Stop being afraid, Zacharias; for your request has been granted. Your wife Elizabeth will bear you a son, and you are to name him John. ¹⁴You will have joy and gladness, and many will rejoice because ofᶠ his birth. ¹⁵Indeed, he will be great in the sight of the Lord. He will never partake of any wine or intoxicating drink, and he will be filled with the Holy Spirit even from his birth. ¹⁶Many of the sons of Israel will he lead back to the Lord their God. ¹⁷In the spirit and power of Elijah, he will go before Him to turn fathers' hearts to [their] children, and disobedient persons to the prudence of the righteous, to make ready for the Lord a people adequately prepared."

¹⁸Then Zacharias asked the angel, "How can I be sure of this? I am now an old man, and my wife is far advanced in years." ¹⁹The angel answered him, "I am indeed Gabriel. I stand in God's presence, and I was commissioned to speak to you and bring you this good news. ²⁰Now, listen! You will be silent and not able to speak until the day when these things take place, because you did not believe my words, which will be fulfilled at the proper time."

²¹Meanwhile, the people were waiting for Zacharias, and they wondered why he stayed so long in the Sanctuary. ²²When he did emerge, he was not able to speakᵍ to them. They concluded that he had seen a vision in the Sanctuary, for he was making signs to them, and he remained speechless. ²³When his term of Temple service was completed, he returned home.

²⁴After these days his wife Elizabeth conceived and, for five months, kept herself secluded, saying, ²⁴"The Lord has done this for me in the days when He looked upon me to take away my humiliation at being childless."ʰ

²⁶In the sixth month [of Elizabeth's pregnancy] the angel Gabriel was sent from God to a town in Galilee called Nazareth, ²⁷to a virgin who had been promised in marriageⁱ to a man named Joseph, a descendant of David; and the virgin's name was Mary. ²⁸The angel came into her presence and said,

---

ᵈThe priests were so numerous that lots were cast to determine their periods of duty.
ᵉCf. Exod. 30:1-8.
ᶠCausal use of Greek preposition *epi*.
ᵍThe usual procedure was to pronounce the benediction. Cf. Num. 6:23-26.
ʰLiterally, "to remove my reproach among men."
ⁱThe ceremony of the betrothal took place about a year before a marriage was consummated. If a bride was unfaithful, she and her paramour were stoned to death as decreed by Deut. 22:23-24. See note on Matt. 1:18.

"Greetings, highly favored one! The Lord is with you!" [29]Mary was much disturbed by these words, and wondered what such a salutation might mean.

[30]Then the angel said to her, "Stop being afraid, Mary, for you have found favor with God. [31]Listen! You will become pregnant and bear a son, and you shall name Him Jesus. [j] [32]He will be great, and will be called the Son of the Most High. The Lord God will give Him the throne of His forefather David, [33]and He will reign over the house of Jacob forever, and His kingdom will have no end."

[34]Mary asked the angel, "How can this be, since I do not know intimately a man?" [35]The angel answered her, "The Holy Spirit will come upon you, and the power of the Most High will over-shadow you. Because the conception will take place by divine influence,[k] the Holy Offspring will be called the Son of God.[l] [36]And listen to this: Elizabeth your kinswoman, has herself conceived a son in her old age. It was thought she was incapable of motherhood, but she is now in the sixth month [of her pregnancy]. [37]For no promise from God ever goes unfulfilled."[m] [38]And Mary replied, "Behold, [I am] the Lord's servant-girl. Let it happen to me as you have said." Then the angel departed from her.

[39]Soon afterwards[n] Mary set out and went hurriedly to the hill country, to a town in Judaea, [40]and entered the house of Zacharias and greeted Elizabeth. [41]When Elizabeth heard Mary's greeting, the babe in her womb leaped. Elizabeth was filled with the Holy Spirit, [42]and with a loud outcry she exclaimed, "Fortunate are you among women, and blessed is the Child you are to bear! [43]But why am I so honored,[o] that the mother of my Lord should visit me? [44]For the moment the sound of your greeting reached my ears, the babe in my womb leaped with gladness. [45]How fortunate is she who has believed, for the things spoken to her by the Lord will be brought to completion."

[46]Mary said, "My soul declares the Lord's greatness, [47]and my spirit rejoiced in God my Savior [48]because He has looked [with favor] upon the lowliness of His servant-girl. Just think of it—from now on all generations will consider me fortunate [49]because the Mighty One has done great things for me! Holy is His Name [50]and His mercy [is shown] from generation to generation upon those who reverence Him. [51]He has performed mighty deeds with His arm. He has confused persons who are haughty and presumptuous in their thoughts. [52]He has brought down potentates from [their] thrones, and

---

[j]Cf. Matt. 1:21.

[k]Indicated by *dio,* inferential conjunction, and context.

[l]Or, the Child to be born will be called Holy, the Son of God.

[m]Literally, "For no saying from God is without power."

[n]Or, without delay. Literally, "In those days."

[o]Literally, "And whence this to me?"

He has exalted humble people. [53]He has filled the hungry with good things, and the rich He has sent away empty. [54]He has come to the aid of Israel His servant, remembering to show mercy [55]even as He spoke to our forefathers, to Abraham and to his descendants forever." [56]Mary remained with Elizabeth about three months, and then returned home.

[57]When the time came for Elizabeth's child to be born, she gave birth to a son. [58]Her neighbors and relatives heard that the Lord had demonstrated His great kindness to her, and they rejoiced with her.

[59]On the eighth day[p] they came to circumcise the child, and they were going to name[q] him "Zacharias," after his father. [60]But his mother objected. "No, indeed!" she said. "He shall be called John." [61]They said to her, "But none of your relatives is called by that name." [62]Then by means of signs they asked[r] the [child's] father what he wished him to be called. [63]He asked for a small writing-board and, to the amazement of all, he wrote, "His name is John." [64]And instantly, Zacharias' power of speech was restored and he began to talk, giving praise to God. [65]Deep reverence came upon all their neighbors, and throughout the hill country of Judaea all these matters were discussed back and forth. [66]And everyone who heard [about these happenings] kept [them] in mind. "What, indeed, will this child become?" people asked. For the hand of the Lord was surely upon him.

[67]Then Zacharias, his father, was filled with the holy Spirit and spoke with special insight,[s] saying, "Blessed be the Lord, the God of Israel, because He has visited His people and accomplished their redemption. [69]He has raised up for us a mighty Savior[t] in the lineage of His servant David, [70]just as He promised long ago through the lips of His holy prophets, [71]that He would save us from our enemies and from the hand of all who hate us, [72]to show mercy to our forefathers and to remember His holy covenant, [73]the solemn pledge which He affirmed to Abraham our forefather, [74]that we should be delivered from the hand of our foes and serve Him without fear [75]in holiness and righteousness in His sight all our days. [76]And you, child, will be called a prophet of the Most high, for you will go in advance of the Lord to make ready His ways, [77]to tell His people how they can be saved through the forgiveness of their sins,[78]because of the tender mercies of our God, by which the Dawn from the height will shine on us, [79]to give light to those who sit in darkness and in death's shadow, to guide our feet into the way of peace."

[80]And the child kept growing and gaining strength in spirit,[u] and he lived in the rugged desolate places until the time for his appearance to Israel.

---

[p]Cf. Gen. 17:12; Lev. 12:3.
[q]Greek conative imperfect.
[r]Cf. v. 22.
[s]Literally, "he prophesied."
[t]Literally, "a Horn of salvation." Horn, as a metaphor denoting power or strength, is frequent in the Old Testament. Cf. 1 Sam. 2:10; 2 Sam. 22:3; Ps. 18:2; 75:10; 132:17.
[k]Or, by the Spirit.

Chapter 2

And it happened in those days that an order went out from Caesar Augustus that a census [for taxation] should be taken of the whole Empire.[a] [2]This first census took place while Quirinius was ruling Syria. [3]Everyone was going to be registered, each person to his own town. [4]So Joseph went up from Galilee, out of the town of Nazareth, into Judaea to David's city which is called Bethlehem—because he belonged to the house and lineage of David—[5]to be enrolled together with Mary his betrothed wife[b] who was expecting a child.

[6]It happened that while they were there, the time came for Mary's child to be born. [7]So she brought forth her first-born Son, wrapped Him in bands of cloth, and laid Him down in a manger because there was no place for them in the lodging-house.

[8]There were shepherds nearby, living in the open fields and keeping guard over their flock during the night. [9]Suddenly an angel of the Lord stood by them, and the splendor of the Lord shone around them, and they were seized with great fear.

[10]"Stop being afraid," the angel told them, "for, behold, I announce to you good news of great joy which is to be shared by all people; [11]for this very day in the city of David there was born for you a Savior, who is Christ the Lord.[c] [12]And this is how you will identify Him: you will find a babe wrapped in bands of cloth and lying in a manger."

[13]Suddenly there appeared with the angel a multitude of heaven's army, praising God and saying, [14]"Glory to God in the highest realms, and on earth peace among men of good will!"

[15]When the angels had departed from them [and returned] to heaven, the shepherds kept saying to one another, "Let us go on to Bethlehem at once and see this event of which the Lord has told us." [16]So they went hurriedly and found both Mary and Joseph, and [saw] the Baby lying in the manger.

[17]After they had seen [Him] they made known the message which had been revealed to them concerning this Child. [18]And all who heard it were amazed at what the shepherds told them. [19]But Mary cherished all these things, and kept thinking about them in her heart. [20]Then the shepherds returned, giving glory and praise to God for everything they had heard and seen, [for it was] just as they had been told.

[21]Eight days after the birth of the Child, when it was time for his circumcision,[d] He was named Jesus,[e] the name given by the angel before His conception.[f]

---

[a]Greek *oikoumene,* "the inhabited earth."
[b]Cf. Matt. 1:18-25.
[c]Or, who is the Lord Messiah.
[d]See note on 1:59.
[e]See note on Matt. 1:21.
[f]Luke 1:31.

When the time came for their purification according to the Law of Moses,[s] Joseph and Mary took Him up to Jerusalem to present Him to the Lord—[23]just as it stands written in the Law of the Lord, "Every first-born male offspring[h] shall be considered as consecrated to the Lord"—[24]and to offer the sacrifice designated by the Law of the Lord. "A pair of turtle doves or two young pigeons."[i]

[25]Now a man named Simeon lived in Jerusalem, and this man was righteous and devout. He was expecting Israel's consolation, and the Holy Spirit was upon him. [26]It had been revealed to him by the Holy Spirit that he would not experience death before he had seen the Lord's Christ.[j] [27]Directed by the Spirit, he came into the Temple precincts just as the parents brought in the Child Jesus to do for Him what was customary according to the Law.[28]Then Simeon took the Child in his arms and praised God and said, [29]"Supreme Master, now Thou art permitting Thy servant to depart in peace according to Thy promise, [30]for my eyes have beheld Thy salvation [31]which Thou has prepared for all peoples to see—[32]a light for revelation to the Gentiles and for glory to Thy people Israel."

[33]While the Child's father and mother[k] were wondering at what was being said concerning Him, [34]Simeon blessed them and said to Mary His mother, "Remember, this One is appointed for the falling and rising of many in Israel, and He will be an object of much enmity;[l] [35]for the thoughts of many hearts will be exposed, and a sword will pierce even your own soul."

[36]Also present was Anna, a prophetess, daughter of Phanuel of the tribe of Asher. She was of great age, having been married for seven years [37]and a widow for eighty-four years.[m] She never left the Temple area but served [God] night and day, fasting and praying. [38]At that very hour, she came up and began giving thanks to God and talking about the Child[n] to all who were looking for the redemption of Jerusalem.

[39]When [Joseph and Mary] had completed everything required by the Law of the Lord, they returned to Galilee, to their own town of Nazareth. [40]And the Child continued growing and gaining strength, being filled with wisdom, and God's gracious favor was upon Him.

[41]Now it was the practice of His parents to go to Jerusalem each year to celebrate the Passover. [42]So when Jesus was twelve years of age, they went up as usual to the festival. [43]After their visit was completed and they started for

[g]Cf. Lev. 12:1ff.

[h]The neuter, *pan arsen*, "every male," includes the first-born male of both man and beast. Cf. Exod. 13:2; Numb. 18:15.

[i]Cf. Lev. 12:6-8.

[j]Or, Messiah, i.e., the Lord's Anointed.

[k]Some manuscripts read, And Joseph and His mother.

[l]Literally, "a sign opposed by many."

[m]Or, she was now a widow eighty-four years old.

[n]Literally, "about Him."

home, the boy Jesus stayed behind in Jerusalem but His parents were not aware of it. [44]Supposing that He was in the caravan, they went a day's journey before they began to look for Him among their relatives and acquaintances. [45]But they could not find Him, so they turned back to Jerusalem, searching carefully for Him. [46]After three days, they found Him in the temple precincts, among the scholars, both listening to them and asking questions. [47]And all who heard Him were amazed at His intelligence and His answers.

[48]When [Mary and Joseph] saw Him, they were astonished, and His mother said to Him, "My Son, why have you treated us like this? See how your father and I, greatly distressed, have been searching for You!" [49]He replied to them, "Why were you searching for Me? You knew, did you not, that I must be concerned about the things of My Father?"[o] [50]But they did not grasp the meaning of what He said.

[51]Then He went back with them to Nazareth, and lived [there] in obedience to them. His mother carefully treasured all these matters in her heart. [52]And Jesus kept advancing in wisdom and in stature, and in favor with God and man.

Chapter 3

Now in the fifteenth year of the reign of Tiberius Caesar,[a] when Pontius Pilate[b] was governor of Judaea, and Herod[c] was tetrarch of Galilee, and his brother Philip was tetrarch of the region of Ituraea and Trachonitis, and Lysanias was tetrarch of Abilene, [2]during the high-priesthood of Annas[d] and Caiaphas, the word of God came to John, the son of Zacharias, in the rugged desolate region.

[3]Then John went into all the valley of the Jordan,[e] proclaiming a baptism, characterized by repentance,[f] based upon the forgiveness of sins, [4]as it stands written in the book of the words of Isaiah the prophet, "A voice calling in the wilderness: 'Prepare ye the way of the Lord, make His paths straight. [5]Every

---

[o]Or, that it is necessary for Me to be in the places of My Father?

[a]Tiberius, stepson of Augustus, was the second Roman emperor. He reigned A.D. 14-37.

[b]See note b on Mark 15:1.

[c]That is, Herod Antipas, who ruled Galilee 4 B.C. to A.D. 39.

[d]As a former high priest Annas, the father-in-law of Caiaphas, continued to wield considerable influence. Cf. John 18:13.

[e]John preached on both sides of the Jordan River. Cf. John 10:40.

[f]Descriptive genitive.

ravine must be filled up, and every mountain and hill must be brought down, and the crooked places [changed] into straight ones and the rough roads made smooth. [6]And all people will see the salvation wrought by God.' "[g]

[7]John went on to say to the crowds who kept coming out to be baptized by him, "Broods of serpents! Who has suggested to You to flee from the coming wrath? [8]Produce fruit[h] indicative of repentance, and do not presume to say within yourselves, 'We have Abraham as our father.' For I tell you that out of these stones God is able to raise up descendants for Abraham. [9]As a matter of fact, the axe is already facing the root of the trees. Therefore, every tree that does not produce good fruit will be chopped out and thrown into the fire."

[10]In response, the crowds were asking John, "What, then, are we to do?" [11]He answered them, "Let the man who has two tunics[i] share with him who has none; and let him who has food share it with the hungry."[j]

[12]Tax collectors also came to be baptized, and they asked him, "Teacher, what should we do?" [13]And to them he said, "Collect no more than the amount designated for you." [14]Some soldiers also were asking him, "What are men like us to do?" He told them, "Do not intimidate anyone, nor take money by extortion, but be satisfied with your pay."

[15]As the people were in constant expectation, and all were wondering in their hearts concerning John, if perhaps he himself, might be the Christ,[k] [16]John definitely told them all, "I do, indeed, baptize you with water, but the One who is mightier than I is coming. I am not worthy to unfasten His sandal-thong. He, Himself, will baptize you with the Holy Spirit, and[l] with fire. [17]His winnowing fork is in His hand, that He may thoroughly cleanse His threshing floor and gather the wheat into His granary, but the chaff He will burn up with fire that cannot be extinguished."

[18]With these and many other exhortations[m] John continued proclaiming the good news to the people. [19]But when John reproved Herod the tetrarch for taking Herodias, his brother's wife, and for all [his other] evil deeds, [20]Herod, in addition to everything else he had done, shut up John in prison.

[21]After all the people had been baptized, Jesus also, was baptized, and as He was praying, heaven was opened [22]and the Holy Spirit descended upon Him in bodily form like a dove, and a voice from heaven said, "Thou[m] art My Son, the Beloved. In Thee I am well pleased!"[n]

---

[g]Subjective genitive. Cf. Isa. 40:5 (Septuagint).

[h]Plural. Cf. Matt. 3:8, where the singular sums up all the elements of repentance.

[i]See note on Mark 6:9.

[j]Literally, "Let him do likewise."

[k]Or, the Messiah.

[l]Cf. John 1:29-36; 3:27-36.

[m]Emphatic pronoun.

[n]Greek timeless aorist, as in Matt. 3:17 and Mark 1:11.

²³When Jesus began [His public ministry] He was about thirty years of age⁰
People supposed He was a son of Joseph, the son of Heli,ᵖ ²⁴the son of
Matthat, the son of Levi, the son of Melchi, the son of Jannai, the son of
Joseph, ²⁵the son of Mattathias, the son of Amos, the son of Nahum, the son
of Esli, the son of Naggai, ²⁶the son of Maath, the son of Mattathias, the son
of Semein, the son of Josech, the son of Joda, ²⁷the son of Joanan, the son of
Rhesa, the son of Zerubbabel, the son of Salathiel, the son of Neri, ²⁸the son
of Melchi, the son of Addi, the son of Cosam, the son of Elmadam, the son of
Er, ²⁹the son of Joshua, the son of Eliezer, the son of Jorim, the son of
Matthat, the son of Levi, ³⁰the son of Simeon, the son of Judah, the son of
Joseph, the son of Jonam, the son of Eliakim, ³¹the son of Melea, the son of
Menna, the son of Mattatha, the son of Nathan, the son of David, ³²the son of
Jesse, the son of Obed, the son of Boaz, the son of Sala, the son of Nahshon,
³³the son of Aminadab, the son Admin, the son of Arni, the son of
Esrom, the son of Phares, the son of Judah, ³⁴the son of Jacob, the son of
Isaac, the son of Abraham, the son of Terah, the son of Nahor, ³⁵the son of
Seruch, the son of Reu, the son of Phalek, the son of Eber, the son of Shelah,
³⁶the son of Cainan, the son of Arphaxad, the son of Shem, the son of Noah,
the son of Lamech, ³⁷the son of Methuselah, the son of Enoch, the son of
Jared, the son of Maleleel, the son of Cainan, ³⁸the son of Enos, the son of
Seth, the son of Adam, the son of God.

Chapter 4

Jesus, full of the Holy Spirit, returned from the Jordan and was led by the
Spirit in the wilderness, ²while being tempted forty days by the devil. He ate
nothing during those days, and after they were brought to an end, He became
hungry.ª ³So the devil said to Him, "Inasmuch as You are the Son of God,ᵇ
tell this stone to become bread." ⁴Jesus answered him, "It stands written,
'Man shall not live by bread only.' "ᶜ ⁵Then the devil led Him up and, in a
moment of time, showed Him all the kingdoms of the inhabited earth. ⁶And
the devil said to Him, "I will give you all this authority and their splendor; for
it has been delivered to me, and I can give it to anyone I choose. ⁷So if You

---

⁰Cf. Num. 4:3, 47.

ᵖSome scholars hold that Matthew gives Jesus' legal lineage through Joseph (Matt.
1:1-16), whereas Luke states Jesus' physical lineage through Mary. Thus Joseph was the
son of Jacob according to Matthew, and the son-in-law of Heli according to Luke.

ªIngressive aorist indicative.
ᵇSame idiom as in Matt. 4:3. See note.
ᶜCf. Deut. 8:3.

will make an act of worship to me, it will all be Yours." [8]Jesus answered him, "It stands written, 'You shall worship the Lord your God, and serve Him only.' "[d]

[9]Then the devil led Him to Jerusalem, and placed Him on the highest point of the Temple, and said to him, "Inasmuch as You are the Son of God,[e] throw Yourself down from here; [10]for it stands written, 'He will charge His angels with the responsibility of guarding You,' [11]and 'On [their] hands they will bear You up so that You may not at any time strike Your foot against a stone.' "[f] [12]Jesus answered him, "It has been said, 'You shall not test the Lord your God.' "[g] [13]So, after Satan had finished with every [kind] of temptation, he departed from Jesus until another time.

[14]Then Jesus returned in the power of the Spirit to Galilee. And reports about Him spread throughout all the surrounding countryside. [15]And He began to teach in their synagogues, and everyone was commending Him.

[16]Jesus came to Nazareth where He had been brought up and, as was His custom, He entered the synagogue on the Sabbath day. He stood up to read [the Scriptures] [17]and the book of the prophet Isaiah was handed to Him. He opened the scroll and found the place where it was written, [18]"The Spirit of the Lord is upon Me, because He has anointed Me to preach the good news to the poor. He has sent Me to proclaim release to captives and restoration of sight to the blind, to liberate the oppressed, [19]to proclaim the year of the Lord's favor."[h]

[20]Then He rolled up the parchment,[i] gave it back to the attendant and sat down [which was an indication He was about to address the audience]. The eyes of everybody in the synagogue were fixed intently upon Him. [21]And He proceeded to say to them, "Today this Scripture has been fulfilled in your hearing."

[22]They were all deeply impressed by Him[j] and were amazed because of[k] the manner and content of what He said.[l] Yet they kept remarking, "This man is Joseph's son, is He not?" [23]Then Jesus said to them, "No doubt you will quote to Me the proverb, 'physician, heal yourself!' We have heard about what happened in Capernaum. Do the same things here in Your home town!" [24]He said, "Truly I tell you, no prophet is acceptable in his native place. [25]Let Me emphasize this truth. There were many widows in Israel during the days of Elijah, when the skies were shut up for three years and six months, and there

---

[d]Cf. Deut. 6:13.

[e]A first class condition, as in v. 3.

[f]Cf. Ps. 91:11-12.

[g]Deut. 6:16.

[h]Cf. Isa. 61:1-2.

[i]Literally, the "book," "scroll," or "document."

[j]Literally, "they were all witnessing to Him."

[k]Causal use of Greek preposition, *epi*.

[l]Or, due to His interesting way of speaking. Literally, "because of the gracious words which proceeded out of His mouth."

was a severe famine over all the land; [26]yet Elijah was sent to none of them, except to a widow at Sarepta in the land of Sidon. [27]And during the time of the prophet Elisha there were many lepers in Israel, yet not one of them was cured except Naaman the Syrian.''

[28]When they heard these things, all those in the synagogue were filled with rage. [29]So they rose up and drove Jesus out of the city, and led Him to the edge of the cliff on which their city had been built, intending to hurl Him over [the precipice]. [30]But He passed through their midst and went on His way.

[31]He went down to Capernaum, a city of Galilee. And on the Sabbath He began to teach [those who were in the synagogue[m]]. [32]They were astonished at His teaching, because He spoke with [His own inherent] authority. [33]In the synagogue, there was a man under the control of an unclean demon, and he cried out with a loud voice, [34]''Ah, Jesus the Nazarene, why are You interfering with us?[n] Did You come to ruin us? I know who You are—the Holy One of God.'' [35]But Jesus rebuked him. ''Be silent,''[o] He said, ''and come out from him!'' And the demon, after hurling the man down in their midst, came out from him without injuring him.

[36]Amazement came upon all the people, and they were discussing [the incident] with one another, saying, ''What is this word? With authority and power He gives orders to the unclean spirits and they come out!'' [37]So reports concerning Him began to spread through all the surrounding country.

[38]Jesus left the synagogue and went into Simon's house. The mother-in-law of Simon was held in the grip of a high fever, so they asked Jesus to heal her.[p] [39]He stood over her, and rebuked the fever, and it left her; and at once she arose and began to serve[q] them.

[40]As the sun was setting,[r] all who had any [friends] who were ill with various diseases brought them to Jesus, and He placed His hands on each one of them and healed them. [41]Even demons came out of many people, crying out and saying, ''Thou art the Son of God!'' But He rebuked them, and would not permit them to continue speaking, because they knew He was the Christ.

[42]When morning came, Jesus went out and made His way to a lonely place. But the crowds kept seeking Him until they reached Him. They tried to prevent[s] Him from going away from them [43]but He told them, ''I must

---

[m]Cf. Mark 1:21.

[n]See note on Mark 1:24.

[o]Literally, ''Be muzzled.'' Aorist imperative passive, as in Mark 1:25. Cf. perfect imperative passive of same verb in Mark 4:39.

[p]Literally, ''and they made a request of Him concerning her.''

[q]Inchoative imperfect.

[r]The Sabbath ended at sunset, after which the sick could be carried without violating the Jewish work-rules. Cf. John 5:10.

[s]Conative imperfect.

proclaim the good news of the kingdom of God to the other cities also, because that is what I was sent to do." [44]So He went about preaching[t] in the synagogues of Judaea.[u]

Chapter 5

One day as Jesus was standing beside the Lake of Gennesaret,[a] and the crowd was pressing upon Him and listening to the word of God, [2]He saw two boats close to the shore; the fishermen had gone out of them and were washing the nets. [3]Jesus stepped into one of the boats, the one which belonged to Simon, and asked Him to push out a little distance from the shore. Then He sat down, and continued teaching the crowds from the boat.

[4]When He ceased speaking, He said to Simon, "Shove out into the deep [water], and you men lower your nets for a catch." [5]Simon replied, "Master, we have worked hard through the whole night and caught nothing. Nevertheless, on the basis of Your word, I will lower the nets." [6]And when they did so, they enclosed such a great multitude of fish that the nets started to break.[b] [7]They motioned to their partners in the other boat to come and take hold [of the nets] with them. They did, and filled both the boats [with fish] so that the vessels were about to sink.[c] [8]And when Simon Peter saw [all this], he fell down at Jesus' knees and said, "Depart from me, Lord, because I am a sinful man!" [9]He and all those with him were gripped by astonishment at the catch of fish which they had made. [10]The same was true of James and John, Zebedee's sons, who were business associates with Simon. Then Jesus said to Simon, "Stop being afraid! From now on you will be catching men!" [11]So when they had brought the boats to the shore, they left everything and followed Him.

[12]While Jesus was in one of the towns, there was present a man full of leprosy. When the man saw Jesus, he fell on his face [before Him] and begged Him saying, "Lord, if You will, You are able to cure me." [13]Jesus stretched forth His hand, touched him, and said, "I am willing; be cured!" And immediately, the leprosy left him. [14]Jesus then charged the man to tell no one. "Go and show yourself to the priest," He said, "and make the offering

---

[t]Literally, "and He kept on preaching."

[u]Some manuscripts read, Galilee.

[a]This inland lake is generally called the Sea of Galilee (cf. Matt. 15:29; Mark 1:16; 7:31). Another name for it is the Sea of Tiberias (cf. John 6:1; 21:1).

[b]Inchoative imperfect.

[c]Inchoative present passive infinitive.

concerning your cleansing, just as Moses prescribed,[d] for the certification of a cure.''[e] [15]But more than ever, the report about Jesus continued to spread, and many crowds kept coming together to hear [Him] and to be healed of their diseases. [16]But Jesus, Himself, from time to time, withdrew into lonely places and prayed.

[17]One day as He was teaching, Pharisees and expositors of the Law who had come out of every village of Galilee and from Judaea and Jerusalem, were sitting by; and the power of the Lord was [operative] in Him to heal [the sick]. [18]And behold, some men [approached] carrying a paralyzed man on a stretcher. They tried to bring him in and place him before Jesus. [19]But when they could not find any way to get him in because of the crowd, they went up on the roof, and lowered him and the stretcher [on which he was lying] down through the tiles[f] into the midst [of the crowd] in front of Jesus.

[20]When Jesus saw their faith, He said, ''Man, your sins are forgiven.'' [21]The Law-experts and the Pharisees began to reason, saying, ''Who is this fellow who is speaking blasphemies? Who but God alone is able to forgive sins?''

[22]But Jesus, aware of their thoughts, said to them, ''Why are you reasoning in your hearts? [23]Which is easier to say, 'Your sins are forgiven,' or to say, 'Stand up and walk'? [24]But to let you see that the Son of Man has authority on earth to forgive sins''—He said to the paralytic—''I tell you, Stand up, take your stretcher and go home.'' [25]At once the man stood up before them, took [the stretcher] on which he had been lying, and went away to his house, praising God. [26]Everyone was seized with fear and said, ''We have seen unusual things today!''

[27]After this, Jesus went out and saw a tax collector by the name of Levi[g] sitting at the tax office, and He said to him, ''Follow Me!'' [28]And he left everything, and rose up and kept following Him.

[29]And Levi arranged a great reception for Jesus in his home; and there was a large crowd of tax collectors and others who were dinner-guests along with Jesus and His disciples.[h] [30]But the Pharisees and their Law-experts began complaining to His disciples: ''Why are you eating and drinking in company with these tax collectors and sinners?'' [31]Jesus answered them, ''They who are healthy have no need of a physician, but they who are ill.[i] [32]I have not come to call righteous persons, but sinners to repentance.''

[33]They said to Him, ''The disciples of John fast often and offer prayers, and likewise the disciples of the Pharisees; but Yours do not conform to this practice.''[j] [34]Jesus said to them, ''You cannot make the wedding guests fast

---

[d]Cf. Lev. 13:39; 14:2-32.
[e]Literally, ''for a testimony to them.''
[f]Cf. Mark 2:4.
[g]See note on Matt. 9:10.
[h]Literally, ''with them.''
[i]Literally, ''the ones having it bad.''
[j]Literally, ''but yours keep eating and drinking.''

while the bridegroom is with them, can you? [35]But the time will come when the bridegroom is taken away from them; in those days they will fast."

[36]And He went on to speak a parable to them: "No one tears a piece from a new garment and uses it to patch an old garment. If he does, the new garment will not only be damaged but the piece taken from the new [material] will not match the old. [37]Moreover, no one pours new wine into old wine-skins. If he does, the new wine will burst the skins and run out and the containers will be ruined. [38]But new wine must be poured into new skins. [39]And no one, after drinking old [wine], wants new [wine]. For he says, "The old is good."

Chapter 6

On a certain Sabbath, as Jesus was passing through grainfields, His disciples began to pluck ears of grain,[a] rubbing [out the kernels] with their hands and eating them. [2]Some of the Pharisees asked, "Why are you doing what is not lawful on the Sabbath?" [3]Jesus answered them, "Have you not read what David did when he and those with him were hungry? [4]How he went into God's house and took the Loaves of the Presentation,[b] which he shared with his men and they ate them, even though only the priests were allowed to eat [such consecrated bread]?"[c] [5]And Jesus went on to say to them, "The Son of Man is Lord of the Sabbath."

[6]On another Sabbath, Jesus went into the synagogue and was teaching. And there was present a man whose right hand was withered. [7]And the Law-experts and the Pharisees kept watching Jesus closely [to see] if He would heal the man on the Sabbath—they wanted to find [something] by which to accuse Him. [8]But He was aware of their thoughts; so He said to the man whose hand was withered, "Get up and stand in the center!" So he arose and stood there.

[9]Then Jesus said to them, "I ask you, is it lawful on the Sabbath to do good or to do evil to save a life or to destroy it?" [10]Then He looked around at all of them and said to the man, "Stretch out your hand!" He did so, and his hand was completely restored. [11]But [the Law-experts and the Pharisees[d]] were filled with fury and began discussing[e] with one another what they might do to Jesus.

[12]In those days He went out to the mountain to pray, and He continued all night in prayer to God.[f] [13]When day came, He summoned His disciples and

---

[a]Cf. Deut. 23:25.
[b]Cf. 1 Sam. 21:1-6.
[c]Cf. Lev. 24:5-9.
[d]Cf. v. 7.
[e]Inchoative imperfect.
[f]Objective genitive.

from among them He selected twelve whom He designated apostles: [14]Simon, whom He also named Peter, and his brother Andrew; James and John; Philip and Bartholomew; [15]Matthew and Thomas; James, the son of Alphaeus; Simon called the Zealot;[g] [16]Judas, the son of James; and Judas Iscariot[g] who became a traitor.

[17]Jesus came down with them and stood on a level place. And a large crowd of His disciples, and a great multitude of the people from all Judaea and Jerusalem and from the sea coast of Tyre and Sidon, [18]had come to hear Him and to be cured of their diseases. Even those tormented by unclean spirits were being healed. [19]And the surging crowd[i] was trying to touch Him, because power was going forth from Him and they were all being cured.

[20]Then Jesus looked into the faces of His disciples[j] and proceeded to say, "How fortunate are the beggarly,[k] because yours is the kingdom of God! [21]How fortunate are those who are hungry now, because you will be satisfied! How fortunate are those who weep now, because you will laugh! [22]How fortunate are you when people hate you, and when they exclude you [from their company] and insult you and cast out your name as wicked, on account of the Son of Man! [23]On that day rejoice, and leap with joy. For just think of it—your reward in heaven will be great! For their forefathers used to treat the prophets the same way.

[24]"But how sad it is for you who are rich, because you have all the comfort you are going to get![l] [25]How sad it is for you who have plenty to eat now, because you will be hungry! How sad it is for you who are laughing now, because you will mourn and weep! [26]How sad it is when all men speak well about you, for their forefathers used to treat the false prophets the same way!

[27]"But to you who are listening I say: love[m] your enemies. Practice doing good to those who hate you. [28]Bless those who curse you. Keep praying for those who mistreat you. [29]To the person who strikes you on the cheek, offer him the other [cheek]; and if anyone takes your cloak, do not withhold from him your coat. [30]Give to anyone who asks you, and from the man who takes your belongings do not demand them back. [31]Always treat[n] other persons just as you would like for them to treat you.

[32]"If you love [only] those who love you, what credit is that to you? For even sinners love those who love them. [33]If you do good to those who do good to you, what credit is that to you? Even sinners practice that. [34]If you lend to

---

[g]Cf. Matt. 10:4; Mark 3:18.

[h]See note on Matt. 10:4.

[i]Literally, "all the crowd."

[j]Literally, "And He lifted up His eyes upon His disciples."

[k]Cf. Matt. 5:3.

[l]See note on Matt. 6:2.

[m]See note on Matt. 5:44.

[n]Indicated by Greek present imperative.

those from whom you expect to get something in return, what credit is that to you? Even sinners lend to each other to receive back an equal amount.

[35]"But love your enemies. Do good and lend without expecting [to receive] anything in return. Then your reward will be great, and you will be sons of the Most High; for He is kind to the ungrateful and wicked. [36]Always be compassionate,[o] even as your Father is compassionate.

[37]"Do not have the habit of finding fault [with others] and your faults will not be exposed. Stop condemning [others], and you will in no way be condemned. Maintain the attitude of forgiveness and you will be forgiven. [38]Keep giving, and it will be given to you. Excellent measure, pressed down, shaken together, and running over will they pour into the fold of your garment; for the measure of your giving will be the measure by which you will receive."

[39]He also said to them in a parable: "A blind man is not able to guide a blind man, is he? Will they not both fall into a pit? [40]A pupil is not superior to his teacher, but everyone who is properly trained will be like his teacher.

[41]"Why do you look at the slight imperfection[p] in your brother and not notice the great imperfection in yourself? [42]How can you say to your brother, 'Brother, let me remove the twig from your eye,' when you are ignoring the beam of timber from your [own] eye? You hypocrite! First remove the beam of timber from your [own] eye, and then you can see clearly to remove the twig from your brother's eye.

[43]"No excellent tree produces worthless fruit, nor does a worthless tree produce excellent fruit. [44]Each tree is known by its own fruit. Accordingly, figs are not gathered from thornbushes nor are grapes harvested from brambles. [45]A good man, out of the good that resides in his heart, brings forth that which is good; an evil man, out of the evil [that resides in his heart] brings forth that which is evil. For out of [the] fullness of [what is in a person's] heart his mouth speaks.

[46]"Why do you keep calling Me 'Lord! Lord!' and yet do not practice what I tell you? [47]Everyone who comes to Me and listens to My words and puts them in practice, I will show you whom he is like. [48]He is like a house-builder who dug and went deep and laid the foundation upon the solid rock.[q] When a flood came, the torrent dashed against that house but was not able to shake it, because it had been well built. [49]But he who heard [My words] and did not put them into practice is like a man who built a house on the ground without a foundation. The torrent dashed against it and immediately it collapsed; and the ruin of that house was complete."

---

[o]Linear force of the Greek present imperative.

[p]Literally, "Why do you look at the twig in your brother's eye, and not notice the beam of timber in your own eye?"

[q]Greek, *petra*. See note b on Matt. 16:18.

Chapter 7

After Jesus had finished all His sayings in the hearing of the people, He went into Capernaum. ²Now a certain centurion's servant, who was very dear to him, was seriously ill[a] and was at the point of death. ³When [the centurion] heard about Jesus, he sent some Jewish elders to Him, requesting Him to come and save [the life of] his servant.[b] ⁴When they came to Jesus, they pleaded urgently with Him, saying, "He deserves to have this [favor] done for him, ⁵for he loves our people and it was he who built our synagogue for us."

⁶So Jesus went with them. However, when He was not far from the house, the centurion sent some friends to tell Him, "Lord, trouble Thyself no further; I am not worthy to receive You under my roof. ⁷This is why I did not presume to approach You [in the first place]. But just say a word, and let my servant be cured. ⁸For I, myself, am a man who takes orders and I have soldiers under my command. I say to this one, 'Go!' and he goes, and to that one, 'Come!' and he comes, and to my servant, 'Do this!' and he does it."

⁹When Jesus heard these words, He marvelled at him; and, turning to the crowd that was following said, "I tell you, not even in Israel have I found faith like this." ¹⁰Then the messengers returned to the house and found the servant restored to health.

¹¹Soon afterward, Jesus went to a town called Nain, and His disciples and a large crowd accompanied Him. ¹²As He approached the gate of the town, it happened that a dead youth[b] was being carried out [for burial]. He was the only son of his mother, and she was a widow. A considerable crowd of people from the town were with her. ¹³When the Lord saw her, He was moved with deep compassion for her. "Stop weeping!" He said to her. ¹⁴Then He went forward and touched the stretcher. The bearers stopped and Jesus said, "Young man, I say to you, Arise!" ¹⁵The dead man sat up and began to talk, and Jesus restored him to his mother. ¹⁶Fear took hold of everyone, and they began to praise God. "A great Prophet has appreared among us!", they said. "God has visited His people!" ¹⁷And this account concerning Jesus spread through the whole of Judaea and all the surrounding country.

¹⁸Now John's disciples reported all these things to him. ¹⁹Then John summoned two of his followers and sent them to ask the Lord, "Are you actually the Coming One, or should we look for someone else?" ²⁰So the men came to Jesus and said, "John the Baptizer sent us to You to ask, "Are You actually the Coming One, or should we look for someone else?"

---

[a]Literally, "was having it bad."
[b]Literally, "that He might come and bring his servant safely through [the illness]."

²¹At that very hour Jesus cured many people of diseases and scourges and evil spirits, and granted sight to many who were blind. ²²Then He said to [John's messengers], "Go and report to John what you have seen and heard: Blind men receive sight, lame men are walking, lepers are being cleansed, the deaf are hearing, dead persons are being raised, and the poor have good news preached to them.ᶜ ²³And exceedingly fortunate is the man who finds no offense in Me."ᵈ

²⁴After John's messengers had departed, Jesus began to say to the crowds concerning John: "What did you go out into the desert to see? A reed being swayed by the wind? ²⁵Actually, what did you go forth to see? A man clothed in soft garments? Listen, those who wear gorgeous apparel and live in luxury are in the palaces of kings. ²⁶Well, what did you go out to see? A prophet? Yes, I tell you and far more than a prophet!ᵉ ²⁷This is the man of whom it stands written, 'Behold, I send My messenger ahead of You, and he will prepare the way before You.'ᶠ ²⁸I tell you, among those born of woman, no one is greater than John; yet the lowliest in the kingdom of God is greater than he."

²⁹All the people, including the tax collectors, who heard this, acknowledged the justice of God's requirements, for they had submitted to John's baptism. ³⁰But the Pharisees and the expositors of the Law, by refusing to be baptized by him, rejected God's purpose for themselves.

³¹"To what may I compare the men of this generation?" [Jesus asked]. "What are they really like? ³²They are like children sitting in a market place and calling to one another, 'We played wedding musicᵍ for you but you did not dance. We wailed the funeral dirgeʰ but you did not weep.' ³³For John the Baptizer came neither eating bread not drinking wine and you say, 'He is possessed by a demon.' ³⁴The Son of Man came eating and drinking, and you say, 'Look at Him! He is a glutton and a wine-drinker, a friend of tax collectors and outcasts!' ³⁵Never-the-less wisdom is justifiedⁱ by all who practice her precepts.!"ʲ

³⁶A prominent Pharisee invited Jesus to dine with him. So He entered the Pharisee's house and reclined at the table. ³⁷Now there was in the city a woman who was a notorious sinner. When she learned that Jesus was a dinner-guest in the Pharisee's home she brought an alabaster flask of perfume,

---

ᶜCf. v. 14.

ᵈSee note on Matt. 11:5.

ᵉLiterally, "who does not stumble because of Me."

ᶠJohn himself had been announced by prophecy, and he was the personal forerunner of the Messiah. Cf. Isa. 40:3-5, Luke 3:4.

ᵍCf. Mal. 3:1.

ʰLiterally, "We played the flute."

ⁱLiterally, "We mourned."

ʲGnomic aorist.

[38] and came and stood behind [Him] at His feet,[k] weeping. By her tears His feet were made wet, and with the hair of her head she kept wiping them. She repeatedly kissed His feet as she anointed them with the perfume. [39] When the Pharisee who had invited Jesus saw this, he thought to himself, "If this fellow were a prophet, He would know who is touching Him and what sort of character this woman is, that she is a sinner." [40] In reply [to what Simon was thinking] Jesus told him, "Simon, I have something to say to you." He said, "Teacher say it."

[41] "Two men were in debt to a certain money-lender," said Jesus. "The one owed five hundred denarii,[l] the other fifty. [42] As they had nothing [with which] to repay him, [the creditor] graciously cancelled the debt of both. Which of them, therefore, will love him more?" [43] Simon answered, "I suppose the one for whom the largest debt was cancelled." Jesus told him, "You have judged correctly." [44] Then He turned toward the woman and said to Simon, "Do you see this woman? When I entered your house, you gave Me no water for My feet; but she has wet My feet with her tears and dried them with her hair. [45] You gave Me no kiss [of welcome]; but she, since I came in, has not ceased kissing My feet. [46] You did not pour oil on My head; but she anointed My feet with perfume. [47] I tell you, her sins, although they are many, have been pardoned. That is why she has loved much. But he who is forgiven little, loves little." [48] Then Jesus said to her, "Your sins are forgiven."

[49] At that, the other dinner-guests began to say to themselves, "Who is this man who even forgives sins?" [50] But Jesus said to the woman, "Your faith hath saved you. Go in peace."

Chapter 8

It happened afterward that Jesus was traveling through town after town and village after village preaching and proclaiming the good news about the kingdom of God. The Twelve were with Him, [2] and certain women who had been cured of evil spirits and infirmities: Mary, called the Magdalene, out of whom seven demons had gone; [3] Joanna the wife of Chuza, Herod's administrator; Susanna, and many other women who, out of their resources, were giving assistance to Jesus and the Twelve.[a]

---

[k] Literally, "by all her children."

[l] While dining, persons assumed a reclining posture at the table, with their feet behind them.

[m] See note on Matt. 18:28.

[a] Literally, "who were ministering to them." Some manuscripts read, *to Him.*

[4]As a large crowd was gathering together and people were coming to Him from town after town, He spoke [to them] by a parable: [5]"The sower went forth to sow his seed. While he was sowing, some fell beside the path and was trampled under foot; and the birds of the air devoured it. [6]Other [seed] fell upon rock [covered with only a thin layer of soil] and, after springing up, it was withered because it had no moisture. [7]Other [seed] fell in the midst of thorns, and the thorns grew with it and choked it. [8]But other [seed] fell into good soil, and grew up and produced a hundred times as much [as was sown]." While He was saying these things, He called out repeatedly,[b] "The one who has ears to hear, let him listen!"

[9]Jesus' disciples began asking Him what this parable might mean, [10]and He said, "You have been given [the privilege] of knowing the mysteries of the kingdom of God, but to the rest [they are declared] in parables, so that 'seeing they may not discern, and hearing they may not understand.'[c]

[11]"Now this is the [meaning of the] parable: The seed is the word of God. [12]That beside the path represents people who have heard. Then the devil comes and takes away the word from their heart to prevent them from believing and being saved. [13]The seed on the rock [covered with only a thin layer of soil represents people] who, when they first hear the word, welcome it with joy. But these have no root—they believe for a while but fall away in time of temptation. [14]The seed which fell among the thorns represents people who have heard, but as they go along they are gradually choked[d] by anxieties and riches and pleasures of this life, and they do not reach maturity. [15]But the seed in the good soil represents the people who, with an excellent and good heart, hear the word, hold it fast, and bear fruit with perseverance."

[16]"No one lights a lamp and covers it with a bowl or puts it beneath a couch, but he places it on a lampstand in order that the people who come in may see the light. [17]Indeed, there is nothing hidden which will not become manifest, nothing secret which will not be fully known and exposed. [18]So be careful how you listen; for whoever has will be given more; and whoever has not, even what he thinks he has will be taken from him."

[19]Jesus' mother and His brothers arrived, but they were not able to get near Him on account of the crowd. [20]It was reported to Him, "Your mother and Your brothers are standing outside—they want to see You." [21]But in reply He said, "My mother and My brothers are those who hear the word of God and practice it."

[22]One day He stepped into a boat with His disciples and said to them, "Let us cross over to the other side of the lake." So they put out to sea. [23]As they sailed He fell asleep. A violent storm came down on the lake, and [the boat]

was being filled [with water] and the disciples were in danger. [24]So they came to Jesus and aroused Him, saying, "Master, Master, we are perishing!" Then He woke up and rebuked the wind and the raging waves, and they ceased and there was a calm. [25]Then He asked them, "Where is your faith?" They were frightened and amazed, saying to one another, "Who then is this Man, that He commands even the winds and the water, and they obey Him?"

[26]They reached land in the country of the Gerasenes, which is opposite Galilee. [27]When He stepped ashore a certain demon-possessed man from the city met Him. For a long time [the man] had worn no clothing, and he did not live in a house, but remained among the tombs. [28]As soon as he saw Jesus, he cried out, fell down before Him, and exclaimed in a loud voice, "Why are You interferring with me,[e] Jesus, Son of the Most High God? I beg You, do not torment me." [29]For Jesus was ordering the unclean spirit to come out of the man. Many times it had seized him, and he had been kept under guard, bound with fetters and chains, but he habitually tore apart the bonds and was driven by the demon into the desert places.

[30]Jesus asked him, "What is your name?" And he said, "Legion," because many demons had entered into him. [31]Then they began begging Jesus not to order them to go away into the abyss. [32]Now a large herd of swine was feeding there on the hillside, and so [the demons] asked Jesus for permission to enter into the swine. He gave them permission [to do so]. [33]Then the demons went out of the man and entered into the swine, and the herd stampeded down the precipice into the lake and was strangled.

[34]When the herdsmen saw what had taken place, they fled and reported it in the city and in the country places. [35]The people went out to see what had happened, and they came to Jesus, and found the man from whom the demons had departed sitting at the feet of Jesus, clothed and in his right mind, and they became frightened. [36]Those who were witnesses, told them how the demon-possessed man had been cured. [37]And all the multitude of the region around the Gerasenes asked Jesus to go away from them, because they were held in the grip of a great fear. So He entered into a boat and started back [across the lake].

[38]The man from whom the demons had gone out kept begging Jesus to allow him to remain with Him. But He sent him away, saying, [39]"Go back home and tell what things God has done for you." So the man went and proclaimed through all the city what things Jesus had done for him.

[40]Now when Jesus returned the crowd welcomed Him, for they were all eagerly waiting for Him. [41]Just then, a man named Jairus, who was a leader of the synagogue, came and fell at the feet of Jesus and began to plead with Him

---

[b]Indicated by Greek imperfect tense.
[c]Cf. Isa. 6:9-10.
[d]Greek present passive indicative.
[e]Cf. Mark 1:24; Matt. 8:29.

to come to his house, [42]because his only daughter, who was about twelve years of age, was dying. As Jesus was going, the crowds kept pressing upon Him. [43] [Among them was] a woman who had suffered from a flow of blood for twelve years, and who could not be cured by anyone. [44]She came up behind [Jesus] and touched the tassel[f] of His robe, and at once her bleeding stopped. [45]Jesus said, "Who touched Me?" When they all denied [that they had touched Him] Peter said, "Master, the crowds are pressing upon You and crushing You." [46]But Jesus said, "Someone touched Me, for I was aware of power going out from Me." [47]When the woman saw that she had not escaped notice, she came trembling and fell before Him and declared in the presence of all the people why she had touched Him, and how she had been instantly healed. [48]Jesus said to her, "Daughter, your faith has saved you; go in peace."

[49]While He was still speaking, someone arrived from the [house[g] of the] synagogue leader and said, "Your daughter has died. Do not trouble the Teacher any further." [50]But Jesus heard it, and He said to the man, "Stop being afraid! Only believe, and she will be healed."

[51]When Jesus reached the house, He did not allow anyone to go in with Him except Peter and John and James and the girl's father and mother. [52]All [the people] were weeping and beating their breasts with grief for her. But Jesus said, "Stop weeping. She is not dead but is asleep." [53]And they began to laugh scornfully at Him, knowing that she was dead. [54]But Jesus took her by the hand and called to her, "Little girl, get up!" [55]Her spirit returned, and she stood up at once. Then Jesus commanded them to give her something to eat. [56]Her parents were amazed, but He ordered them not to tell anyone what had happened.

Chapter 9

Jesus called the Twelve together and gave them power and authority over all the demons and to heal diseases. [2]Then He sent them forth to proclaim the kingdom of God and to cure [the sick]. [3]And He said to them, "Take nothing for the journey—neither staff,[a] nor provision-bag, nor bread, nor money, nor an extra tunic for anyone.[b] [4]Into whatever house you enter, there remain [for the duration of your stay] and from such a center evangelize the area.[c] [5]And as many as do not welcome you, when you leave that town shake off the dust from your feet as a testimony against them." [6]So they went out and kept going through village after village, proclaiming the good news and healing everywhere.

[7]Herod the tetrarch heard all the things that were happening, and he was

---

[f]See note on Matt. 9:20.
[g]Cf. v. 41.

[a]Cf. Mark 6:8, except a staff.
[b]Literally, "nor each to have two tunics." See note on Mark 6:9.
[c]Literally, "from there keep going out."

perplexed because some people said that John had risen from the dead, [8]some that Elijah had appeared, and others that one of the ancient prophets had arisen. [9]"I beheaded John," said Herod. "But who is this about whom I keep hearing such reports?" And he was eager to see Him.

[10]Now the apostles returned and gave to Jesus a full report of all they had done. Then He took them and withdrew privately to a city called Bethsaida. [11]But the crowds found out [about it] and followed Him. He welcomed them, and began to speak to them about the kingdom of God, and to cure those who needed healing.

[12]As the day began to decline, the Twelve approached and said to him, "Dismiss the crowd in order that they may go into the neighboring villages and farms to find lodging and provisions, for here we are in a desert place." [13]But He told them, "You, yourselves, give them [something] to eat." They replied, "We do not have more than five bread-cakes and two fish—unless we ourselves are to go and buy food for all these people." [14]Actually, there were about five thousand men. But He told His disciples, "Have them to sit down[d] in groups of about fifty each. [15]They did so, and made them all sit down. [16]Then taking the five bread-cakes and the two fish, Jesus looked up to heaven, blessed them and broke [them] and kept giving [them] to the disciples to distribute to the crowd. [17]They all ate and were satisfied, and the excess of the broken pieces there was taken up for them, twelve wicker-baskets.

[18]Now it happened, that while Jesus was praying apart from the people,[e] the disciples were with Him and He asked them, "Who do the crowds say I am?" [19]They replied, "John the Baptizer; and others Elijah; but others, that one of the ancient prophets has risen up." [20]Then He said to them, "But you—who do you say I am?" Peter responded, "The Christ of God!" [21]Then Jesus admonished them strongly and charged them not to tell this to anyone. [22]He said, "The Son of Man must suffer many things, and be rejected by the elders and chief priests and scribes, and be killed. But He will be raised up on the third day."

[23]Jesus went on to say to all of them, "If anyone wishes to come after Me, let him disregard himself and take up his cross each day and keep on following Me. [24]For whoever desires to save his life will lose it, but whoever loses his life for My sake will save it. [25]For what shall it profit a man if he gains the whole world but loses or forfeits himself? [26]For whoever is ashamed of Me and My words, of him will the Son of Man be ashamed when He comes in His glory and [in the glory] of the Father and of the holy angels. [27]I tell you truly, there are some of those standing here who will by no means experience death until they see the kingdom of God.

[28]Now about eight days after making these statements, Jesus took Peter and John and James and went up into the mountain to pray. [29]And while He was praying, the appearance of His countenance was changed and His clothing became white—dazzling.[f] [30]Suddenly, two men—Moses and Elijah in

---

[d]Literally, "to recline, as at meal-time."

[e]Literally, "alone."

[f]Literally, "flashing forth," implying an inward source of light.

fact—were talking with Him. [31]They had appeared in a glorified state[g] and were speaking of His departure, which He was about to accomplish at Jerusalem.

[32]Peter and those with him had been weighed down by sleep; but on getting fully awake they saw Jesus' glory and the two men standing with Him. [33]As they were being parted from Jesus, Peter said to Him, "Master, it is excellent for us to be here! Let us make three booths—one for You, one for Moses, and one for Elijah," not realizing what he was saying. [34]But while he was speaking these things, a cloud came and overshadowed them; and they were afraid as they entered the cloud. [35]Then out of the cloud came a voice which said, "This is My Son, the Chosen One. Keep listening to Him!" [36]And after the voice had spoken,[h] Jesus was found alone. [The disciples] kept silent and told no one in those days anything of what they had seen.

[37]On the following day when they had come down from the mountain, a large crowd met Him. [38]Suddenly, a man from the crowd cried out, saying, "Teacher, I beg you to consider my son, because he is my only [child]. [39]A spirit seizes him, and suddenly, he shrieks and it throws him into a foaming convulsion; and with difficulty it withdraws, leaving him badly bruised. [40]I begged Your disciples to drive it out, but they could not."

[41]Jesus replied, "O faithless and perverse generation! How long shall I be with you and put up with you? Bring your son here." [42]While [the boy] was approaching, the demon threw him down and convulsed him violently. But Jesus rebuked the unclean spirit and cured the boy and gave him back to his father. [43]And the people were all amazed at the majesty of what God[i] had done.

While everyone was marvelling at all the things Jesus was doing, He said to His disciples, [44]"Listen carefully and remember these words:[j] The Son of Man is about to be given over into the hands of men." [45]But they did not understand this saying. Actually, [its meaning] was kept hidden from them, so that they might not grasp it. And they were afraid to question Him about it.

[46]A discussion arose among them as to which of them might be greatest. [47]But Jesus, who knew the attitude of their heart, took a little child and placed it beside Himself. [48]Then He said to them, "Whoever receives this child in My Name receives Me; and whoever receives Me receives Him who sent Me. For the one who is lowliest among you all, that person is [the one who is] great."

[49]John remarked, "Master, we saw someone driving out demons in Your name, and we tried to stop[k] him, because he does not follow with us." [50]But

---

[g]Literally, "in glory."

[h]Literally, "After the voice had come."

[i]Subjective genitive.

[j]Literally, "Put these words into your ears."

[k]Conative imperfect.

Jesus said to him, "Cease trying to stop him, for whoever is not against you is for you."[1]

[51]Now it happened that, as the days for His ascension were drawing near,[m] He set His face firmly to go to Jerusalem. [52]So He sent messengers ahead of Him. And they went forth and entered into a village of the Samaritans to prepare for Him. [53]But [the Samaritans] would not receive Jesus, because His direction indicated He was going to Jerusalem. [54]When the disciples James and John saw this, they said, "Lord, do You want us to command fire to come down from heaven and destroy them?"[n] [55]But Jesus turned and rebuked them. [56]And they went to a different village.

[57]While they were going along the road someone said to Him, "I will follow You wherever You go." [58]But Jesus told him, "The foxes have dens and the birds of the sky have roosting-places, but the Son of Man has nowhere to lay His head." [59]Jesus said to another man, "Follow Me." He replied, "Permit me first to go back and bury my father." [60]But Jesus told him, "Let the [spiritually] dead bury their own dead. You go forth and keep proclaiming the kingdom of God." [61]Another man said, "I will follow You, Lord; but first let me say farewell to those at my home." [62]Jesus said to him, "No one, who puts his hand to the plough and keeps looking at the things behind him, is fit for the kingdom of God."

Chapter 10

Now after these things, the Lord commissioned seventy others and sent them forth by twos to go ahead of Him into every city and place where He, Himself, intended to visit. [2]And He told them, "The harvest is indeed abundant, but the laborers are few. So ask the Lord of the harvest to thrust out laborers into His harvest. [3]Go on your way. Remember that I am sending you forth like lambs in the midst of wolves. [4]Do not take a purse, nor a provision-bag, nor [extra] sandals, and do not [stop to] greet[a] anyone along the way. [5]And into whatever house you enter, first say, 'Peace [be] to this house.' [6]And if there is someone there who is peaceable in character,[b] your peace will rest upon him; if not, it will come back to you. [7]Stay at the same house, eating and drinking what they provide;[c] for the worker deserves his pay. Do not be moving around from one house to another.[d]

---

[1]Cf. Mark 9:39.
[m]Literally, "were being fulfilled."
[n]Cf. 2 Kings 1:10-14; Mark 3:17.

[a]Eastern greetings were elaborate and time-consuming. Cf. 2 Kings 4:29.
[b]Literally, "And if a son of peace is there."
[c]Literally, "the things from them."
[d]Cf. 9:4.

[8]"When you enter a city and the people receive you, eat what is placed before you. [9]Heal the sick who are there, and tell them, 'The kingdom of God has drawn near to you.' [10]But if you enter a town and they do not receive you, go out into its streets and say, [11]'Even your town's dust that sticks to our feet we shake off [as a testimony] against you. Nevertheless, be certain of this, the kingdom of God has drawn near.' [12]I tell you, it will be less severe for Sodom in the day of judgment[e] than for that town.

[13]"Woe to you, Chorazin! Woe to you, Bethsaida! For if the mighty works which have been done among you, had occurred in Tyre and Sidon, they would have repented long ago, sitting in sackcloth and ashes. [14]Nevertheless, it will be less severe for Tyre and Sidon in the judgment than for you. [15]And you, Capernaum, you do not expect to be exalted to the sky, do you? You will be brought down to Hades!

[16]"Whoever listens to you, listens to Me, and he who rejects you, rejects Me. And whoever rejects Me, rejects Him who sent Me."

[17]The seventy returned with joy, saying, "Lord, even the demons are subject to us in Your name." [18]He said to them "I was watching Satan fall[f] like a flash of lightning from the sky. [19]Yes, I have given you the authority to tread on serpents and scorpions, and over all the power of the enemy; hence nothing can harm you in any way whatever.[g] [20]However, do not rejoice because the spirits are subject to you; instead, keep on rejoicing because your names are inscribed in heaven."

[21]At that moment, Jesus rejoiced greatly in the Holy Spirit and said, "I make acknowledgement to Thee, Father, Lord of heaven and earth, because Thou hast hidden these things from wise and clever persons, and revealed them to little children. Yes, Father, because it was pleasing to Thee to do so. [22]All things have been given over to Me by My Father; and no one knows who the Son is except the Father, and who the Father is except the Son, and [he] to whom the Son chooses to reveal [Him]."

[23]Jesus turned to the disciples and said privately, "How fortunate are the eyes that see what you are seeing! [24]Indeed, I tell you that many prophets and kings desired to see the things you see, but did not see [them]; and to hear the things which you hear but did not hear [them]."

[25]A certain professional expositor of the [Mosaic] Law stood up to test Jesus, saying, "Teacher, what must I have done to gain eternal life?" [26]Jesus replied, "What stands written in the Law? How do you interpret it?" [27]The lawyer replied, "You must love the Lord your God with all your heart, and with all your soul, and with all your strength, and with all your mind; and [you

---

[e]Literally, "in that day." Cf. Matt. 10:15.
[f]Cf. John 12:31; 16:11.
[g]Force of Greek triple negative.

must love] your neighbor as [you love] yourself." [h] [28]Jesus said to him, "You have answered correctly. Practice this and you will live."

[29]But the lawyer, wishing to justify himself, said to Jesus, "And who is my neighbor?" [30]Jesus took up that point and said, "A certain man was on his way from Jerusalem to Jericho and he was attacked by bandits who, after stripping and beating him, went away leaving him half dead. [31]It happened that a certain priest was going down that road. He saw [the wounded man] but passed by on the opposite side. [32]A Levite came along and reacted the same way—he looked at the man and passed by on the other side. [33]But a certain Samaritan, who was on a journey, approached. When he saw the man, he was moved with deep compassion. [34]He went over to him, treated his wounds with oil and wine, [i] and carefully bandaged them. Then he placed him upon his own riding-animal, and brought him to a public lodging-place, and cared for him. [35]The next day he took out two denarii, [j] and gave them to the inn-keeper. 'Take care of him,' he said, 'and whatever you may spend [on him] in addition, I will, myself, repay you when I return.' [36]In your opinion, which of these three became a neighbor to the man who fell among the bandits?" [37][The lawyer] replied, "The one who showed mercy to the man." Then Jesus told him, "You go and make it your practice to do likewise."

[38]As they continued their travels, Jesus entered a certain village where a woman named Martha welcomed Him into her house. [39]She had a sister named Mary, who seated herself beside the Lord, at His feet, and was listening to His word. [40]But Martha, anxiously preoccupied with preparing a meal, [k] approached Jesus and said, "Lord, do You not care that my sister has left it to me to do the serving alone? Tell her to take hold at the other end [l] [of the table] together with me." [41]But the Lord replied to her, "Martha, you are worried and disturbed about many things, [42]but only a few things are needful—actually just one. Indeed, Mary has chosen the better portion, and it will not be taken away from her."

---

[h]Cf. Deut. 6:5; Lev. 19:18.

[i]Ancient remedies for wounds. Olive oil was soothing, and wine had disinfectant qualities.

[j]A denarius was the usual daily wage of an ordinary laborer. Cf. Matt. 20:2. Two denarii would pay for a considerable period at the inn, possibly for a stay as long as two months.

[k]Literally, "distracted about much serving."

[l]Indicated by the aorist subjunctive of the double compound, *sunantilambanomai.* Cf. The present indicative of this verb in Rom. 8:26.

Chapter 11

Jesus was in a certain place praying and, when He ceased, one of His disciples said to Him, "Lord, teach us to pray, even as, also, John taught his disciples." [2]So He told them, "When you pray, say, 'Father, may Thy name be held in reverence. May Thy kingdom come. [3]Keep giving us day by day the bread we need.[a] [4]And forgive us our sins, for we, also, ourselves are maintaining an attitude of forgiveness toward everyone who is indebted to us. And do not bring us into testing.' "[b]

[5]And Jesus said to them, "Suppose one of you has a friend to whom he goes in the middle of the night and says, 'Friend, lend me three loaves of bread, [6]because a friend of mine just came to my house after a journey, and I have nothing to set before him.' [7]And [suppose] he from the inside answers 'Stop troubling me! The door has already been closed and locked for the night,[c] and my children are with me in bed. I cannot get up and give you anything.'

[8]"I tell you, even if the man will not get up and give him anything because of friendship, yet on account of his persistence[d] he will rise up and give him as much as he needs.

[9]"So I tell you, keep asking, and it will be given to you. Keep searching, and you will find. Keep knocking, and [the door] will be opened to you. [10]For everyone who continues asking, continues receiving, and the one who continues searching, continues finding, and to the one who continues knocking, [the door] will be opened. [11]Would any one of you who is a father give his son a serpent if he asked for a fish? [12]Or if he asks for an egg, he will not hand him a scorpion, will he? [13]If you then, imperfect as you are[e] know how to give good things to your children, how much more will the Heavenly Father give the Holy Spirit to those who ask Him?"

[14]And Jesus was casting out a demon which had rendered a man speechless.[f] And when the demon had gone out, the man who had been speechless spoke. The crowds were amazed. [15]But some of them said, "He drives out the demons in connection with Beezeboul,[g] the chief of the demons." [16]But others, testing Him, were demanding of Him a sign from heaven. [17]But He, knowing their thoughts, said to them, "Every kingdom divided against itself is brought to ruin: households attack each other [as such a kingdom] collapses.[h] [18]So if Satan has been divided against himself, how

---

[a]See note on Matt. 6:11.
[b]Cf. Matt. 6:13.
[c]Perfect passive indicative, *shut to stay.*
[d]Or, shamelessness.
[e]Or, in your poor condition.
[f]Literally, "and it was speechless."
[g]See note on Matt. 10:25.
[h]Literally, "and house falls against house."

can his kingdom stand? Yet you say that I drive out the demons in connection with Beezeboul. [19]Now if I by means of Beezeboul expel the demons, by whom do your sons expel them? Therefore, they will act as your judges. [20]But if by means of God's power I expel the demons, you may be sure[i] that the kingdom of God has reached you.

[21]"When a strong man, fully armed, guards his palace, his possessions are safe. [22]But when someone stronger than he appears and overcomes him, [the conqueror] takes all the weapons on which [the vanquished] had relied, and distributes the plunder. [23]He who is not with Me is against Me, and he who does not gather with Me scatters.

[24]"When the unclean spirit goes out of a man, it goes through waterless places in search of rest but does not find it. So it says, 'I will go back to my house which I left.' [25]And having returned, it finds it swept and set in order. [26]Then it goes and takes with it seven other spirits more wicked than itself; and they enter in and dwell there. And the last condition of that man is worse than the first."

[27]While Jesus was saying these things, a certain woman from the crowd lifted up her voice and said to Him, "Blessed is the womb that bore You and the breasts from which You nursed!" [28]However He said, "Yes indeed, but more blessed are those who listen to the word of God and obey it!"

[29]As the crowds were pressing upon Jesus, He proceeded to say, "This generation is a wicked generation. It seeks a sign, but no sign will be given to it except the sign exemplified by Jonah.[j] [30]For as Jonah became a sign to the Ninevites, so the Son of Man will be to this generation. [31]The queen of the South will be raised up in the judgment together with the men of this generation and condemn them, because she came from the extremities of the earth to hear the wisdom of Solomon,[k] and just think of it, something greater than Solomon is here! [32]The men of Nineveh will stand up in the judgment together with the present generation and condemn it, because they repented on the basis of Jonah's proclamation,[l]; and just think of it, something greater than Jonah is here!

[33]"No one lights a lamp and places it in a secret place, or under a bowl,[m] but on the lamp-stand in order that the people who come in may see the light. [34]The lamp of the body is your eye. When your eye is sound,[n] your entire body is full of light; but when [your eye] is diseased,[o] your body is in

---

[i]Rendering *ara,* Greek inferential particle.

[j]Subjective genitive. Cf. Matt. 12:39.

[k]Cf. 1 Kings 10:1-13.

[l]Jonah 3:5-10.

[m]See note on Matt. 5:15.

[n]Literally, "without fold," i.e., without duplicity or mixed motives; hence, focused on what is good.

[o]Bad, or impaired; focused on wickedness.

darkness. [35]So make sure that the light in you is not darkness. [36]If therefore, you entire body is full of light, with no part in darkness, it will be as fully illumined as when a lamp shines upon you with its brilliance.''

[37]As Jesus finished speaking, a Pharisee invited Him to breakfast with him. So He went in and reclined at the table. [38]But the Pharisee noticed with surprise that Jesus did not first wash [His hands ceremonially][p] before eating. [39]But the Lord said to him, ''Now you Pharisees cleanse the outside of the cup and the dish, but within yourselves you are full of greed and wickedness. [40]You foolish people! Did not He who made the outside make the inside, also? [41]Give to the poor the contents[q] [of the cup and the dish] and, behold, all things are clean to you.

[42]''But how sad for you Pharisees[1] You pay tithes of mint and rue and every [kind of] garden plant[r] but disregard justice and the love of God. You should have practiced these [major obligations] without neglecting those [lesser things]. [43]Woe to you Pharisees, because you value highly the chief seat[s] in the synagogues and greetings of honor in the market-places. [44]Woe to you, because you are like unmarked tombs over which people walk without knowing it.''

[45]At that, one of the official Law interpreters said to Him, ''Teacher, by saying these things You are insulting us, also.'' [46]But He replied, ''Woe to you Law-experts too, because you load men with burdens difficult to bear but you yourselves will not lift one of your fingers [to lighten] the burdens. [47]Woe to you, because you build memorials for the prophets, whom your fathers killed. [48]Accordingly you bear witness to what your fathers did, and you approve fully their deeds, because they put to death [the prophets] and you build [their monuments].

[49]''That is why God in His wisdom said,[t] 'I will send to them prophets and apostles, some of whom they will kill and [others they will] persecute,'[u] [50]so that the blood of all the prophets, shed since the foundation of the world, may be charged to the present generation; [51]from the blood of Abel to the blood of

---

[p]The Pharisees regularly dipped their hands in water as a religious rite before meals. Cf. Matt. 15:2; Mark 7:2.

[q]Literally, ''But give as alms the things that are within.'' That is, give from the heart. The emphasis is upon inward righteousness. Cf. Matt. 23:26.

[r]Cf. Matt. 23:23.

[s]This was a semi-circular bench at the front of the synagogue, facing the congregation.

[t]Literally, ''the Wisdom of God said.'' Cf. 7:35.

[u]Cf. Matt. 23:34.

Zachariah[v] who perished between the Altar and the Sanctuary. Yes, I say to you, it will be required of this generation!

[52]"Woe to you interpreters of the Law, for you have taken away the key of knowledge. You, yourselves, have not gone in, and you have prevented those who are trying to enter."[w]

[53]When Jesus went out from the Pharisees' house,[x] the Law-experts and the Pharisees began to set themselves vehemently against Him, to draw out from Him answers concerning many questions, [54]plotting against Him, in an effort to get hold of some statement they could use against Him.[y]

Chapter 12

In the meantime, when a crowd of tens of thousands had come together, so that the people were stepping on one another, Jesus proceeded to say first to His disciples: "Be careful and avoid the leaven—the hypocrisy—of the Pharisees. [2]For there is nothing covered up which will not be revealed, and nothing hidden which will not become known. [3]Therefore, whatever you have said in the darkness will be heard in the light, and what you whispered to the ear in the inner rooms, will be proclaimed from the roof-tops.

[4]"But I tell you who are My friends, do not be afraid of those who kill the body, and after that can do nothing more. [5]I will show you the One you should fear: Fear Him who, after killing you, has the authority to cast you into Gehenna.[a] Yes, I say to you, fear Him! [6]Are not five sparrows sold for two pittances?[b] Yet, not one [little bird] has been forgotten in the sight of God. [7]actually, even the hairs of your head have all been counted. Stop being afraid. You are of more value than many sparrows.

[8]"Furthermore I tell you, whoever acknowledges Me before men, him also the Son of Man will acknowledge before God's angels. [9]But whoever denies Me before men will be denied before God's angels. [10]Anyone who speaks a word against the Son of Man, it shall be forgiven him; but to him who blasphemes against the Holy Spirit it will not be forgiven.

---

[v]In the Jewish canon, the books of Chronicles stood last. From this viewpoint, the slaying of Abel (Gen. 4:10) and of Zechariah the son of Jehoiada (2 Chron. 24:20-22) represent all the martyrs of the Old Testament period.

[w]Greek conative present participle.

[x]Literally, "from there."

[y]Literally "to catch something out of His mouth."

[a]See note on Matt. 5:22.

[b]Two *assarions*. Cf. Matt. 10:29. Apparently when four of the little birds were purchased, a fifth was thrown in free, which shows their trivial market value.

[11]"Whenever they take you before the synagogues and the ruling powers and the authorities, do not worry about how you will defend yourselves or what you will say; [12]for the Holy Spirit will teach you at the very moment what you ought to say."

[13]Someone out of the crowd said to Jesus, "Teacher, tell my brother to give me my share of our inheritance." [14]And Jesus asked him, "Man, who appointed Me a judge or an arbitrator over you?" [15]Furthermore, He said to them, "Be careful, and guard yourselves against every [kind of] greed, for a person's life does not consist in the abundance of his possessions."

[16]Then Jesus told them this parable: "The land of a certain wealthy man was very productive. [17]So he began reasoning with himself, saying, 'What shall I do, because I do not have enough space to store my crops?' [18]So he said, 'This is what I will do: I will tear down my barns and build larger ones and in them I will store all my grain and goods. [19]Then I will say to my soul, 'Soul you have many good things stored up for many years. Relax, take life easy. Eat, drink, and have a merry time!' [20]But God said to him, 'Foolish man! This very night your soul will be demanded of you. Then the things you have accumulated—whose will they be?' [21]So [it is with] the person who stores up [material things] for himself, and is not rich in God."

[22]Jesus said to His disciples, "Therefore I tell you, stop worrying about your [present] life—what you are to eat; or about your body—what you are to wear. [23]For life is more than food, and the body is more than clothing. [24]Look at the ravens—they neither sow nor reap; they have no storehouses or barns—yet God feeds them. How much more important are you than the birds!

[25]"As a matter of fact, who of you, by means of worry, can add to the span of his life?[c] [26]If, therefore, you are not able to do the least thing, why worry about the other matters? [27]Consider the lilies,[d] how they neither spin nor weave; yet I tell you, even Solomon in all his splendor was never dressed like one of these. [28]Now if God clothes [in such beauty] the grass of the meadow, which exists today and tomorrow is thrown into the furnace, how much more [will He clothe] you, men of little faith!

[29]"So do not be concerned about what you are to eat and what you are to drink; and stop wavering with apprehension, [30]For all the nations of the world seek after these things; but your Father knows that you need them. [31]Strive for His kingdom, and these things will be added to you. [32]Have no fear, little flock, because your Father has been pleased to give you the kingdom.

[33]"Sell your possessions and give [the money] to the poor. Make for yourselves purses that never wear out—inexhaustible treasure in

---

[c]See not on Matt. 6:27.

[d]Jesus may have used *krina,* "lilies," in a generic sense, referring to all the colorful wild flowers that adorn the fields of Palestine in the spring.

heaven—where no thief comes near and no moth works destruction. [34]For where your treasure is, there, also, your heart will be.

[35]"Keep your belts fastened [in readiness for action][e] and your lamps burning. [36]And be like men waiting for their master to return from wedding festivities, so that, when he arrives and knocks, they may open [the door] for him at once. [37]Fortunate are those servants whom the master finds watching when he comes. Truly I tell you, he will dress himself [as one who serves], and make them recline at table, and he will come around and serve them.[f] [38]And if he happens to come in the second or in the third watch and finds those servants alert,[g] they are fortunate. [39]But be sure of this: if the housemaster had known what time the thief was coming, he would not have allowed him to break into his house. [40]So you yourselves must keep prepared, because in an hour when you are not expecting [Him], the Son of Man will come."

[41]Peter asked, "Lord, are you giving this illustration to us, or to everybody else also?" [42]And the Lord replied, "Who then is the faithful and sensible administrator whom the master appoints over his household attendants, to give them at the proper time their portion of food? [43]Fortunate is that servant whom his master will find so doing when he comes. [44]Truly I tell you, that he will place him in charge of all his possessions.

[45]"But if that servant says in his heart, 'My lord delays His coming,' and begins to beat the menservants and the maidservants, and to eat and drink and get drunk, [46]that servant's master will come on a day when he does not expect [him], at an hour which he does not know, and will punish him with extreme severity,[h] and put him with the unfaithful.

[47]"Now that servant who knows the will of his master and does not get ready or carry out the requirements will be beaten with many lashes; [48]while the one who does not know [his master's will] but deserves punishment for what he has done, will be beaten with few [lashes]. For everyone to whom much has been given, much will be required; and to whom much has been entrusted, much more will be expected.

[49]"I come to cast fire upon the earth, and how I wish it were already set ablaze! [50]But I have a baptism to undergo, and how distressed I am until it is accomplished! [51]Do you suppose that I came to bring peace to the earth? Not at all, I tell you, but rather division.[i] [52]For from now on five in one house will be divided, three against two and two against three. [53]Father will be divided against son and son against father, mother against daughter and daughter against mother, mother-in-law against daughter-in-law and daughter-in-law against mother-in-law."

---

[e]Otherwise quick movement would be impeded by the loose-flowing robes worn by Eastern peoples.
[f]Cf. Rev. 3:20; 19:9.
[g]Literally, "and finds [them] thus."
[h]Literally, "he will cut him in two."
[i]Cf. Matt. 10:34-36.
[j]Greek, *leptos*, the smallest coin in use. See note on Mark 12:42.

[54]Jesus went on to say to the crowds, "When you see a cloud rising in the west, immediately you say, 'A shower of rain is coming,' and it happens that way. [55]When a south wind blows, you say, 'There will be hot weather,' and it happens that way. [56]You hypocrites! You know how to discern the appearance of the earth and the sky, but why can you not discern [the signs of] this time?

[57]"Moreover, why can you not decide for yourselves what is right? [58]For example, when you are going with your opponent to the magistrate, work diligently to reach a settlement with him on the way, lest he drag you before the judge, and the judge hand you over to the court officer, and the court officer throw you into prison. [59]I tell you, you will never get out from there until you pay even the last mite."[j]

Chapter 13

Now, at that very time some were present who told Jesus about the Galileans whose blood Pilate[a] had mingled with [that of] their sacrifices. [2]Jesus asked, "Do you think that these Galileans had become sinners beyond all the [other] Galileans because they suffered these things? [3]Not at all. But I tell you that unless you repent, You will all likewise perish. [4]Or those eighteen upon whom the tower at Siloam collapsed and killed them, do you think they had become more guilty than all the [other] people dwelling in Jerusalem? [5]Certainly not! But I tell you, unless you repent you will all perish in a similar manner."

[6]Jesus went on to speak this parable: "A certain man had a fig tree growing[b] in his vineyard. He came seeking fruit on it but did not find any. [7]So he said to the vinedresser, 'Listen, for three years I have kept coming[c] to look for fruit on this fig tree, and I find none. Cut it down. Why should it impoverish even the soil?' [8]The vinedresser replied, 'Master, leave it yet this year until I dig around it and fertilize it. [9]After that, perhaps it may bear fruit. If not, you can have it cut down.' "

[10]Jesus was teaching in one of the synagogues on the Sabbath. [11]And behold, there was present a woman who for eighteen years had been under the influence of a spirit that caused an infirmity,[d] so that she was bent over and was utterly unable to stand up straight. [12]When Jesus saw her, He summoned her and said, "Woman, you are released from your infirmity." [13]Then He placed His hands upon her, and immediately, she stood up straight and began to praise God.

---

[a]Cf. 23:12.
[b]Literally, "having been planted."
[c]Literally, "it is three years since I continue coming."
[d]Objective genitive.

¹⁴But the ruler of the synagogue, indignant because Jesus had healed on the Sabbath, said to the crowd, "There are six days on which work may be done. Come on those days and be healed, but not on the Sabbath day." ¹⁵But the Lord replied to him, "You hypocrites! Does not each one of you loose his ox or his donkey from the stall and lead it away to water it on the Sabbath day? ¹⁶And was it not expedient that this woman, a daughter of Abraham, whom Satan had bound for these eighteen years, be loosed from her bondage on the Sabbath day?"

¹⁷As Jesus was saying these things, all His adversaries were put to shame, while the entire crowd kept rejoicing because of all the glorious things being done by Him.

¹⁸"What is the kingdom of God like," Jesus went on to ask, "and to what may I compare it? ¹⁹It is like a grain of mustard seed which a man took and planted in his garden. It grew and became a tree, and the birds of the sky lodged in its branches." ²⁰And again He asked, "To what may I compare the kingdom of God? ²¹It is like yeast which a woman took and mixed into three portions of flour until it was all leavened."

²²And Jesus continued His journey through town after town and village after village, teaching as He made His way toward Jerusalem. ²³And someone asked Him, "Lord, will only a few people be saved?" He said to them, ²⁴"Put forth every effortᵉ to get in through the narrow door because many, I tell you will try to enter but will not be able. ²⁵When once the Master of the house gets up and closes the door, then you may find yourselvesᶠ standing outᵍ and knocking repeatedly on the door, calling, 'Lord, open for us!' But He will answer and say to you, "I do not know you, or where you came from.'²⁶Then you will begin to say, 'We ate and drank in Your company, and You taught in our streets!' ²⁷But He will reply, 'I tell you, I do not know where you come from. Depart from Me, all you workers of unrighteousness!'" ²⁸There will be weeping and the grinding of teeth when you see Abraham and Isaac and Jacob and all the prophets in God's kingdom but you, yourselves, being thrown outside. ²⁹People will come from east and west, and from north and south, and sit down to feast at the table in the kingdom of God. ³⁰Think of it! Some who are last will be first, and some who are first will be last!'"

ᵉPresent imperative of *agonizomai*, "agonize."
ᶠAorist middle subjunctive.
ᵍLiterally, "you may begin to stand outside."

[31]At that very hour some Pharisees approached, saying to Him, "Leave and get away from this place, because Herod[h] intends to kill You." [32]Jesus answered them, "You go and tell that fox, 'Look, I continue driving out demons and performing cures today and tomorrow, and on the third [day] my work will be completed. [33]Nevertheless, today and tomorrow and the following day I must continue My journey, because it is not permissible for a prophet to perish outside Jerusalem!

[34]"O Jerusalem, Jerusalem, you who habitually slay the prophets and stone the [messengers] sent to you! How often have I longed to gather your children the way a bird [gathers] her brood under her wings, but you refused! [35]As a consequence, your house is abandoned to you. And I say to you, by no means will you see Me until you say, 'Blessed is He who comes in the name of the Lord.' "[l]

Chapter 14

One Sabbath day, Jesus went to eat at the house of a leader of the Pharisees, and they were watching Him closely. [2]There in front of Him was a certain man who was suffering from dropsy. [3]"Is it lawful to heal on the Sabbath or not?" Jesus asked the Law-experts and Pharisees. [4]They remained silent. So Jesus took hold of the man, cured him, and sent him away. [5]Then He asked them, "Which of you, if your son or your ox falls into a pit, will not at once pull him out even on a Sabbath day?" [6]To these things they were not able to reply.

[7]When Jesus noticed how the ones who had been invited were choosing for themselves the chief places at the table, He told them this parable: [8]"When you are invited by anyone to wedding festivities, do not seat yourself at the best place. Someone considered more honorable than you may have been invited by him. [9]And he who invited you and him will come and say to you, 'Give the place to this man,' and then you will proceed with embarrassment to take the lowest place. [10]But when you are invited, go and take the lowest place, so that when the host appears he will say to you, 'My friend, come up higher!' Then you will be honored in the presence of all your fellow-guests. [11]For everyone who exalts himself will be humbled, and whoever humbles himself will be exalted."

[12]Then Jesus went on to say to the man who had invited Him, "Whenever you give a morning meal or a dinner, do not keep inviting your friends or your

---

[h]The reference is to Herod Antipas. See note on Matt. 14:1. Jesus was now in Herod's territory, probably in southern Perea.
[l]Cf. Ps. 118:26; Matt. 23:37-39.

[a]Or, all at once.
[b]Or, a farm building.

brothers or your relatives or your rich neighbors; for they may invite you in return and you will be repaid. [13]Instead, when you prepare a banquet, make it a practice to invite the poor, the crippled, the lame, and the blind. [14]Then you will truly be happy because they have nothing with which to pay you back. Actually, it will be repaid to you at the resurrection of the righteous.''

[15]On hearing this, one of the fellow-guests said to Him, ''Fortunate is he who will eat bread in the kingdom of God!'' [16]Jesus told him, ''A certain man planned a great dinner, to which he invited many guests. [17]When it was time for the dinner, he sent his servant to tell those who had been invited, 'Come, for everything is ready now!' [18]But they all alike[a] began to make excuses. The first said to him, 'I have bought some land, and I must go out and look at it. Please consider me excused.' [19]Another said, 'I bought five yoke of oxen, and I am on my way to test them. Please consider me excused.' [20]And the next said, 'I have just married a wife, and that is why I cannot come.'

[21]''The servant returned and reported these things to his lord. Then the owner of the house became angry and said to his servant, 'Go out quickly into the streets and alleys of the city and bring in here the poor and the crippled and the blind and the lame.' [22]The servant reported, ''Lord, what you commanded has been carried out, and yet there is room.' [23]Then the lord said to the servant, 'Go out to the main roads and the footpaths along the hedges and urge [people] to come in, so that my house may be filled. [24]For I tell you that not one of those who were [first] invited will taste of my dinner.' ''

[25]Great crowds were going along with Jesus, when He turned and said to them, [26]''If any man comes to Me and does not hate his father and mother, and wife and children, and his brothers and sisters, and even his own life, he cannot be a disciple of Mine. [27]Whoever does not bear his own cross and follow Me cannot be my disciple.

[28]''Indeed, who of you, when he intends to build a tower,[b] does not first sit down and calculate the cost, [to see] if he has enough [resources] to complete it? [29]Otherwise, after the foundation has been laid, and he is not able to finish [the structure], all those watching will begin to make fun of him, [30]and say, 'This man began to build but was not able to finish!' [31]Or what king marches into battle against another king without first sitting down to consider whether with ten thousand men he is strong enough to encounter the one who is coming against him with twenty thousand? [32]If he cannot, then while the other is still far away, he sends a delegation requesting the terms for peace.

[33]''So it is, every one of you who does not forsake all his possessions cannot be a disciple of Mine. [34]Salt is useful. But if it loses its character as salt, how can the saltness be restored? [35]It is unfit for the ground or for the manure heap. People just throw it away. Whoever has ears to hear, let him listen!''

Chapter 15

The tax-collectors and the outcasts were all drawing near to Jesus to listen to Him. [2]But the Pharisees and the Law-experts began to complain. "This man keeps receiving outcasts and dines with them!", they said. [3]So Jesus told them this parable: [4]"What man among you, if he has a hundred sheep and loses one of them, does not leave the ninety-nine in the open pasture and go after the lost one until he finds it? [5]And when he has found it, with joy he puts it on his shoulders; [6]and when he gets home he calls together his friends and his neighbors, and says to them, 'Rejoice with me, for I have found the sheep that was lost.' [7]So, I tell you, there will be more joy in heaven over one outcast[a] who repents than over ninety-nine righteous persons who have no need of repentance.

[8]"Or what woman, if she has ten silver coins[b] and loses one, does not light a lamp, and sweep the house and keep searching carefully until she finds it? [9]And when she has found it, she calls together her women-friends and her neighbors, and says, 'Rejoice with me, because I have found the coin which I lost.'' [10]So, I tell you, there is joy in the presence of God's angels over one sinful person who repents."

[11]Jesus also said, "A certain man had two sons. [12]And the younger of them said to his father, 'Father, give me the share of the estate that is going to be mine.[c] So the father divided his property between them. [13]A few days later the younger son sold his share of the possessions[d] and went away into a distant country, and there wasted his money in reckless living. [14]After he had spent all he had, there came a severe famine throughout that country and he began to be in need. [15]So he went and attached himself to one of the citizens of that land, who sent him into his fields to herd swine. [16]Often he was hungry enough to eat the carob pods from which the swine were feeding; and no one gave him anything. [17]But when he came to his senses he said, 'How many of my father's hired servants have an abundance of food, and here I am starving to death! [18]I will arise and go to my father and I will say to him, "Father, I have sinned against heaven and before you. [19]No longer do I deserve to be called your son. Make me as one of your hired servants.' "

[20]"So he arose and started back to his father. But while he was still a long way off, his father saw him and was filled with deep compassion for him and he ran, and fell upon his neck and kissed him fervently. [21]The son said to him,

---

[a]Cf. v. 1.

[b]Literally, "ten Drachmas." The Greek drachma was a silver coin equal in value to the Roman denarious. See note on Matt. 18:28.

[c]Cf. Deut. 21:17.

[d]Literally, "gathered together everything."

'Father, I have sinned against heaven and before you. No longer do I deserve to be called your son.' ²²But the father said to his servants, 'Bring quickly the best robe and put it on him. Put a ring on his finger and sandals on his feet. ²³Bring the fattened calf, butcher it and let us eat and rejoice! ²⁴For this my son was dead and he has come back to life! He was lost and is found!' So they began to celebrate.

²⁵"Now the elder son was in the field. And as he drew near the house, he heard music and dancing. ²⁶He called one of the servant-lads and inquired eagerly what these things meant. ²⁷The servant told him, 'Your brother has come back home and your father has butchered the fattened calf, because he has him back safe and sound.'

²⁸"But the elder son became angry and refused to go in. His father came out and kept pleading with him [to come in]. ²⁹But he answered and said to his father, 'Look, all these years I have served you and never did I transgress one of your commands. Yet never once did you give me even a small goat, so that I might enjoy a feast with my friends. ³⁰But as soon as this son of yours arrived, after wasting your livelihood with harlots, you killed for him the fattened calf.'

³¹"The father replied, 'My son, you are always with me, and everything I have is yours. ³²But we had to celebrate and rejoice, for this your brother was dead and has come to life again. He was lost but he has been found.' "

Chapter 16

And Jesus went on to say to His disciples, "There was a certain wealthy man who was informed that his estate-manager was misappropriating his property. ²So he called him and said, 'What is this I hear about you? Prepare a final report of your stewardship, for you can no longer manage my business.'

³"The manager said to himself, 'My lord is going to take my job away from me. What shall I do? I am not strong enough to dig [for a living] and I am ashamed to beg. ⁴I know what I will do! I will act in such a way that when I am removed from the managership, people will receive me into their homes!' ⁵So he summoned each one of his lord's debtors. 'What is the amount you owe my master?' he asked the first. ⁶The man replied, 'A hundred containers of olive-oil.' He said to him, 'Here is your note; sit down quickly and reduce the amount to fifty.'ᵃ ⁷Then he asked another, 'How much do you owe?' The

---

ᵃLiterally, "write fifty."

man answered, 'A hundred measures of wheat.' He told him, 'Here is your note; reduce the amount to eighty.'[b]

[8]"The landlord commended the dishonest estate-manager because he acted shrewdly. Actually, the sons of this age are more clever than the sons of light in dealing with their own kind. [9]So I, myself, say to you, in your own interest make friends for yourselves by your use of the mammon characterized by unrighteousness,[c] so that when the wealth comes to an end[d] you may be received into a lasting home.[e]

[10]"He who is faithful in a very little is faithful also in much; and the man who is dishonest in very little is dishonest also in much. [11]If therefore, you have not been trustworthy in regard to the wealth of this world, who will trust you with the genuine [riches]? [12]And if you have not been faithful with what belongs to someone else, who will give you that which is your own?

[13]"No household worker can serve two masters; for either he will hate the one and love the other, or he will hold firmly to one and despise the other. You cannot serve God and mammon."[f]

[14]Now the Pharisees, who were fond of money, began to scoff at Jesus when they heard these things. [15]So He said to them, "You are the ones who try to justify[g] yourselves before men, but God knows your hearts. For what [is considered] lofty among men is detestable in the sight of God. [16]The Law and the Prophets [were in force] until John [the Baptizer]. Since then the kingdom of God is being preached and all sorts of people[h] are forcing their way[i] into it. [17]It is easier for Heaven and earth to pass away than for one small part[j] of the Law to fall.

[18]"Everyone who divorces his wife and marries another commits adultery, and the man who marries a woman whose husband has divorced her commits adultery.[k]

[19]"There was a certain rich man who used to dress in purple and costly linen, and live in luxury day after day. [20]And a certain beggar, named Lazarus, covered with sores, was placed at his gate. [21]There he lay, longing to satisfy his hunger with the scraps that fell from the rich man's table. Furthermore, the scavenger dogs used to come and lick his sores.

[22]"It happened that the beggar died and was carried away by the angels to [a place of honor in] the close presence of Abraham. The rich man also died

---

[b]Literally, "write eighty."

[c]Descriptive genitive.

[d]Literally, "when it fails."

[e]Cf. v. 4.

[f]Or, money.

[g]Greek conative present participle.

[h]Literally, "everyone."

[i]Rendering *biazetai* as middle voice. Cf. Matt. 11:12.

[j]Literally, "a little horn." The tip or minute projection on some Hebrew letters which distinguishes them from similar-shaped letters.

and was buried; [23]and in Hades,[k] where he was tormented, he lifted up his eyes and saw Abraham far off and Lazarus in the folds of his robe.[l] [24]And the rich man called and said, 'Father Abraham, take pity on me and send Lazarus to dip the tip of his finger in some water[m] and cool my tongue, because I am tormented in this flame.' [25]But Abraham said, 'Son, remember that you received to the full[n] good things in your life, and Lazarus on the other hand [received] the bad things. But now he is being conforted here, and you are suffering. [26]Furthermore, between us and you a great chasm is permanently established,[o] so that those who want to pass from here to you cannot, nor can any cross over from you to us.'

[27]"And he said, 'Then I beg you, father, to send Lazarus to my father's house, [28]for I have five brothers. Let him solemnly warn them, so that they also may not come to this place of torment.' [29]But Abraham said, 'They have [the writings of] Moses and the Prophets. Let them listen to them!' [30]He replied, 'No, father Abraham, but if someone from the dead goes to them, they will repent.' [31]But Abraham told him, 'If they refuse to listen to Moses and the Prophets, they would not be convinced even if someone rose from the dead.' "

Chapter 17

Jesus said to His disciples, "Occasions that cause stumbling must inevitably come, but woe to the person who causes them. [2]It would be better for him to be hurled into the sea with a mill-stone around his neck than for him to cause one of these little ones to stumble.

[3]"Keep watch on yourselves. If your brother commits an act of sin, reprove him; and if he repents, forgive him. [4]Even if he sins against you seven times a day, and seven times turns to you and says, 'I repent,' forgive him."

---

[k]Cf. Matt. 5:32, which indicates that if an innocent wife is discarded she is blameless.
Hades is the realm of disembodied spirits. Here it refers to the abode of the lost between death and the resurrection. Gehenna is the ultimate destiny of the wicked after the day of judgment. See not on Matt. 5:22.

[l]The expression denotes intimate communion. Note the singular in this sense in v. 22 and in John 1:18, 13:23. In Luke 6:38, the singular is used literally of *the fold* of a garment.

[m]Partitive genitive.

[n]Indicated by Greek preposition *apo*, in composition with the verb *lambano*, "to receive."

[o]Indicated by Greek perfect passive indicative.

[5]The apostles said to the Lord, "Increase our faith." [6]The Lord replied, "If you have faith as a grain of mustard, you might say to this mulberry tree, 'Be rooted up and planted in the sea,' and it would obey you.

[7]"Which of you who has a servant plowing or herding sheep, will say to him when he returns from the field, 'Come at once and recline at the table'? [8]Will he not rather say to him, 'Prepare something for my supper. Make yourself ready to serve me while I eat and drink; and after that you, yourself, may eat and drink'? [9]He does not express thanks to the servant because he did what he was ordered to do, does he? [10]So also you, when you have done all the things you have been commanded to do, say, 'We are undeserving servants. We have done what it was our duty to do.' "

[11]On His way to Jerusalem, Jesus was traveling along the border between Samaria and Galilee. [12]And as He was entering a certain village, He was met by ten leprous men who stood at a distance,[a] [13]and lifted up their voices and cried out, "Jesus, Master, have pity on us!" [14]When He saw them He said, "Go and show yourselves to the priests."[b] And it happened that while they were going they were cleansed.

[15]One of them, realizing that he was cured, turned back, praising God in a loud voice; [16]and he fell on his face at Jesus' feet, thanking Him. And that man was a Samaritan. [17]In response Jesus said, "Were not ten cleansed? The [other] nine—where are they? [18]Could none be found to return and give praise to God, except this foreigner?"[b] [19]Then He said to the man, "Stand up and go your way; your faith has made you well!"

[20]When Jesus was asked by the Pharisees when the kingdom of God would come, He told them, "The kingdom of God does not come with outward display. [21]No one will remark 'Look, here it is! or 'There it is!' For, as a matter of fact, the kingdom of God is within you!"[c]

[22]He said to the disciples, "A time is coming when you will long to see one of the days of the Son of Man but you will not see it. [23]And some people will say to you, 'See, there [He is]!' or 'See, here [He is]!' But do not go forth or follow them. [24]For just as the lightning flashes from [one part] of the sky across to the other, so will be the [manifestation of the] Son of Man in His day. [25]But first He must suffer many things and be rejected by the present generation.

[26]"Just as things were in the days of Noah,[d] so they will be in the days of the Son of Man: [27]people were eating, drinking, marrying, and giving in marriage right up to the day Noah went into the ark—then came the flood and destroyed them all. [28]Similarly, things will be like they were in the days of

---

[a]Cf. Lev. 13:46.
[b]To be pronounced clean. Cf. Luke 5:14.
[c]Or, is in your midst [in the person and ministry of Jesus].
[d]Cf. Gen. 6:1ff.
[e]Cf. Gen. 19:1ff.

Lot:[e] they were eating, drinking, buying, selling, planting, and building. [29]But on the very day Lot left Sodom, it rained fire and brimstone from heaven and destroyed them all.

[30]"It will be like that on the day when the Son of Man is revealed. [31]On that day if a man is on the housetop and his goods are in the house, let him not go down to get them; and whoever is in the field likewise—let him not turn back to the things behind. [32]Remember Lot's wife![f]

[33]"Whoever tries to preserve his life for himself will lose it, but whoever loses it will find it anew. [34]I tell you, on that night two persons will be in the same bed; one will be taken away and the other left. [35]Two women will be grinding [grain] together; one will be taken away but the other will be left."

[37g]In response they asked Him, "Where [will this take place] Lord?" And He said to them, "Where the body is, there also the eagles[h] will be gathered together."

Chapter 18

Jesus spoke a parable to His disciples,[a] to emphasize the necessity of always praying and not losing heart: [2]"There was in a certain city a judge who had no reverence for God and no regard for man. [3]And in that city there was a widow who kept coming to him and saying, 'Deliver me from the oppression of my adversary.' [4]For a time the judge refused [her request] but afterward he said to himself, 'Even though I do not reverence God nor regard man, [5]yet because this widow is continually troubling me I will vindicate her, or she will keep coming and wear me out completely.' "

[6]And the Lord said, "Listen to the remark of the unrighteous judge. [7]Now, will not God, certainly, bring about justice for His chosen ones, who cry to Him day and night? Will He be slow to avenge them? [8]I tell you that He will vindicate them without delay. Nevertheless, when the Son of Man comes, will He actually find any faith[b] on the earth?"

[9]To some people who were confident that they themselves were righteous, and looked with contempt on everyone else, Jesus spoke this parable: [10]"Two men went up into the Temple precincts to pray; one was a Pharisee, and the

---

[f]Cf. Gen. 19:26.

[g]Verse 36 is placed in the margin here by Nestle. But the essence of the verse is found in Matt. 24:40.

[h]Or, vultures. Cf. Job 39:27-30.

[a]Literally, "to them."

[b]The Greek is *ten pistin*, "the faith."

other a tax-collector. ¹¹The Pharisee stood [in a conspicuous place] and prayed these things about himself: 'O God, I thank Thee that I am not like the rest of men—robbers, unjust, adulterers—or even like the tax-collector over there.^c ¹²I fast twice a week. I pay tithes on everything I acquire.' ¹³Meanwhile, the tax-collector stood at a distance and would not even lift up his eyes toward heaven, but he kept striking his breast and saying, 'O God, be merciful to me, a great sinner!'^d ¹⁴I tell you, this man, and not the other, went home justified [before God]. For everyone who exalts himself will be humbled, but he who humbles himself will be exalted.''

¹⁵People were bringing the little children to Jesus that He might touch them. When the disciples saw it, they began to turn them away. ¹⁶But Jesus called [the little ones] to Him and said, ''Permit the children to keep coming to me. Stop hindering them, ¹⁷for whoever does not receive the kingdom of God as a little child will by no means enter into it.''

¹⁸One of the rulers asked Jesus, ''Good Teacher, what must I have done to gain eternal life?'' ¹⁹''Why do you call Me good?'' Jesus said to him. ''No one is good except One—God, Himself. ²⁰You know the commandments: 'Do not commit adultery,' 'Do not kill,' 'Do not steal,' 'Do not bear false witness,' 'Honor your father and mother.' ''^e ²¹He replied, ''I have observed all these since I was a boy.'' ²²When Jesus heard this He told him, ''There is still one thing you lack: Sell everything you have and distribute [the money] to the poor—and you will have treasure in heaven—then come and follow me!'' ²³But when the ruler heard these requirements he became very sad, because he was exceedingly wealthy. ²⁴When Jesus saw [his reaction] He said, ''How difficult it is for those who have riches to get into God's kingdom! ²⁵Actually, it is easier for a camel to go through a needle's eye than for a rich man to enter the kingdom of God.''

²⁶His listeners asked, ''Then who can be saved?'' ²⁷Jesus replied, ''Things that are impossible with men are possible with God!'' ²⁸Peter said, ''What about us? We left everything we had,^f and followed You.'' ²⁹Jesus said to them, ''Truly I tell you, there is no man who has given up home or wife or brothers or parents or children, for the sake of the kingdom of God, ³⁰who will not receive back many times as much in this present time, and in the age to come, eternal life.''^g

³¹Jesus took the Twelve aside and said to them, ''Now we are going up to Jerusalem, and everything written by the prophets concerning the Son of Man

---

^cLiterally, ''as this tax-collector.''
^dLiterally, ''the sinner.''
^eCf. Exod. 20:12-16; Deut. 5:16-20.
^fLiterally, ''We left our own things,'' or ''our homes.''
^gCf. Mark 10:29-30.

will be accomplished. [32]He will be handed over to the Gentiles and be mocked and insulted and spit upon; [33]and they will scourge Him and put Him to death; but on the third day He will rise again." [34]The apostles[h] understood none of these things; the meaning remained hidden from them, and they were not able to grasp [the significance of] what was said.

[35]As Jesus approached Jericho, a certain blind man was sitting by the side of the road, begging. [36]When he heard the crowd going along, he began inquiring what it meant. [37]They told him, "Jesus the Nazarene is passing by." [38]So he called out, "Jesus, Son of David, have pity on me!" [39]The people who were walking in front began to reprimand him and told him to get quiet. But he kept crying out all the more, "Son of David, have pity on me!" [40]Jesus stopped and ordered them to bring the man to Him. When he drew near, Jesus asked him, [41]"What do you want Me to do for you?" And he said, "Lord, that I may see again!" [42]Jesus said to him, "Receive your sight! Your faith has cured you." [43]And instantly he received his sight, and he began to follow Jesus, giving God the glory. And all the people who witnessed [what had happened] gave praise to God.

Chapter 19

Jesus entered Jericho and was passing through [that city]. [2]And a man was there whose name was Zacchaeus. He was the supervisor of tax collectors [for the district] and was wealthy. [3]And he was trying to catch a glimpse[a] of Jesus, what sort of person He was; but he was not able [to do so] on account of the crowd, because he was small in stature. [4]So he ran on ahead and climbed up into a fig-mulberry tree in order that he might get a view of Jesus, for He was about to pass that way.

[5]When Jesus came to the place, He looked up and said to him, "Zacchaeus, come down quickly, for today I must stay at your house." [6]So Zacchaeus came down quickly, and welcomed Jesus joyfully. [7]When the people saw this they all began to complain, saying, "With a sinful man, He went in to be a guest."

[8]But Zacchaeus stood up and said to the Lord, "Look, Lord, I give half of my possessions to the poor; and if[b] I have exacted wrongfully anything from anyone, I will pay back [to him] four times as much." [9]And Jesus said to him, "Today salvation has come to this house, because this man in a real sense is a

---

[h]Cf. v. 31.

[a]Force of Greek aorist infinitive.

[b]A first-class condition which, in the mind of the speaker, indicates a fact. See note on Matt. 4:3.

son of Abraham.[c] [10]For the Son of Man came to seek and to save that which was lost.''

[11]While they were listening to these things Jesus went on to speak [to them in] a parable, because He was near Jerusalem and they were thinking that the kingdom of God was going to be made manifest immediately. [12]Therefore He said, ''A certain nobleman went into a distant country to receive for himself a kingdom and then return. [13][Before leaving] he summoned ten of his servants and gave each of them a mina[d] and told them 'Develop these resources[e] while I am on my journey.' [14]But his citizens hated him, and sent a delegation after him to say, 'We are not willing for this man to reign over us.'

[15]''When the nobleman had received the kingdom and returned, he ordered summoned those servants to whom he had given the money, in order that he might see what each one had gained by trading. [16]The first came and said, 'Lord, your mina has gained ten minas.' [17]He said to him, 'Well done, good servant! Because in a small matter you proved faithful, you shall have authority over ten cities.'

[18]''The second came and said, 'Lord your mina has made five minas.' [19]And he told him, 'You take charge of five cities.'

[20]''Then the other came and said, 'Lord, here is your mina, which I have been keeping laid away in a handkerchief. [21]I was afraid of you because you are a strict man. You gather what you did not plant, and you reap what you did not sow.' [22]The nobleman said to him, 'By your own words I will judge you, wicked servant! You know that I am a strict man, gathering what I did not plant, and reaping what I did not sow? [23]Then why did you not put my money to use, so that on my return I could have claimed it with interest?' [24]Then to the bystanders he gave orders, 'Take from him the mina and give it to the man who has the ten minas.' [25]They said to him, 'Lord, he [already] has ten minas.' [26][The Lord replied] 'I tell you, that more will be given to everyone who [makes good use of what he] has, but the one who makes no use of his opportunities[f] will lose what he has. [27]Now, as for my enemies, who did not want me to become king over them, bring them here and slay them in my presence.' ''

[28]After saying these things, Jesus continued on ahead [of the disciples] on His way up to Jerusalem. [29]When He came near Bethphage and Bethany at the Mount of Olives,[g] Jesus sent two of His disciples, saying, [30]''Go into the

---

[c]Cf. Rom. 4:12-13; Gal. 3:7, 29.

[d]Literally, ''gave to them ten minas.'' The mina was a Greek coin which would be equivalent to about twenty dollars.

[e]Literally, ''Carry on business,'' or ''Trade with these.''

[f]Literally, but from the one who does not have even what he has will be taken away.

[g]Literally, ''the hill called Olive-orchard.''

village straight ahead of you, and as you enter it you will find tied there a colt on which no man ever yet sat. Untie it, and bring it [to Me]. [31]And if anyone asks you, 'Why are you untying [the colt]?' say, 'The Lord needs it.' ''

[32]The men whom Jesus had appointed went and found [everything] just as He had told them. [33]While they were untying the colt, its owners asked them, 'Why are you untying that colt?' [34]They replied, 'The Lord needs it.' [35]So they brought the colt to Jesus, threw their cloaks on its back and placed Jesus upon it.

[36]As He moved along, the people kept spreading their garments under [Him] on the way. [37]When He drew near the place where the road starts down[h] from the Mount of Olives, the whole multitude of the disciples began rejoicing and praising God with loud voices for all the powerful deeds they had seen. [38]They shouted, "Blessed is the One who comes—the King—in the Name of the Lord! Peace in heaven and glory in the highest realms!"

[39]Some of the Pharisees from the crowd said to Jesus, "Teacher, warn Your disciples to be quiet!" [40]But He replied, "I tell you, if these men become silent, the stones will cry out."

[41]When Jesus drew near and beheld the city, He wept over it [42]and said, "If you only knew, even today, the things that lead to peace! But now they are hidden from your sight. [43]Yet the time will come upon you when your enemies will throw a battle line against you and surround you and hem you in on all sides. [44]They will dash to the ground you and the inhabitants within your walls,[j] and will not leave one stone upon another[j] among you, because you failed to take advantage of the time of your opportunity."[k]

[45]And Jesus went into the Temple courts, and began to drive out those who were selling. [46]He told them, "It stands written, 'My house shall be a house of prayer', but you have made it 'a den of robbers.' ''[l]

[47]And Jesus continued teaching day after day in the Temple area, but the chief priests and the Law-experts and the leaders of the people were seeking to destroy Him; [48]but they could find no way to do it, because all the people kept crowding around Him to hear His words.[m]

Chapter 20

One day while Jesus was teaching the people in the Temple area and proclaiming the good news, the chief priests and the Law-experts,

---

[h]Literally, "near to the descent."
[i]Literally, "and your children within you."
[j]Cf. 21:6.
[k]Or, you did not realize the time of [God's gracious] visitation. Cf. 1:68.
[l]Cf. Isa. 56:7; Jer. 7:11.
[m]Literally, "were hanging upon Him, listening."

accompanied by the elders, confronted Him [2]and said, "Tell us by what kind of authority You are doing these things, or who gave You this authority?" [3]In reply Jesus said to them, "Let Me ask you a question. Now you tell Me: [4]The baptism proclaimed by John[a]—was it from heaven or from men?"

[5]They reasoned among themselves, "If we say, 'From heaven,' He will ask, 'Why did you not believe him?' [6]But if we say, 'From men,' we will be stoned by the people, for they are convinced that John was a prophet." [7]So they answered that they did not know its origin. [8]Then Jesus said to them, "Neither will I tell you by what kind of authority I am doing these things."

[9]Then Jesus went on to tell the people this parable: "A man planted a vineyard and leased it to vine-dressers and went abroad for a considerable time. [10]In due season[b] he sent the vinedressers a servant to receive from them a share of the fruit of the vineyard. But the vine-dressers beat him and sent him away empty-handed. [11]He proceeded to send another servant, but him also they beat and insulted and sent away with nothing. [12]Furthermore he sent a third, whom they likewise wounded and threw out. [13]Then the owner of the vineyard said, 'What shall I do? I will send my beloved son. Surely, they will respect him.'

[14]"But when the vine-dressers saw the son, they began reasoning with one another, saying, 'This is the heir. Let us put him to death in order that the inheritance may become ours!' [15]So they threw him outside the vineyard and killed him. Now what will the lord of the vineyard do to those tenants? [16]He will come and destroy them, and give the vineyard to others."

[17]When His listeners heard this they said, "Such conduct is unthinkable!"[c] But He looked straight at them and asked, "What, then, is [the meaning of] this which stands written, 'The stone which the builders rejected has become the Keystone of the building'?[d] [18]Everyone who falls on that Stone will be broken, but the man on whom it falls will be crushed to dust."

[19]The Law-experts and the chief priests wanted to seize Him that very moment, for they realized that He had directed this parable at them; but they feared the people. [20]So they watched [Him] closely,[e] and appointed spies, who posed as honest persons, to trap Jesus in [His] speech[f] and deliver Him to the jurisdiction and authority of the governor.

[21]They asked Jesus, "Teacher, we know that You speak and teach what is right and You are not partial to anyone, but on [the basis of] truth You teach God's way. [22]Is it right for us to pay tribute-money to Caesar or not?" [23]Being aware of their cunning, Jesus said to them, [24]"Show Me a denarius.

---

[a]Subjective genitive
[b]Cf. Lev. 19:23-25.
[c]Literally, "May it never happen!"
[d]Cf. Ps. 118:22.
[e]Or, *they watched carefully for their chance.*
[f]Literally, "by a word."

Whose likeness and title are on it?'' ''Caesar's,'' they replied. [25]He said to them, ''Then give to Caesar the things that belong to Caesar and to God the things that belong to God.'' [26]So they were not able to ensnare Him by anything He said in the presence of the people; and, marvelling at His answer, they became silent.

[27]Some Sadducees—those who deny there is a resurrection—came forward and questioned Him. [28]''Teacher,'' they said, ''Moses wrote to us, 'If a married man dies and leaves no children, his brother should marry the widow and raise up children for his brother.'[g] [29]Now there were seven brothers. The first took a wife and died without children. [30]The second [married the widow] [31]and so did the third. The [rest of the] seven did likewise—they all died, leaving no children. [32]Finally, the woman also died. [33]Now then, at the resurrection whose wife will she be? For she had been the wife of all seven.''

[34]Jesus said to them, ''In this age men and women marry and are given in marriage, [35]but those considered worthy of attaining the age to come and the resurrection from the dead neither marry nor are given in marriage. [36]Nor can they die any more, for they are like angels, and are God's children because they share in the resurrection. [37]But that the dead are raised, even Moses made known [in the passage] about the bush, where he calls the Lord 'The God of Abraham and the God of Isaac and the God of Jacob.'[h] [38]He is not the God of the dead but of the living, for all men are alive to Him.''

[39]Some of the Law-experts answered, ''Teacher, You have spoken well.'' [40]In fact, they did not dare to question Him any further. [41]But Jesus said to them, ''How can people say that the Messiah is David's son? [42]For David himself says in the book of Psalms, 'The Lord said to My Lord, Sit at My right [43]until I make Your enemies a footstool for Your feet!'[i] [44]So David calls Him 'Lord'. Then how can [the Messiah] be David's son?''

[45]Now, while all the people were listening, Jesus said to His disciples, [46]''Beware of the Law-experts, who like to walk around in flowing robes and love to be greeted with expression of respect in public places, to sit in the front seats in the synagogues, and to occupy the places of honor at dinners; [47]who take advantage of helpless widows, yet pretend [to be religious] by making long prayers. They will receive the more severe condemnation.''

Chapter 21

Jesus looked up and saw wealthy people casting their gifts into [the chest of] the Temple treasure.[a] [2]And He noticed a certain poor widow dropping in two

---

[g]Cf. Deut. 25:5-10.
[h]Cf. Exod. 3:2-6.
[i]Cf. Ps. 110:1.

[a]See note on Mark 12:41.

small coins.[b] [3]He said, "Truly, I tell you that this destitute widow has put in more than all the rest. [4]For all these from their abundance contributed to the gifts, but this woman out of her poverty has put in everything she had for her life's support.

[5]As some were talking about the Temple, how it was adorned with beautiful stones and costly gifts, Jesus said, [6]"As for these things that you are observing, the days are coming when there will not be left one stone upon another that will not be thrown down." [7]They questioned Him, saying "Teacher, when will these things happen? And what will be the sign to indicate that they are about to take place?" [8]He replied, "See to it that you are not led astray. For many will claim to be the Christ,[c] saying, 'I am He,' and 'The time is at hand.' Do not follow them. [9]And when you hear of wars and disturbances, do not be terrified; for it is necessary that these things occur first, but the end will not follow immediately."

[10]Then Jesus went on to tell them, "Nation will rise against nation and kingdom against kingdom. [11]There will be great earthquakes and pestilences and famines in various places; and there will be fearful sights and mighty signs in the sky. [12]But before all this happens, people will seize you and persecute you, and hand you over to synagogues and prisons. You will be brought before kings and governors for the sake of My name. [13]This will be an opportunity for you to give [your] testimony. [14]So determine in your hearts not to meditate in advance about what you will say in your defense. [15]For I Myself will give you words and wisdom which none of your opponents will be able to resist or refute.

[16]"You will be betrayed even by your parents and brothers and relatives and friends, and they will put some of you to death. [17]And you will be hated by all men because of My name. [18]Yet not a hair of your head will by any means perish.[d] [19]In your endurance you will realize your salvation.[e]

[20]"But when you see Jerusalem being surrounded by armies,[f] then be certain that its devastation is at hand.[g] [21]Then let those who are in Judaea flee to the mountains, and let those inside the city[h] leave it. Let those who are in the fields [near Jerusalem] not try to take refuge within the city walls;[i] [22]for those will be days characterized by vengeance, when all the things that have been written [in the Scriptures] will be fulfilled.

[23]"Woe to the pregnant women and to mothers with nursing babies in those days, for there will be great anguish upon the land, and wrath against this

---

[b]Greek *lepta*. A *leptos* (the word means "thin," "slight," or "tiny") was the current coin smallest in size and value. Cf. Mark 12:42.

[c]Literally, "many will come in My name."

[d]In the light of v. 16, this must be understood in a spiritual sense.

[e]Literally, "gain your souls."

[f]Cf. Matt. 24:15; Mark 13:14.

[g]Cf. Luke 19:42-44.

[h]Literally, "in the midst of her."

[i]Literally, "enter not into it."

people. [24][Some of the defenders of the city] will be slain by the edge of the sword and [others] will be led away as prisoners of war among all the nations. And Jerusalem will remain crushed[j] under the feet of heathen peoples until the times of the Gentiles are completed.

[25]"There will be signs in sun and moon and stars; and on the earth distress of nations in perplexity at the roaring and agitation of the sea; [26]men fainting from fear and dread of what is coming upon the inhabited earth. For the heavenly bodice[k] will be shaken, [27]and then they will see the Son of Man coming in a cloud[l] with great power and glory. [28]Now when these things begin to happen, look up and raise your heads, because your deliverance is drawing near."

[29]Then Jesus gave them this illustration: "Look at the fig tree and all the trees. [30]When they put forth [their leaves], you see for yourselves and you know that summer is near. [31]So when you see these things happening, you can be certain that the kingdom of God is near. [32]Truly I tell you, that this generation[m] will by no means come to an end until all things are accomplished. [33] Sky and earth will pass away, but My words will never pass away.

[34]"Keep yourselves alert to prevent your hearts from becoming dulled with self-indulgence and drunkenness and worldly anxieties, and that day catch you suddenly like a trap. [35]For [that is the way] it will come upon all the inhabitants of the entire earth. [36]But you stay awake at all times and pray that you may be strong enough to make it through all these things that are about to happen, and to stand in the presence of the Son of Man."

[37]During the days, Jesus continued teaching in the Temple area but at night He went out [of the city] and lodged on the Mount of Olives. [38]And all the people kept coming to Him early in the morning to listen to Him in the Temple precincts.

Chapter 22

The Festival of Unleavened Bread, called the Passover,[a] was drawing near. [2]The chief priests and the Law-experts were trying to find some way to destroy Jesus, but they were afraid of the people. [3]Then Satan entered into Judas,[b] called Iscariot, who was numbered with the Twelve, [4]and Judas went and conferred with the chief priests and the commanders [of the Temple guards] as

---

[j]Durative force of Greek periphrastic future passive participle.
[k]Literally, "the powers of the heavens."
[l]Cf. Acts. 1:9-11.
[m]See note on Matt. 24:34.
[a]Cf. Exod. 12:3-7.
[b]Cf. John 6:70.

to how he might betray Jesus to them. [5]They were glad and agreed to give him money. [6]So Judas concurred and began looking for an opportunity to hand Jesus over to them without the people knowing it.[c]

[7]Then came the day of Unleavened Bread, on which it was necessary to sacrifice the Passover lamb.[d] [8]Jesus sent Peter and John, saying, "Go and make preparations for us to eat the Passover meal." [9]They asked Him, "Where do You want us to prepare it?" [10]And He told them, "As soon as you enter the city, a man[e] carrying a jar of water will meet you. Follow him into the house which he enters, [11]and say to the owner of the house, 'The Teacher says to you, "Where is the guest-room, in which I may eat the Passover meal with My disciples?" ' [12]And he will show you an upstairs room, spacious and properly furnished. Make preparations there." [13]So they went and found [everything] just as Jesus had told them; and they made ready the Passover supper.

[14]When the hour came, Jesus reclined at [the] table, and the apostles with Him. [15]He said to them, "I have earnestly desired to eat this Passover with you before I suffer. [16]For I tell you, I will never eat it again until it is fulfilled in the kingdom of God."

[17]And He took a cup, when He had given thanks, and said, "Take this and share it among yourselves; [18]for I tell you, I will not by any means, after now, drink from the fruit of the vine until the kingdom of God comes."

[19]Then Jesus took bread and, after giving thanks, He broke it and gave it to them, saying, "This is My body which is being given for you. Do this from time to time[f] in remembrance of Me." [20]In like manner [He handed them] the cup, after supper, saying "This cup is the new covenant in My blood which is being poured out for you. [21]Actually, the hand of My betrayer is with Me at the table. [22]Indeed, the Son of Man goes according to what has been determined, but woe to that man by whom He is betrayed!" [23]Then they began to ask each other which of them might be the one who was about to do this thing.

[24]A contention arose among [the disciples] as to which of them should be regarded as the greatest. [25]Jesus said to them, "The kings of the Gentiles govern their people by force, and those who exercise authority over the subjects are called[g] benefactors. [26]But it is not to be like that with you! Let the greatest person among you become like the younger, and the leader like the one who serves. [27]As a matter of fact who is greater, he who reclines at table

---

[c]Literally, "apart from a crowd."

[d]The original Passover lamb was typical of Christ. Cf. 1 Cor. 5:7.

[e]Carrying water-jars was usually the work of slaves or of women. Cf. Gen. 24:11; John 4:7, 15.

[f]Durative force of Greek present imperative.

[g]Or, call themselves (middle voice).

or he who serves? Is it not he who reclines at table? But I am among you as the one who serves!

²⁸"You are the men who have continued with Me in My temptations. ²⁹So I assign to you, just as My Father has assigned to Me, a kingdom, ³⁰that you may eat and drink at My table in My kingdom; and you will sit on thrones judging the twelve tribes of Israel.

³¹"Simon, Simon, I tell you, Satan has begged permission to sift [all of] you^h like wheat; ³²but I have prayed especially for you that your faith may not fail. And you, when you have come back, strengthen your brothers."ⁱ

³³"Lord" said Peter, "with You I am ready to go both to prison and to death!" ³⁴Jesus replied, "I tell you, Peter, a rooster will not crow today until you deny three times that you know Me!"

³⁵Then Jesus asked the disciples, "When I sent you forth without a purse, or a provision bag, or [extra] sandals, you did not lack anything, did you?" They replied, "Nothing." ³⁶Then He said to them, "But now, let him who has a purse take it along, and likewise also a provision bag. And let him who has no sword sell his outer garment and buy one. ³⁷For I tell you that this [Scripture] which stands written must be accomplished in Me: 'And He was counted among lawless men.'^j For, indeed, that which concerns Me is reaching its fulfillment." ³⁸And they said, "Lord, look, here are two swords." He said to them, "That is enough."

³⁹And Jesus went out and made His way as usual to the Mount of Olives. And the disciples followed Him. ⁴⁰When He reached the place, He said to them, "Pray that you may not enter into temptation." ⁴¹He withdrew from them about a stone's throw, and knelt down and prayed ⁴²in these words: "Father, if Thou art willing, take this cup away from Me; nevertheless let not My will but Thine be done." ⁴³Then an angel from heaven appeared to Him, and gave Him strength. ⁴⁴And being in agony, He prayed more intensely, and His sweat became like drops of blood falling upon the ground.

⁴⁵After praying, Jesus arose and came to the disciples and found them asleep, because they were exhausted from grief. ⁴⁶"Why are you sleeping?" He asked them. "Stand up, and keep praying that you may not enter into temptation."

⁴⁷While He was still speaking, suddenly a crowd appeared, lead by the man named Judas, one of the Twelve. As he approached Jesus to kiss Him, ⁴⁸Jesus said to him, "Judas, are you betraying the Son of Man with a kiss?"

⁴⁹When the men around Jesus saw what was about to happen, they said, "Lord, shall we strike with our swords?" ⁵⁰And one of them did strike at the

---

^hThe Greek pronoun is plural. In v. 32 the pronouns are singular.
ⁱCf. John 21:15-17.
^jCf. Isa. 53:12.

high priest's servant and cut off his right ear. [51]But Jesus answered, "Let them proceed!"[k] And He touched the [servant's] ear, and healed him.

[52]Then Jesus said to the chief priests and the commanders of the Temple police and elders who had come to arrest Him, "Have you come out with swords and clubs as if I were a bandit? [53]Day after day I was with you in the Temple area, and you never raised your hands against me. But this is your hour and [yours is] the dominion characterized by darkness."[l]

[54]Those who had seized Jesus led Him away and brought Him to the house of the high priest. And Peter was following at a distance. [55]After they had kindled a fire in the center of the courtyard, and had sat down together, Peter was sitting among them. [56]Presently, a certain maidservant noticed him as he sat facing the fire. She looked intently at him and said, "This fellow also was with Him." [57]But he denied it, saying, "I do not know Him, woman!" [58]After a short time another person saw him and said, "You too, are one of them." But Peter said, "Man, I am not!" [59]About an hour later, another man began to insist, "Certainly this fellow was with Him, for he is also a Galilean." [60]But Peter said, "Man, I do not know what you are talking about!" And immediately, while he was yet speaking, a rooster crowed. [61]Then the Lord turned and looked at Peter, and Peter was reminded of the Lord's word, how He had said to him, "Before a rooster crows today, you will deny me three times." [62]And he went outside and wept bitterly.

[63]Meanwhile, the Temple police[m] who were holding Jesus in custody were mocking and beating Him. [64]And they blindfolded Him and questioned Him, saying, "Prove You are a prophet! Name the person who struck You!" [65]And in many other ways they kept insulting Him.

[66]As soon as daylight came, the entire Sanhedrin—the elders, the chief priests, and the Law-experts—met and brought Jesus before their council [67]and said, "If You are the Messiah, tell us." But He said to them, "If I tell you, you surely will not believe. [68]And if I ask you a question, you surely will not answer. [69]But from now on, the Son of Man will be sitting at the right hand of the power of God."[n] [70]Then they all asked, "Are You then, Yourself, the Son of God?" And He said to them, "It is you who are saying[o] that I am." [71]Then they said, "What further evidence do we need? We ourselves have heard it from His own lips."

---

[k]Literally, "Permit until this!"
[l]Descriptive genitive. Cf. Col. 1:13.
[m]Literally, "the men."
[n]Cf. Ps. 110:1.
[o]An affirmative answer. Cf. Matt. 26:25, 64; Mark 14:62.

Chapter 23

Then the whole company [of the Sanhedrin][a] rose up and brought Jesus before Pilate. [2]And they began to accuse Him, saying, "We found this fellow perverting our nation, opposing payment of tribute to Caesar, and claiming that He Himself, is a Messiah-king."

[3]Pilate questioned Him saying, "Are You, Yourself, the king of the Jews?" And Jesus answered and said to him, "You are correct."[b] [4]Then Pilate said to the chief priests and the crowds, "I do not find any guilt in this man."[c] [5]But they became more violent, saying "He is stirring up the people, teaching through all Judaea,[d] and beginning from Galilee, even to here."

[6]When Pilate heard that, he asked if the man were a Galilean. [7]On learning that Jesus was under Herod's jurisdiction, Pilate sent Him up to Herod who also was in Jerusalem at that time.

[8]Herod was very glad when he saw Jesus, for he had been wanting to see Him for a long time, because he had been hearing about Him, and was hoping to see some sign performed by Him. [9]So Herod questioned Jesus at length,[e] but He gave him no reply at all.

[10]Meanwhile, the chief priests and the Law-experts were standing by, accusing Jesus vehemently. [11]Then Herod, with his soldiers, treated Jesus with contempt—he mocked Him, threw a shining garment around Him, and sent Him back to Pilate. [12]And on the same day Herod and Pilate became friends with each other, for previously they had been enemies.

[13]Pilate called together the chief priests and the leading men and the people[f] [14]and said to them, "You brought this man before me, alleging that He is agitating the people. Now, look, I, myself, have examined Him in your presence and have found Him not guilty of any of the charges you make against Him. [15]And neither did Herod, for he sent Him back to us. Clearly, nothing deserving [the] death [penalty] has been done by Him. [16]Therefore, I will have Him scourged and let Him go." [18g]But the whole crowd shouted together, "Do away with this fellow! Release Barabbas for us!" [19]Barabbas

---

[a]Apparently not including Nicodemus and Joseph of Arimathea. Cf. 23:51; John 7:50f; 19:38f.

[b]Literally, "You are saying it." See note on Matt. 27:11.

[c]Cf. John 18:33-38.

[d]In this context, Judaea means the land of Palestine.

[e]Literally, "with many words."

[f]Cf. v. 1

[g]The Nestle text places v. 17 in the margin. But see Matt. 27:15; Mark 15:16.

had been thrown into prison on account of a revolt that had occurred in the city and [because of] murder.

[20]Pilate, wishing to release Jesus, again appealed to them. [21]But they kept shouting, "Crucify, crucify Him!" [22]Pilate spoke to them a third time. "Why, what wrong has this Man done?" he asked. "I have found Him guilty of nothing deserving death. So I will have Him scourged and let Him go."

[23]But they kept urging with loud outcries, insisting that Jesus be crucified. And their outcries began to prevail. [24]Then Pilate gave sentence that their request should be carried out. [25]He set free the man they wanted—the one who because of revolt and murder had been thrown into prison—and he handed Jesus over to them, to be treated as they wished.[h]

[26]As they led Jesus away, they took hold of Simon, a certain Cyrenian who was coming in from the country, and they put on his shoulders the cross, for him to carry it behind Jesus.

[27]Large numbers of people followed Him, including women who were mourning[i] and lamenting for Him. [28]But Jesus turned and said to them, "Daughters of Jerusalem, weep not for Me; but weep for yourselves and for your children; [29]because the days will surely come when people will say, 'Fortunate are the women who are barren, and those who have never brought forth children, and the breasts that have never nourished infants!' [30]At that time people will begin to say to the mountains, 'Fall upon us!' and to the hills, 'Cover us!'[j] [31]For is they are doing these things to a green tree, what will happen to one which is withered?"[k]

[32]And two others, who were evil doers, were also led away to be put to death with Jesus. [33]When they came to the place which is called the Skull, there they crucified Him and the evil doers, one at His right and the other at His left. [34]Then Jesus said, "Father, forgive them, for they do not realize what they are doing." And they divided His garments among themselves by casting lots.[l]

[35]Meanwhile, the people stood and watched. The leaders sneered [at Jesus]. "This fellow saved others!" they said. "Let Him save Himself, if He is the Christ of God, the Chosen One!" [36]The soldiers, also, ridiculed Him. They came up, offered Him sour wine[m] [37]and said, "If you are the king of the Jews, save Yourself!" [38]Above Him there was an inscription, THIS IS THE KING OF THE JEWS.

---

[h]Literally, "over to their will." Cf. Acts 3:14.
[i]Literally, "smiting their breasts."
[j]Cf. Hosea 10:8.
[k]That is to say, If an innocent person is treated so cruelly, how much more will be the fate of the guilty when judgment comes upon them!
[l]Cf. John 19:23-24; Ps. 22:18.
[m]See note on Matt. 27:48.

[39]One of the crucified criminals began to scoff at Jesus: "So You are the Christ, are You?" Save Yourself and us!" [40]But the other one reproved [the first] and said, "Do you not fear God, since you received the same sentence? [41]And me, on our part [are condemned] justly, for we are receiving back what we deserve for what we did; but this Man has done nothing out of place. [42]And he went on to say, "Jesus,[n] remember me when You come into[o] Your kingdom." [43]Jesus said to him, "Truly I say to you, today you will be with Me in Paradise."

[44]It was now about the sixth hour,[p] and darkness came over the whole land until the ninth hour, [45]the sun's light failing; and the curtain in the Sanctuary was torn down the middle. [46]Then Jesus, with a loud cry said, "Father, into Thy hands I commit My spirit."[q] And with these words He breathed out His life.

[47]When the centurion saw what had happened, he began to praise God, and declared, "Certainly this man was innocent."[r] [48]And all the crowds that had gathered to view this sight, after beholding the things that occurred, began to return, striking their breasts [in grief]. [49]But all Jesus' friends,[s] including the women who had accompanied Him from Galilee, had been standing at a distance, watching what was going on.

[50]Now there was a good and upright man by the name of Joseph. He was a member of the Council,[t] [51]but he had not agreed with the decision and action of the others. He was from Arimathea, a city of the Jews, and was waiting for the kingdom of God. [52]This man went to Pilate and asked for the body of Jesus. [53]Then he took the body down [from the cross],[u] wrapped it in linen and placed it in a rock-hewn tomb,[v] in which no one had ever yet been buried.

[54]It was Preparation Day[w] and the Sabbath was drawing near.[x] [55]The women, who had come with Jesus out of Galilee, followed closely and noted the tomb and the position of His body.[y] [56]Then they went away and prepared aromatic spices and perfumes. During the Sabbath they rested, as the Law designated.[z]

---

[n]Some manuscripts read, *Kurie, Lord.*

[o]Or, in.

[p]The sixth hour, according to Jewish reckoning, would be about noon.

[q]Cf. Ps. 31:5.

[r]Or, righteous.

[s]Literally, "all those known to Him."

[t]Joseph was a member of the Sanhedrin, as was Nicodemus. Cf. Mark 15:43; John 7:50.

[u]Cf. John 19:39f.

[v]Cf. Mark 15:46.

[w]Friday, the day before the Sabbath. Cf. Mark 15:42.

[x]The Jewish Sabbath began at sundown on Friday.

[y]Literally, "how His body was placed."

[z]Cf. Exod. 20:8-11.

Chapter 24

But on the first day of the week,[a] very early,[b] the women[c] came to the tomb, bringing the aromatic spices they had prepared. [2]They found the stone rolled back from the [entrance of the] tomb; [3]but when they went inside they did not find the body of the Lord Jesus. [4]While they were greatly perplexed about this, two men in dazzling apparel suddenly stood beside them. [5]As the women became terrified and bowed their faces to the ground, the men asked them, "Why are you searching among the dead for the One who is alive? [6]He is not here! He has been raised! Remember what He told you, while He was still in Galilee, [7]that the Son of Man must be delivered into the hands of sinful men, and be crucified, and on the third day rise again."[d]

[8]Then they recalled His words, [9]and they returned from the tomb, and reported all these things to the Eleven and to all the rest. [10]It was Mary the Magdalene and Joanna and Mary the [mother] of James,[e] and the other women with them who were telling these things to the Apostles. [11]But what they said seemed like delirious talk to the Apostles,[f] and they did not believe the women. [12][g]Peter, however, arose and ran to the tomb; but when he stooped down and looked in he saw only the grave cloths.[h] Then he went away by himself, wondering what had happened.

[13]That same day, two of Jesus' disciples[i] were going to a village called Emmaus, sixty stadia[j] from Jerusalem. [14]And they were talking together about all the things that had taken place. [15]During their conversation and discussion, Jesus Himself[k] drew near and went along with them; [16]but their eyes were prevented from recognizing Him. [17]He asked them, "What are these matters which you are discussing with each other as you walk along?"

They stood still, their faces sad. [18]Then one of them, whose name was Cleopas, answered Him, 'Are You alone as a stranger in Jerusalem and do not know about the things which have occurred there during the last few days?" [19]"Exactly what things?" He asked. And they told Him, "The things concerning Jesus the Nazarene, a man who was a prophet mighty in deed and word before God and all the people; [20]and how the chief priests and our

---

[a]Or, on the first day following the Sabbath. Cf. Matt. 28:1.
[b]Literally, "at deep dawn."
[c]Cf. 23:55f.
[d]Cf. 9:22, 44; 17:25; 18:32f.
[e]This James was perhaps the son of Alphaeus. Cf. 6:15.
[f]Literally, "before them."
[g]The Nestle text places this verse in brackets, but it is similar to the account given in John 20:3-10.
[h]Or, the linen cloths by themselves. That is, the body was not in the wrappings.
[i]Literally, "two of them."
[j]About seven miles.

leaders delivered Him up to be sentenced to death, and crucified Him. [21]We were hoping that He was the One who was about to liberate Israel. As a matter of fact, we have come to the third day since these things happened. [22]Furthermore, some women of our company have astounded us. After going early [this morning] to the tomb [23]and not finding His body, they came back to tell us they had seen a vision of angels who declared He is alive. [24]And certain men[l] of our number went to the tomb and found everything just as the women had reported, but Him they did not see."

[25]Then Jesus said to them, "O how dull of thought you are, and slow in heart to believe all that the prophets have spoken! [26]Was it not necessary for the Messiah[m] to suffer these things and thus to enter into His glory?" [27]Then beginning with Moses and all the Prophets, He interpreted to them in all the Scriptures the passages that referred to Himself.

[28]When they drew near the village, to which they were travelling, Jesus acted as if He were going further. [29]But they urged Him strongly, "Remain with us, for it is toward evening and the day is almost gone." So He went in to stay with them. [30]And when He reclined at table with them, He took the bread, blessed it and broke it, and as He handed it to them [31]their eyes were opened and they recognized Him. Then He vanished from their sight.[n]

[32]They said to each other, "Did not our hearts burn within us as He was talking to us on the road, as He was making plain[o] the Scriptures for us?" [33]And they rose up, immediately, and returned to Jerusalem and found that the Eleven and their associates[p] had been gathered together, [34]and were saying, "The Lord has actually been raised and has appeared to Simon!"[q] [35]Then [the two from Emmaus] related their own experience of what had happened on the road, and how He was recognized by them in the breaking of the bread.

[36]While they were talking about these things, Jesus, Himself, stood in their midst and said to them, "Peace to you!" [37]They were startled and terrified, supposing they were seeing a spirit. [38]But Jesus said to them, "Why are you so troubled and why are doubts arising in your hearts? [39]Look at My hands and My feet! Here I am—Myself! Handle Me and see! For a spirit does not have flesh and bones as you see that I have." [40]And as He said this, He showed them His hands and His feet.[r]

---

[k]The Jesus of history is the Christ of faith.
[l]Obviously a reference to John and Peter. Cf. John 20:2-10.
[m]Or, the Christ.
[n]Literally, "He became invisible to them."
[o]Literally, "opening up."
[p]Literally, "those with them." Cf. v. 9; Acts 1:14f.
[q]Cf. 1 Cor. 15:5.
[r]Thus Jesus gives the disciples empirical verification of His identity.

⁴¹While they still could not believe it because of joy, and were wondering, He said to them, "Have you any food here?" ⁴²They handed Him a piece of broiled fish. ⁴³And He took it and ate it while they watched Him.ˢ

⁴⁴Then Jesus said to them, "This is what I told you when I was still with you—that all the things written about Me in the Law of Moses and in the Prophets and in the Psalms must be fulfilled." ⁴⁵Then He opened their understanding, so they could grasp the [meaning of the] Scriptures. ⁴⁶And He said to them, "Thus it stands written that the Christᵗ must suffer, and rise from the dead on the third day; ⁴⁷and that, in His name, repentance which brings the forgiveness of sins should be preached to all the nations, beginning from Jerusalem. ⁴⁸You are witnesses of these things. ⁴⁹Now listen, I am sending forth upon you what My Father has promised. But you remain [here] in the city until you are clothed with power from on high."

⁵⁰Jesus led them out until they were in the neighborhood of Bethany.ᵘ He raised His hands and assured them of God's favor.ᵛ ⁵¹And while He was blessing them, He stood apart from them and was taken up into heaven. ⁵²They worshipped Him, and with great joy they returned to Jerusalem. ⁵³And they were continually in the Temple area, praising God.

ˢLiterally, "He ate before them." Cf. Acts. 10:41.
ᵗOr, the Messiah.
ᵘCf. Acts. 1:12.
ᵛLiterally, "and blessed them."

John

Chapter 1

In the beginning was the Word,[a] and the Word was face to face[b] with God, and the Word in His essential character[c] was God. [2]This One was in the beginning face to face with God. [3]All things came into existence through Him, and apart from Him not one thing which exists came into being. [4]In Him was life, and the life was the Light of men. [5]The Light keeps shining in the darkness, and yet the darkness has never overcome it.[d]

[6]There came a man named John, who was commissioned from God. [7]He came as a witness, to bear testimony concerning the Light, in order that all might believe through him. [8]He himself was not the Light, but [came] that he might testify concerning the Light.

[9]He was the true Light, which illumines every man, coming into the world.[e] [10]He was in the world, and through Him the world came into existence, yet the world did not recognize Him. [11]He came to His own things, but His own

---

[a]The Greek expression, *Logos,* may be rendered "Reason," "Speech," or "Word." John uses the term of the pre-existent Son of God who became incarnate in Jesus of Nazareth. Cf. v. 14.

[b]The Greek preposition, *pros,* "near" or "facing," pictures the *Logos* in communion and quality with the Father.

[c]Indicated by the anarthros construction. The non-use of the Greek article with *theos,* "God," emphasizes the qualitative aspect of the noun. The *Logos* is not "a God," but in His very essence He is God.

[d]Or, did not lay hold of, apprehend, perceive, or appreciate it.

[e]Or, He was the real Light which illumines every man who comes into the world.

people did not receive Him. [12]But as many as received Him, to them He gave authority to become God's children—those who believe in His Name.[f] [13]They received the new life not by natural generation,[g] not by human desire, not by the will of a man, but from God.

[14]And the Word became flesh and dwelled among us, and we beheld His glory—glory as of the Father's unique[h] Son—full of grace and truth.

[15]John gave witness concerning Him when he cried out, "This was He of whom I said, 'The One who is coming after me ranks ahead of me because He existed before I ever lived.' "

[16]We have all received of His fulness—grace following upon grace. [17]For the Law was given through Moses, but grace and truth came through Jesus Christ. [18]No man has ever at any time seen God. The Unique One, who is God, who dwells with the Father in intimate nearness[i]—He has revealed Him.

[19]Now this was the testimony given by John,[j] when the Jews sent to him from Jerusalem priests and Levites to ask him, "Who exactly are you?" [20]He spoke directly, without any hesitation, and acknowledged, "I, myself, am not the Christ!"[k] [21]They asked him, "Then what are you? Are you Elijah?"[l] And He said, "I am not." "Are you the Prophet?"[m] He replied, "No."

[22]Finally, they said to him, "Tell us who you are, that we may give an answer to those who sent us. What do you say concerning yourself?" [23]He said, "I am the voice of one proclaiming in the wilderness, 'Make a straight road for the Lord,' as said by Isaiah the prophet."[n]

[24]Some of the Pharisees had been sent; [25]and they questioned him, saying, "Then why are you baptizing if you are neither the Christ, nor Elijah, nor the Prophet?" [26]John answered, "I, for my part, baptize with water. In your midst stands One whom you, yourselves, do not recognize—[27]the One who is coming after me. I, myself, am not worthy to loosen the thong of His sandal." [28]These things happened in Bethany, beyond the Jordan, where John was engaged in baptizing.

[29]The next day John saw Jesus coming toward him and he exclaimed, "Look! The Lamb of God who takes away the sin of the world! [30]This is He on behalf of whom I said, 'A man is coming after me who ranks ahead of me, because He existed before I ever lived. [31]Even I did not recognize Him [as the Messiah] but in order that He might be made known to Israel, I came baptizing with water." [32]And John declared further, "I saw the Spirit descending out of

---

[f]Literally, "those who believe into His name." See note on Matt. 28:19.

[g]Literally, "not of bloods."

[h]The Greek term, *monogenes*, means "the only one of his kind." Cf. 1:18; 3:16, 18; Heb. 11:17.

[i]Literally, "the One who is in the Father's bosom."

[j]Subjective genitive.

[k]Or, the Messiah.

[l]Cf. Mal. 4:5.

[m]Cf. Deut. 18:15.

[n]Cf. Isa. 40:3.

heaven like a dove, and remain upon Him. [33]I certainly would not have known Him, but He who sent me to baptize with water, told me 'The One upon whom you see the Spirit descending and remaining, He it is who baptizes with the Holy Spirit.' [34]I have seen this and have testified[o] that He is the Son of God.''

[35]Again, the following day John was standing with two of his disciples, [36]when he saw Jesus walking along, he exclaimed, "Look! The Lamb of God!" [37]The two disciples heard him say this and they followed Jesus. [38]Then Jesus turned and noticed them following. He asked them, "What are you seeking?" And they replied, "Rabbi"—which translated means Teacher—"where do You live?" [39]He said to them, "Come and you will see. So they came and saw where He was staying, and they remained with Him that day. It was about the tenth hour.[p]

[40]One of the two men who heard what John said and followed Jesus was Andrew, the brother of Simon Peter.[q] [41]The first thing Andrew did was to find his own brother Simon and say to him, "We have found the Messiah!"—a term which means the Christ, [42]and he brought him to Jesus. Jesus looked intently at him and said, "You are Simon the son of John. You will be called Cephas"[r]—which means Peter, a Rock.[s]

[43]The next day Jesus decided to go into Galilee. He found Philip and said to him, "Follow Me." [44]Now Philip was from Bethsaida, the town of Andrew and Peter. [45]Philip sought out Nathaniel and told him, "We have found the One of whom Moses wrote in the Law, and the One about whom the Prophets spoke—Jesus, Joseph's son from Nazareth." [46]Nathaniel said to him, "Can anything good come out of Nazareth?" Philip replied, "Come and see!"

[47]Jesus saw Nathaniel coming toward Him and said concerning him, "Look, here is a true Israelite[t]—a man in whom there is no deceit." [48]Nathaniel asked Him, "How do you know me?" "Before Philip called you," replied Jesus, "I saw you under the fig tree." [49]Nathaniel answered Him, "Rabbi, You, Yourself, are the Son of God! You are, indeed, the King of Israel!" [50]Jesus answered him, "Do you believe because I told you that I saw you under the fig tree? You will see greater things than that." [51]Furthermore He said to him, "Truly, truly I tell you all,[u] you will see heaven opened wide, and the angels of God ascending and descending upon the Son of Man."

---

[o]Or, I have become and remain a witness-bearer. Force of Greek perfect tense.

[p]Ten hours after sunrise [about 4:00 o'clock in the afternoon], according to the Jewish method of reckoning time. Cf. Matt. 20:1ff.

[q]The appelation, Peter [Greek, *Petros*, "a stone"] is here proleptic. Cf. vs. 42.

[r]Aramaic word for Rock, or Stone.

[s]See notes on Matt. 16:18.

[t]Cf. Rom. 9:6.

[u]Indicated by the Greek plural personal pronoun.

Chapter 2

On the third day there was a wedding at Cana in Galilee, and the mother of Jesus was there. [2]Jesus also, and His disciples had been invited to the festivities. [3]When the wine ran out Jesus' mother said to Him, "They have no more wine." [4]Jesus replied, "Woman, what is that to Me and to you? My hour has not yet come." [5]His mother told the servants, "Whatever He tells you, do it."

[6]Now there were six stone water-jars standing there, for the purification ceremonies[a] of the Jews. Each jar had a capacity of about twenty gallons. [7]Jesus told the attendants, "Fill the jars with water." So they filled them up to the brim. [8]He said to them, "Now dip out some, and bring it to the steward in charge of the feast." They did so. [9]And when the steward tasted the water that had become wine, and did not know where it came from—although the attendants who had dipped out the water knew—he called the bridegroom [10]and told him, "Every one serves the good wine first, and then after [the guests] have had plenty to drink the inferior [wine is served]. But you have kept the good wine until now!"

[11]This first of His signs Jesus performed in Cana of Galilee and manifested His greatness.[b] And His disciples believed in Him.

[12]After this, Jesus and His mother and His brothers and His disciples went down to Capernaum and remained there for a few days.

[13]The Jewish Passover was near, so Jesus went up to Jerusalem. [14]In the outer courts of the Temple, He found the people who were selling oxen and sheep and pigeons; also the money-changers were sitting there. [15]So He made a whip of small cords[c] and drove them out of the Temple precincts, with their sheep and oxen. He poured out the coins of the money-changers and over-turned their tables. [16]And to those who were selling pigeons He said, "Take these things away from here! Stop making My Father's house a place of merchandise." [17]His disciples remembered that it is written in Scripture,[d] "The zeal for Thy house will consume Me."[e]

[18]Therefore, the Jews answered and said to Him, "What sign can You show us that You [have authority] to do these things?" [19]Jesus answered them, "Destroy this Sanctuary, and within three days I will raise it up." [20]Then the Jews said, "It took forty-six years to build this Sanctuary, and You—will You raise it up within three days?" [21]But the Sanctuary of which Jesus spoke was His body. [22]Later, after He had risen from the dead, His disciples recalled that

---

[a]Cf. Mark 7:3.
[b]Or, His glory.
[c]Or, rushes.
[d]Literally, "that it stands written."
[e]Cf. Ps. 69:9.

He had said this, and they believed the Scripture and the word that He had spoken.

²³Now while Jesus was in Jerusalem during the Passover Feast many believed in His Name, when they saw the signs which He was doing. ²⁴But Jesus did not have confidence in them,[f] because He knew all men. ²⁵He did not need to be told about anyone, for He, Himself, knew what was in man.

Chapter 3

There was a man of the Pharisees, named Nicodemus, a ruler among the Jews.[a] ²He came to Jesus by night and said to Him, "Rabbi, we know You are a teacher come from God, for no one can do these signs which You are doing unless God is with him."

³Jesus answered him, "Truly, truly, I say to you, unless a person—whoever he may be[b]—is born from above,[c] he cannot see the kingdom of God." ⁴Nicodemus said to Him, "How can a man be born when he is old? He cannot enter his mother's womb a second time and be born, can he?" ⁵Jesus replied, "Truly, truly, I tell you, unless a person—whoever he may be—is born of water, even[d] of the Spirit, He cannot enter into the kingdom of God. ⁶What is born of the physical nature is physical, and what is born of the Spirit is spirit. ⁷Do not wonder that I said to you, 'It is necessary for all of you[e] to be born from above.' ⁸The wind blows where it chooses, and you hear the sound of it, but you do not know where it comes from or where it is going. It is like that with everyone born of the Spirit."

⁹Nicodemus asked Him, "How can these things come about?" ¹⁰Jesus replied to him, "Are you the teacher of Israel and no not know these things? ¹¹Truly, truly I say to you, we[f] speak what we know, and bear witness to what we have seen, and yet you people do not receive our witness. ¹²If I have told you[e] earthly things and you do not believe, how will you believe if I tell you heavenly things?

---

[f]Literally, "He did not trust Himself to them."

[a]He was a member of the Sanhedrin. Cf. 7:50.

[b]Indicated by *Tis*, Greek indefinite pronoun.

[c]Or, anew.

[d]Ascensive use of the Greek conjunction *kai*, common in the New Testament. Cf. Mark 1:27; 4:41; 10:45; Matt. 7:12; 13:12. In the present context, Jesus' emphasis is upon spiritual birth, as shown by verses 3, 7, 8.

[e]The Greek pronoun is plural.

[f]The plural seems to refer to Jesus and John the Baptizer. It may include the disciples, or it could be the *rhetorical* "we."

[13]"No one has gone up into heaven except the One who came down from heaven—the Son of Man.[g]

[14]"Just as Moses lifted up the serpent in the wilderness,[h] so must the Son of Man be lifted up, [15]in order that everyone who believes in Him may have life eternal. [16]For God loved the world so much that He gave His Son—the only one of His kind—that everyone who believes in Him should not be lost but have life eternal. [17]For God did not send His Son into the world to condemn the world, but in order that the world might be saved through Him.

[18]"He who believes in Him is not condemned. He who does not believe stands condemned already, because he has not believed in the Name of the unique Son of God. [19]Now the reason for this condemnation is that the light has come into the world, and men loved the darkness rather than the light, because their deeds were wicked. [20]For everyone who practices evil things hates the light and does not come to the light—he is afraid his deeds will be exposed. [21]But the person who is practicing the truth comes to the light, so that it may be made manifest that his works have been done in relation to God."

[22]After these things, Jesus and His disciples went into the rural districts of Judaea, and there He spent some time with them and baptized.[i] [23]John, also, was baptizing at Aenon, near Salim, because much water was there, and people kept coming and were being baptized. [24]For John had not yet been cast into the prison.

[25]A discussion arose between some of John's disciples and a Jew about the matter of purification. [26]So they came to John and said to him, "Rabbi, the One who was with you beyond Jordan, to whom you have given witness—He is baptizing,[j] and everyone is going to Him."

[27]John answered, "A man is not able to receive anything unless it has been given to him from heaven. [28]You, yourselves, are witnesses that I said, 'I am not the Christ,' but 'I was sent before Him.' [29]The One who has the Bride is the Bridegroom. The friend of the Bridegroom, the one who stands by and listens to him, rejoices greatly because of the voice of the Bridegroom. So this is my joy, and it is complete. [30]He must continue to increase but my importance must diminish.[k]

[31]"He who comes from above is above all. He who is of the earth belongs to the earth and speaks of the earth. He who comes from heaven is above all. [32]He bears witness to what He has seen and heard, and yet no one accepts His

---

[g]Some manuscripts add, *who is in heaven.* Cf. 1:18.
[h]Cf. Num. 21:7ff.
[i]Jesus' disciples did the actual baptizing. Cf. 4:2.
[j]See note on v. 22.
[k]Literally, "I must be made less."

testimony. [33]The man who has received his witness has attested that God is truthful. [34]He whom God has sent speaks God's sayings, for [God] gives Him the Spirit without measure. [35]The Father loves the Son and has put all things into His hand. [36]Whoever keeps believing in the Son has eternal life, but whoever rejects the Son will not see life, but God's wrath remains on him.''

Chapter 4

When the Lord knew that the Pharisees had heard that Jesus was making and baptizing more disciples than John—[2]although Jesus personally was not doing the baptizing, but His disciples were—[3]He left Judaea and went back again into Galilee.

[4]Now it was necessary for Him to go through Samaria. [5]So He came to a town in Samaria, called Sychar, near the piece of land which Jacob gave his son Joseph. [6]And Jacob's well was there. Jesus, tired as a result of His journey, was sitting at the well. It was the sixth hour.[a] [7]A woman of Samaria came to draw water. Jesus said to her, "Give Me a drink." [8]For His disciples had gone away into the town to buy food. [9]Then the Samaritan woman said to Him, "How can You, a Jew, ask me, a Samaritan woman, for a drink?" For Jews do not associate with Samaritans.[b]

[10]Jesus answered, "If you knew God's gift, and who it is that says to you, 'Give Me a drink,' you[c] would have asked Him and He would have given you living water." [11]The woman said to Him, "Sir, you have nothing with which to draw and the shaft is deep. Where can you get such living water? [12]Are you greater than our forefather Jacob, who gave us the well, and drank from it himself, along with his sons and his cattle?" [13]Jesus answered, "Everyone who drinks from this water will thirst again; [14]but whoever takes one drink[d] of the water that I shall give him will never again be thirsty. As a matter of fact, the water which I shall give him will become in him a fountain of water leaping up into eternal life."

[15]The woman said to Him, "Sir, give me this water, in order that I may not continue thirsting or keep coming to this place to draw water." [16]Jesus said to her, "Go, call your husband, and come back here." [17]The woman replied, "I do not have a husband." Jesus said to her, "You have well said, 'I have no husband,' [18]for you have had five husbands, and the man you are living with now is not your husband. In that sense, what you said is true." [19]The woman

---

[a]That is, about noon. Regarding time, see note on 1:39.
[b]Cf. 2 Kings 17:24-41.
[c]The Greek pronoun is emphatic.
[d]Punctiliar force of the aorist subjunctive.

replied, "Sir, I am beginning to perceive that You[e] are a prophet. ²⁰Our fathers worshipped on this mountain,[f] and you people say that Jerusalem is the place where it is necessary to worship."

²¹Jesus said to her, "Believe Me, woman, the time is coming when you will worship the Father neither on this mountain nor in Jerusalem. ²²You people are worshipping what you do not know; we know what we worship, for salvation is of the Jews. ²³Yes, the hour is coming, and now is, when the true worshippers will worship the Father in spirit and in truth. Indeed, the Father is searching for such persons to worship Him. ²⁴God in His essential nature[g] is spirit, and those who worship [Him] must worship in spirit and in truth."

²⁵The woman said to Him, "I know that the Messiah, the One who is called Christ, is coming. When He comes, He will tell us everything." ²⁶Jesus said to her, "I, Myself,—the One talking to you—am He."

²⁷Just then His disciples came back, and they were astonished that He was speaking with a woman. However, no one asked, "What is it that You want?" ²⁸The woman left her water-jar and went off into the town, and kept saying to the people, ²⁹"Come, see a man who told me everything I ever did! Could it be that He is the Christ?" ³⁰The people left the town and were making their way toward Him.

³¹In the meantime, the disciples urged Jesus, saying, "Rabbi, eat!" ³²But He said to them, "I have food to eat of which you do not know." ³³At that the disciples said to each other, "No one has brought Him anything to eat, has he?" ³⁴Jesus said to them, "My food is to do the will of the One who sent Me, and to complete His work. ³⁵Do you not say, 'There are yet four months until the harvest?' Look, I tell you, raise your eyes and see the fields, that they are already white for harvest. ³⁶Already the reaper is receiving wages and gathering fruit for eternal life so that the sower and the reaper may rejoice together. ³⁷For this corroborates the saying, 'One person sows and another reaps.' ³⁸I sent you to reap a harvest for which you did not toil. Others have done the hard work, and you have benefited from their labor."

³⁹Many Samaritans of that town believed in Him because of the report of the woman who testified, "He told me everything I ever did!" ⁴⁰So when the Samaritans came to Him, they asked Him to stay with them; and He remained there two days. ⁴¹Then many more believed because of His own word, ⁴²and they said to the woman, "We no longer believe [just] because of what you said; but we have heard for ourselves, and we know that this Man is truly the Savior of the world."

⁴³After the two days, He left there and went into Galilee. ⁴⁴Jesus, Himself, had declared that a prophet receives no honor in his own native place. ⁴⁵When

---

[e]The Greek pronoun is emphatic.

[f]That is, Mount Gerizim, at those base Jacob's well is located.

[g]Indicated by anarthrous construction. The non-use of the article emphasizes the qualitative aspect of the noun. Of, same idiom in 1 John 1:5; 4:8.

He arrived in Galilee, the Galileans welcomed Him, having seen all that He did in Jerusalem at the festival, for they too had attended the festival.

⁴⁶Again He went to Cana in Galilee, where He had changed the water into wine. And there was a certain royal official, whose son was ill at Capernaum. ⁴⁷When this man heard that Jesus had come from Judaea into Galilee, he went to Him and requested Him to come down and heal his son, who was about to die. ⁴⁸Then Jesus said to him. "Unless you people see signs and wonders, you will not believe at all." ⁴⁹The official said to Him, "Sir, please come down at once[h] before my child dies." ⁵⁰Jesus said to him, "Go home. Your son will live." The man believed the word which Jesus said to him, and started on his way. ⁵¹As he was going down to Capernaum,[i] his servants met him with the news that his boy was recovering. ⁵²Then he asked them what time it was when he began to improve. They told him, "Yesterday at the seventh hour[j] the fever left him." ⁵³Then the father realized that was the very time in which Jesus had told him, "Your son will live." And he and his entire household became believers. ⁵⁴This was the second sign that Jesus did after He returned from Judaea to Galilee.

Chapter 5

After these things, there was a feast of the Jews, and Jesus went up to Jeusalem. ²Now, there is in Jerusalem near the Sheep-Gate a pool which in Hebrew is called Bethzatha,[a] having five porticoes. ³In them were lying a multitude of sick people—blind, lame, and those whose bodies were ravaged by disease.

⁵ᵇA certain man was there who had been an invalid for thirty-eight years. ⁶When Jesus saw him lying there, and knew that he had been in that condition a long time, He asked him, "Do you want to be healed?" ⁷The invalid answered Him, "Sir, I have no one to lower me into the pool when the water has been stirred. While I am trying to reach it,[c] someone else steps down ahead of me." ⁸Jesus said to him, "Stand up! Take up your pallet and walk." ⁹Instantly, the man was healed, and he took up his pallet and began walking.

---

[h]The Greek aorist imperative expresses urgency.

[i]Cf. v. 46.

[j]About 1:00 P.M.

[a]This Hebrew or Aramaic name means, House of Olives. A variant is Bethesda, House of Mercy.

[b]The latter part of v. 3 and all of v. 4 are not in the best Greek manuscripts, a fact indicated by the Nestle text.

[c]Literally, "While I am coming."

¹⁰That day was the Sabbath. Therefore, the Jews were saying to the man who had been healed, "It is the Sabbath, so it is not lawful for you to carry the pallet." ¹¹But he answered them, "The Man who made me well was the One who told me, 'Take up your pallet and walk.' " ¹²They questioned him, "Who is the fellow that told you to take it up and walk?" ¹³But the healed man did not know who He was. A crowd was in the place and Jesus had slipped away. ¹⁴Later Jesus found the man in the Temple precincts and said to him, "Look, you have been made well. Sin no more, so that something worse may not happen to you." ¹⁵The man went back and told the Jews that it was Jesus who had made him whole.

¹⁶For this reason the Jews were persecuting Jesus, because He kept doing such things on the Sabbath. ¹⁷But Jesus answered them, "My Father never stops working,ᵈ and I, Myself, am continually at work." ¹⁸Consequently, the Jews were even more determined to kill Him, not only because from time to time He was violatingᵉ the Sabbath but He was also calling God His own Father, making Himself equal with God. ¹⁹In reply Jesus said to them, "Truly, truly I tell you, the Son can do nothing by Himself—He does only what He observes the Father doing. Whatever that One does, the Son also does in like manner. ²⁰Indeed, the Father loves the Son and shows Him everything He Himself is doing. And He will show Him greater works than these, so that you will wonder. ²¹For just as the Father raises the dead and gives them life, so also the Son gives life to whom He wills. ²²Furthermore, the Father judges no one, but has given all judgment to the Son, ²³that all men may honor the Son just as they honor the Father. Anyone who does not honor the Son does not honor the Father who sent Him.

²⁴"Truly, truly I say to you, the person who listens to My word and believes in Him who sent Me has eternal life; he does not come into condemnation but has [already] passed from death into life. ²⁵Truly, truly I say to you, the hour is coming and now is, when the dead will hear the voice of the Son of God, and those who obey it will live. ²⁶For just as the Father has life in Himself, so He has granted the Son to have life in Himself. ²⁷And the Father gave Him authority to execute judgment because He is the Son of Man. ²⁸Do not be surprised at this, because the hour is coming in which all who are in the graves will hear His voice ²⁹and they will come forth—those who have done good things to resurrection characterized by life,ᶠ and those who have practiced worthless things to resurrection characterized by condemnation.ᶠ

³⁰"I can do nothing by Myself. I judge just as I hear, and My judgment is right, because I do not seek My own will but the will of Him who sent Me.

ᵈLiterally, "is working until now."
ᵉGreek imperfect tense.
ᶠDescriptive genitive.

³¹If I witness concerning Myself, My witness is not valid.^g ³²But there is Another who bears witness concerning Me; and I know that the testimony He bears concerning Me is valid. ³³You, yourselves, sent [a delegation] to John [the baptizer], and he has given witness to the truth. ³⁴However, I do not depend on the testimony from any human source, but I say these things in order that you, yourselves, may be saved. ³⁵John^h was a lamp burning and shining, and for a time you were willing to rejoice in his light. ³⁶But the testimony I have is greater than John's. Indeed, the works which the Father has given Me to finish—the very works which I am doing—are evidence concerning Me, that the Father has sent Me. ³⁷And the Father who sent Me, He Himself has given testimony concerning Me. You have never at any time heard His voice or seen His form; ³⁸and you do not have His word abiding in you, because you yourselves do not believe the One whom He sent.

³⁹"Search the Scriptures,ⁱ because you think that by means of them you have eternal life; yet the Scriptures themselves testify concerning Me. ⁴⁰But you are not willing to come to Me, in order that you may have life. ⁴¹I do not accept glory from men. ⁴²I have known you, that in yourselves you do not have love for God.^j ⁴³I have come in My Father's name, but you do not receive Me. If someone else comes in his own name, you will receive him. ⁴⁴How can people like you^k ever believe, since^l you receive glory from each other but do not seek the glory that comes from the only God?^m

⁴⁵"Do not think that I will accuse you before the Father. Your accuser is Moses, on whom you have placed your hope. ⁴⁶For if you had really believed Moses, you would have believed Me; because he wrote about Me. ⁴⁷But if you do not believe his writings, how will you believe My words?"

Chapter 6

After these things, Jesus went away to the other side of the Sea of Galilee, which is also called the Lake of Tiberias. ²A large crowd was following Him, because they saw the signs He was doing on those that were ill. ³Then Jesus

---

^gCf. vv. 36-38; 8:14-18. See Deut. 17:6; 19:15; Matt. 18:16; 2 Cor. 13:1.
^hLiterally, "that one," or "that man."
ⁱRendering *eraunate* is imperative. It may be the indicative, You are searching.
^jOr, it may be the subjective genitive, the love imparted by God.
^kEmphatic personal pronoun *humeis.*
^lCausal use of present participle, *lambanontes, receiving.*
^mCf. Deut. 6:4.

went up into the mountain, and was sitting there with His disciples. [4]And the Jewish Festival of the Passover was near.

[5]When Jesus looked up and saw a great multitude coming toward Him, He said to Philip, "Where can we buy bread, in order that these people may eat?" [6]Actually, He was saying this to test Philip, for He, Himself, knew what He was gong to do. [7]Philip answered Him, "Two hundred denarii[a] would not buy enough bread for each of them to receive even a little."

[8]Another of His disciples, Andrew, Simon Peter's brother, told Him, [9]"There is a little boy here who has five loaves of barley bread and two small fish—but what are these for so many?" [10]Jesus said, "Make the people sit down." There was much grass in the place, so the men, about five thousand in number, sat down.

[11]Then Jesus took the loaves, gave thanks, and distributed them to those who were sitting there. He did the same with the dried fish, giving the people as much as they wanted. [12]When they were satisfied Jesus said to His disciples, "Gather together the broken portions which are left over, so that nothing may be wasted." [13]So they gathered [them] and filled twelve wicker-baskets with broken portions from the five loaves of barley bread left over by those who had eaten.

[14]When the people saw the sign which Jesus did, they began to say, "This man is surely the Prophet[b] who was to come into the world." [15]Then Jesus, realizing that they were about to come and take Him by force to make Him king, withdrew again into the mountain by Himself alone.

[16]When evening came, His disciples went down to the lake, [17]stepped into a boat and started across the lake toward Capernaum. It was already dark and Jesus had not yet come to them. [18]A strong wind was blowing, and the lake was becoming rough. [19]After rowing about twenty-five or thirty stadia,[c] they saw Jesus walking on the lake and coming near the boat, and they were frightened. [20]But He said to them, "It is I! Stop being afraid!" [21]Then they were glad to take Him into the boat, and immediately the boat arrived at the shore to which they had been going.

[22]The next day the crowd that had remained on the opposite side of the lake realized that only one boat had been there, and that Jesus had not entered it with His disciples, but that the disciples had departed without Him. [23]However, small boats from Tiberias came ashore near the place where the people had eaten the bread, after the Lord had given thanks. [24]So when the crowd saw that neither Jesus nor His disciples were there, they entered those boats and crossed to Capernaum, searching for Jesus. [25]When they found Him on the other side of the lake, they asked Him, "Rabbi, when did You get

---

[a]See note on Matt. 18:28.
[b]Cf. Deut. 18:15; John 1:21.
[c]Three or four miles. A stadion was about 600 feet.

here?'' [26]Jesus answered them, ''Truly, truly I tell you, you are seeking Me not because you grasped [the significance of] the signs, but because you ate from the loaves and were filled. [27]Stop working for the food which perishes, but [work for] the food which endures to eternal life, which the Son of Man will give you; for on Him the Father—God, Himself—has set His seal of approval!''

[28]Therefore, they asked Him, ''What may we do in order that we may work the works of God?'' [29]In reply Jesus told them, ''This is the work of God, that you believe in Him whom He has sent.'' [30]Then they said to Him, ''Then what sign are You doing that we may see and believe You? What are You accomplishing? [31]Our forefathers ate the manna in the wilderness, just as it stands written,[d] 'He gave them bread from heaven to eat.' '' [32]Jesus answered them, ''Truly, truly I tell you, Moses did not give you the bread from heaven. [33]Indeed, the bread of God is that which[e] comes down from heaven and gives life to the world.''

[34]Therefore, they said to Him, ''Sir, Give us this bread always.'' [35]Jesus said to them, ''I, Myself, am the Bread of Life. He who comes to Me will never be hungry, and he who believes in Me will never be thirsty. [36]But as I have told you, even though you have seen Me, yet you do not believe. [37]All that the Father gives Me will come to Me, and the one who comes to Me I will in no way cast out. [38]For I have come down from heaven not to do My will but the will of Him who sent Me. [39]Now this is the will of Him who sent Me, that of all that He has given Me I should lose nothing, but should raise it up on the last day. [40]For this is My Father's will, that everyone who sees the Son and believes in Him may have eternal life; and I, Myself, will raise him up at the last day.''

[41]At this, the Jews began complaining about Him because He had said, ''I, Myself, am the Bread which came down out of heaven.'' [42]And they were remarking, ''Is this not Jesus, the son of Joseph, whose father and mother we, ourselves, know? Then how can He say, 'I have come down from heaven'?'' [43]Jesus said to them, ''Stop complaining among yourselves! [44]No one can come to Me, unless he is drawn by the Father who sent Me, and I will raise him up at the last day.

[45]''In the Prophets it stands written, 'And they will all be taught by God.'[f] Everyone who has listened to the Father, and learned from Him, comes to Me. [46]Not that anyone has ever seen the Father, except the One who is from God—that One has seen the Father. [47]Truly, truly I say to you, he who continues believing has eternal life. [48]I am the Bread of life. [49]Your forefathers ate the manna in the wilderness, and yet they died. [50]This is the

---

[d]Cf. Exod. 16:4 ff; Deut. 8:3.
[e]Or, He who.
[f]Cf. Isa. 54:13.

Bread that comes down out of heaven, from which a man may eat and not die. [51]I, Myself, am the living Bread which came down from heaven. If anyone eats of this Bread, he will live forever. And the Bread which I will give, in behalf of the world's life, is My flesh.''

[52]Then the Jews began to quarrel vehemently among themselves, saying, ''How can this man give us His flesh to eat?'' [53]So Jesus said to them, ''Truly, truly I tell you, unless you eat the flesh of the Son of Man and drink His blood, you have no life in yourselves. [54]He who eats My flesh and drinks My blood has eternal life, and I, Myself, will raise him up at the last day. [55]For My flesh is true food, and My blood is true drink. [56]Whoever eats My flesh and drinks My blood dwells in Me and I in him. [57]Just as the living Father sent Me, and I have life because of the Father, so he who eats Me will live because of Me. [58]This is the Bread that came down from heaven. It is not like the bread the forefathers ate and died. He who eats this Bread will live forever.''

[59]Jesus said this while He was teaching in a synagogue in Capernaum. [60]After they heard it, many of His disciples said, ''This statement is a difficult one to receive. Who is able to listen to Him?''[g] [61]But Jesus, knowing in Himself that His disciples were complaining about this, He said to them, ''Does this disturb you? [62]What if you see the Son of Man ascending to where He was before? [63]The Spirit is what gives life; the unregenerate nature does not profit anything. The utterances which I have spoken to you,—they are Spirit and they are life. [64]But there are some of you who do not believe.'' For Jesus knew from the beginning who were the ones that did not believe and who was going to betray Him. [65]And He went on to say, ''This is why I told you that no one can come to Me unless the Father has enabled him [to do so].''

[66]From this time,[h] many of His disciples turned back to the things they had left behind and no longer walked with Him. [67]So Jesus said to the Twelve, ''You, yourselves, do not intend to go away, also, do you?'' [68]Simon Peter answered Him, ''Lord, to whom shall we go away? You have the words that bring eternal life! [69]And we on our part have come to believe and to know that You[i] are the Holy One of God.'' [70]Jesus answered them, ''Did not I select the Twelve of you for Myself? Yet one of you is a devil.'' [71]Now He was speaking about Judas, son of Simon Iscariot.[j] For this man—one of the Twelve—was going to betray Him.

---

[g]Or, who is able to obey it?
[h]As a result of this.
[i]The Greek pronoun is emphatic.
[j]See note on Mark 14:10.

Chapter 7

After these things Jesus went about in Galilee. He did not wish to travel in Judaea because the Jews there were eager to kill Him. [2]When the Jewish Feast of Tabernacles[a] drew near, [3]His brothers said to Him, "Leave this place and go to Judaea, so that Your disciples also may see the works You are doing. [4]For no one does anything in secret if he desires to be widely known. If You do things like these[b] show Yourself to the world." [5]For even His brothers did not believe in Him.

[6]Jesus said to them, "'My time has not yet come, but your time is already. [7]The world cannot hate you; but it hates Me because I testify concerning it, that its works are evil. [8]Go up yourselves to the festival. I am not yet going up to this festival, because My time has not fully come."

[9]And having said these things to them, Jesus remained in Galilee. [10]But after His brothers had gone up to the festival, He too went up, not openly but without any publicity.

[11]Now the Jews at the festival were looking for Him and kept inquiring, "Where is He?" [12]Among the crowds there was a great deal of whispering about Him. Some were saying, "He is a good man." Others declared, "No! For He is leading the people astray." [13]However, no one spoke openly about Him, for fear of the Jews.

[14]When the Festival week[c] was already half over, Jesus went up into the Temple area and began to teach. [15]The Jews were amazed. "How does this man know the Scriptures?"[d] they asked. "He has not been trained." [16]Jesus answered them, "My doctrine is not My own, but His who sent Me. [17]If anyone is willing[e] to do God's will,[f] he will know concerning the doctrine, whether it is from God or whether I am expressing My own ideas. [18]Whoever expresses his own ideas[g] seeks glory for himself. But the man who seeks the glory of The One who sent him is trustworthy, in him there is nothing false.[h] [19]Did not Moses give you the Law? Yet not one of you practices the Law. Why are you seeking to kill Me?"

[20]"You are possessed by a demon! the crowd replied. "Who is trying to kill You?" [21]Jesus answered them, "I did one deed,[i] and you are all amazed.

---

[a]That is the Feast of Booths, or Tents. Cf. Lev. 23:34, 43; Deut. 16:13.

[b]Or, Inasmuch as you are doing these things. A condition of the first class. See note on Matt. 4:3.

[c]The Feast of Tabernacles lasted for seven days, and was followed by a day of holy convocation. Cf. Lev. 23:34-43.

[d]Literally, "Know letters?"

[e]Linear force of Greek present subjunctive.

[f]Literally, "His will."

[g]Literally, "He who speaks from himself."

[h]Or, in him there is no unrighteousness.

[i]Cf. John 5:8-9.

²²Because Moses gave you the [rite of] circumcision—althought it did not originate with Moses but with the patriarchs—even on the Sabbath you administer it.ʲ ²³If a person is circumcised on the Sabbath, in order that the Law of Moses may not be violated, are you angry with Me because I made a man completely well on the Sabbath? ²⁴Stop judging according to appearance, but render righteous judgment."

²⁵Then some of the people of Jerusalem said, "Is not this the Man they are trying to put to death? ²⁶Look! He is speaking openly, and they say nothing to Him! Can it be that the authorities have realized that He is the Messiah? ²⁷However, we know where this man is from, but when the Messiah appears, no one will know where He is from."

²⁸Jesus, while He was teaching in the Temple area, called out and said, "You know Me and you know where I am from. But I came not on My own initiative, but the One who sent Me is trustworthy, whom you, yourselves, do not know. ²⁹I know Him because I am from Him and He, Himself, commissioned Me."

³⁰At that they tried to seize Him, but no one laid hands on Him, for His hour had not yet come. ³¹However, many of the crowd believed in Him. "When the Messiah comes," they said, "He will perform no greater signs than this man has done, will He?"

³²The Pharisees heard the crowd whispering these things about Him, so the chief priests and the Pharisees together sent Temple police to arrest Him. ³³Then Jesus said, "Only a little longer am I with you, and then I am going back to Him who sent Me. ³⁴You will search for Me but you will not find Me, and where I am you, yourselves, cannot come."

³⁵At that, the Jews said to one another,"Where can this fellow go that we cannot find him? He is not going to the Dispersion among the Greeks and teach the Greeks, is He? ³⁶What does he mean by saying 'You will search for me but you will not find me, and where I am you yourselves cannot come'? "

³⁷Now on the last and greatest day of the Festival, Jesus stood up and called out, "If anyone is thirsty, let him come to Me and drink. ³⁸The person that believes in Me, just as the Scripture says,ᵏ from his inward being will flow rivers of living water." ³⁹He said this about the Spirit whom those who believed in Him, were about to receive. For the Spirit was not yet [given in His fullness] because Jesus had not yet been glorified.ˡ

⁴⁰Some of the crowd, on hearing these words, said, "This man is really the Prophet!"ᵐ ⁴¹Others said, "Certainly the Christ does not come out of Galilee,

---

ʲCf. Gen. 17:12; Lev. 12:3; Luke 2:21.
ᵏCf. Isa. 44:3; 55:1; 58:11; Zech.14:8; Joel 3:18.
ˡCf. John 12:23-33; 14:15-21, 26; 16:7, 13-14; Acts 1:5, 8.
ᵐCf. Deut. 18:15; John 1:21; 6:14.

does He? [42]Does not the Scripture[n] declare that the Christ is a descendant of David and comes from Bethlehem, the town where David lived?" [43]So on account of Him, a division developed among the crowd. [44]Some wanted to seize Him, but no one laid hands on Him.

[45]When the Temple police returned to the chief priests and Pharisees, they were asked, "Why did you not bring Him?" [46]The Temple police replied, "Never at any time has a man spoken as this man speaks!" [47]The Pharisees answered, "You, too, have not been deceived, have you? [48]Not a single one of the rulers or of the Pharisees has believed in Him, has he? [49]As for this crowd, who do not know the Law, they are accursed!"

[50]Nicodemus, the one who had come to Jesus previously,[o] being one of their number, said, [51]"Does our Law judge a person without first giving him a hearing and finding out what He has done?"[p] [52]They answered Him, "You are not from Galilee too, are you? Search and see that the Prophet does not arise from Galilee." [53]Then each man went to his own house.

Chapter 8

But Jesus went to the Mount of Olives. [2]Early in the morning, He came again into the Temple area and was met by a crowd of people. He sat down and began teaching them. [3]Then the interpreters of the Law and the Pharisees brought to Him a woman who had been caught in adultery. They stood her in the center, [4]and began questioning Jesus, "Teacher, this woman was taken in the act of committing adultery. [5]In the Law, Moses commanded us that such women should be stoned.[a] So what do You say?" [6]They said this to test Him, in order that they might bring accusation against Him. But Jesus stooped down and began writing on the ground with His finger.

[7]But as they continued questioning Him, He straightened up and said to them, "Whoever among you is without sin, let him be the first to throw a stone at her!" [8]Again, He stooped down and proceeded to write on the ground. [9]When they had heard this, and they started going out one by one, beginning with the older ones to the last ones, until Jesus was left alone, with the woman standing before Him.[b]

[10]When Jesus stood up He saw no one except the woman. He said to her, "Woman, where are the ones that accused you? Has no one condemned you?"

---

[n]Cf. Ps. 89:3-4; Mic. 5:2.

[o]Cf. John 3:1ff. Nicodemus was a member of the Sanhedrin, the highest Jewish tribunal.

[p]Cf. Deut. 1:16.

[a]Cf. Deut. 22:21ff.

[b]Literally, "in the midst."

¹¹"No one, Lord," she replied. Then He said, "Neither do I condemn you. Go and no longer practice sin."

¹²Jesus continued speaking, to them, "I, Myself, am the Light of the world. Any person who consistently follows Me will in no way walk in the darkness, but he will have the Light of Life." ¹³Therefore, the Pharisees said to Him, "You are testifying concerning Yourself. Your testimony is not valid." ¹⁴Jesus answered them, "Even if I Myself do testify concerning Myself, My testimony is valid because I know where I came from and where I am going; but you do not know where I came from or where I am going. ¹⁵You judge according to human standards; I, Myself, do not judge anyone. ¹⁶But even if I did exercise judgment, My judgment is valid, because [it is] not I alone [who judges] but I and the One who sent Me. ¹⁷And even in your Law it stands written[c] that the testimony of two witnesses is valid. ¹⁸I am the One who bears witness concerning Myself, and the Father who sent me bears witness concerning Me."

¹⁹"Where is Your Father?" they asked. Jesus answered, "You know neither Me nor My Father. If you had known Me you would also have known My Father."

²⁰These words He proclaimed as He stood by the treasury in the Temple area, but no one seized Him because His time had not yet come.

²¹Then Jesus again spoke to them, "I am going away. You will look for Me but you will die in your sin. Where I am going you cannot come." ²²Therefore the Jews said, "He will not kill Himself, will He, because He says, 'Where I am going you cannot come'?" ²³He went on to say to them, "You[d] are from below; I[d] am from above. You[d] are from this world; I[d] am not from this world. ²⁴That is why I said you will die in your sins. For unless you come to believe that I am [He], you will die in your sins."

²⁵Then they asked Him, "Who are You?" Jesus replied, I am what I tell you at the beginning. ²⁶I have many things to say and to judge concerning you. But He who sent Me is true, and I am telling the world the very words which I heard from Him."

²⁷They did not realize that He was speaking to them of the Father. ²⁸So Jesus said, "When you lift up the Son of Man, then you will realize that I am [He], and I do nothing by Myself, but just as the Father taught Me, these things I declare. ²⁹He who sent Me is ever with Me. He did not leave Me alone, for I always do what pleases Him."

³⁰While He was saying these things, many [persons] came to believe in Him. ³¹To the Jews who had believed in Him, Jesus said, "If you remain in

---

[c]Cf. Deut. 17:6; 19:15.
[d]Emphatic pronouns.

My word, you are truly My disciples, ³²and you will know the truth, and the truth will set you free."

³³They answered Him, "We are descendants of Abraham, and we have never remained enslaved to anyone. What do you mean by saying, 'You will become free'?" ³⁴Jesus answered them, "Truly, truly I tell you, everyone who practices sin is a slave of sin. ³⁵Now the slave does not abide in the house forever, but a son does. ³⁶So if the Son makes you free, you will be free in reality. ³⁷I know that you are descendants of Abraham, yet you are seeking to kill Me, because My word has no place in you. ³⁸I declare what I have seen at the Father's side, and you, accordingly, practice what you heard at your father's side."

³⁹They answered Him, "Abraham is our father!" At this Jesus replied, "If you were Abraham's children, you would be doing the works Abraham did. ⁴⁰But now you are seeking to kill Me, a Man who has told you the truth which God has given Me. Abraham did not act like that. ⁴¹You^e are practicing the deeds of your father." They said to Him, "We were not begotten illegitimately. We have one Father—God!" ⁴²Jesus said to them, "If God were your Father, you would love Me, because I came forth from God. Indeed, I have not come of My own initiative, but He sent Me. ⁴³Why do you not understand what I am saying? It is because you are not able to listen to My word. ⁴⁴You are of your father the devil, and you want to practice the desires of your father. He was a murderer from the beginning, and he does not stand by the truth because there is no truth in him. When he speaks a lie he speaks out of his own nature, for he is a liar and the father of lies. ⁴⁵But because I, Myself, declare the truth, you do not believe Me. ⁴⁶Who of you reproves Me concerning sin? If I declare the truth, why do you not believe Me? ⁴⁷He who is of God listens to the words of God. The reason you are not listening is because you are not of God."

⁴⁸Then the Jews answered Him, "Are we not right in saying that You are a Samaritan and possessed by a demon?" ⁴⁹Jesus answered, "I am not demon possessed. As a matter of fact, I am honoring My Father but you are dishonoring Me. ⁵⁰But I do not seek My glory. There is One who seeks [it] and He is judging. ⁵¹Truly, truly I tell you, If anyone keeps My word he will certainly never experience death.

⁵²The Jews said to Him, "Now, we do know that You are demon possessed. Abraham died, and the prophets died, and You say, 'If anyone keeps My word, he will certainly never taste death.' ⁵³You are not greater than our forefather Abraham, who died, are You? And the prophets died, also. So who are You claiming to be?"

---

^{e}Emphatic pronoun.

⁵⁴Jesus answered, "If I glorify Myself, My glory is nothing. It is My Father—whom you claim is your God—that glorifies Me, ⁵⁵and yet you have not come to know Him, but I know Him. And if I should say that I do not know Him I would be like you, a liar. But I know Him, and I keep His word.

⁵⁶"Abraham, your forefather, rejoiced that he might see My day, He saw [it] and was glad." ⁵⁷At this the Jews said to Him, "You have not yet [lived] fifty years, and have You seen Abraham?" ⁵⁸Jesus said to them, "Truly, truly I tell you, before Abraham came into existence, I AM."

⁵⁹At that they picked up stones to throw at Him, but Jesus hid^f himself and went forth out of the Temple area.

Chapter 9

While He was walking along, Jesus saw a man [who had been] blind from birth. ²And His disciples questioned Him, saying, "Rabbi, who sinned, this man or his parents, that he was born blind?" ³Jesus answered, "Neither did this man sin, nor his parents, but [it happened] in order that the works of God might be manifested in him. ⁴As long as it is day, we must do the deeds of Him who sent Me. The night is coming, when no one can work. ⁵While I am in the world, I am the Light of the world."

⁶Having said these things, He spat on the ground and made mud of the saliva and put the mud on his eyes ⁷and told him, "Go wash in the pool of Siloam" [which means, one who has been sent]. So he went and washed himself, and came [back] seeing.

⁸Then his neighbors and the ones who were accustomed to seeing him as a beggar, said, "Is not this man the one who used to sit and beg?" ⁹Some were saying, "This is he." Others were saying, "No, but he is like him." He, himself, was saying, I am [he]." ¹⁰So they were saying to him, "Then how were your eyes opened?" ¹¹He answered them, "The man by the name of Jesus made clay and spread [it] on my eyes and said to me, "Go to Siloam and wash." So I went and washed and now I see." ¹²And they said to him, "Where is that Man?" He replied, "I do not know."

¹³They brought to the Pharisees the man who formerly had been blind. ¹⁴Now it was on a Sabbath day when Jesus prepared the mud and opened his eyes. ¹⁵The Pharisees questioned him further as to how he received his sight. He said to them, "He put mud upon my eyes, and I washed [them], and I can see." ¹⁶Then some of the Pharisees were saying, "This man is not from God because he does not observe the Sabbath." Others remarked, "How can a man [who is] a sinner perform such signs as this?" So there was a division among them.

---

^fLiterally, "was concealed."

¹⁷Then they asked the blind man again, "What do you say about Him, since He has opened your eyes?" He replied, "He is a Prophet." ¹⁸However, the Jews would not believe that he had actually been blind and that his sight had been restored. They called his parents ¹⁹and asked them, saying, "Is this your son, whom you say was born blind? Then how is it that he can now see?" ²⁰Then his parents answered, "We know that this is our son and that he was born blind. ²¹But how he now sees we do not know, or who opened his eyes we, ourselves, do not know. Ask him. He is of age. Let him speak for himself." ²²His parents said these things because they were afraid of the Jews. For the Jews had already agreed that if anyone should confess Him [to be the] Messiah he would be expelled from the synagogue. ²³That is why his parents said, "He is of age. Ask him."

²⁴So a second time, they called the man who had been blind and said to him, "Give glory to God. We, ourselves, know that this man is a sinner." ²⁵At this the man answered, "Whether He is a sinner [or not] I do not know. One thing I know, that although I was blind, now I see!" ²⁶Then they said to him, "What did He do to you? How did He open your eyes?" ²⁷He replied, "I have already told you but you did not listen. Why do you want to hear again? You, yourselves, do not wish also to become His disciples, do you?" ²⁸Then they reviled him and said, "You, yourself, are a disciple of that fellow, but we, ourselves, are disciples of Moses. ²⁹We, ourselves, know that God has spoken to Moses, but this fellow—we do not know where He comes from."

³⁰The man answered them, "Indeed, in this is the marvelous thing, that you, yourselves, do not know where He comes from, yet He opened my eyes! ³¹We know that God does not listen to sinners, but if any one is God-fearing and consistently does His will, that one He hears. ³²Since the world began, it was never heard that anyone opened the eyes of one who was born blind. ³³If this man were not from God, He could not do anything." ³⁴They answered him, "You, yourself, were altogether born in sins, and are you trying to teach us?" And they threw him out.

³⁵Jesus heard that they had thrown him out and, having found him He said, "Do you believe in the Son of Man?" ³⁶That one answered, "And who is He, Sir, that I may believe in Him?" ³⁷Jesus said to him, "Actually, you have seen Him, and the One who is speaking with you, that One is He." ³⁸And he said, "I believe, Lord." And he worshipped Him.

³⁹And Jesus said, "For judgment I came into this world, that those not seeing might see and those seeing might become blind." ⁴⁰Some of the Pharisees who were near Him heard these things and said to Him, "We are not blind, also, are we?" ⁴¹Jesus said to them, "If you were blind you would not have sin. But now you say, 'We see.' Your sin remains."

Chapter 10

"Truly, truly I say to you, the one who enters not through the door into the sheepfold but climbs over at some other place, that one is a thief and a robber.[a] [2]But he who enters in through the door is the shepherd of the sheep. [3]The doorkeeper opens to him, and the sheep listen to his voice, and he calls his own sheep by name and he leads them out. [4]When he has brought all his own sheep out, he walks in front of them, and the sheep follow him because they know his voice.[5]Under no circumstance, will they follow a stranger, but will run away from him because they do not know the voice of strangers."

[6]Jesus spoke this figurative[b] discourse to them but they did not understand what the things were which He was telling them. [7]Therefore Jesus spoke again, "Truly, truly I tell you, I, Myself, am the door of the sheep. [8]All who came before Me are thieves and robbers, but the sheep did not listen to them. [9]I, Myself, am the door. Through Me, if anyone enters in, he will be saved, and he will go in and out and find a pasture. [10]The thief does not come except to steal and kill and destroy. I, Myself, came that they may have life and have [it] to the full.

[11]"I, Myself, am the Good Shepherd. The good shepherd lays[c] down his life in behalf of the sheep. [12]He who is a hireling[d] and not the shepherd, does not own the sheep, so when he sees the wolf coming he deserts the sheep and flees—and the wolf seizes and scatters the flock—[13]because he is a hireling and does not care for the sheep.

[14]"I, Myself, am the Good Shepherd and I know My own [sheep] and My own [sheep] know Me, [15]even as the Father knows Me and I know the Father; and I lay down My life for the sheep. [16]I have other sheep which are not of this fold. Them also I must lead, and they will hear My voice, and there will become one flock [and] one Shepherd.

[17]"For My Father loves Me because I lay down My life in order that I may receive [it] again. [18]No one took it from Me, but I lay it down voluntarily.[e] I have authority to lay it down, and I have authority to take it up again. This command I received from My Father."

[19]Again a division arose among the Jews on account of these words. [20]And many of them were saying, "He is possessed by a demon and is mad. Why do you listen to Him?" [21]Others were saying, "These are not the words of a demon-possessed man. A demon is not able to open the eyes of the blind, is he?"

---

[a]False Christs or Messiahs.
[b]Parable or allegory.
[c]Gives—sacrifices.
[d]Hired man.
[e]Literally, "of myself."

²²The time came for the Feast of the Dedication[f] in Jerusalem. It was winter, ²³and Jesus was walking in the Temple area, in Solomon's Portico. ²⁴So the Jews surrounded Him and were saying, "How long will You hold us in suspense? If You are the Messiah, tell us plainly!" ²⁵Jesus replied to them, "I have told you but you do not believe. The works which I am doing in My Father's name, these are testifying concerning Me, ²⁶but you do not believe because you are not of My sheep. ²⁷My sheep listen to My voice, and I know them and they follow Me. ²⁸And I give them eternal life and they will certainly never perish, and no one will snatch them out of My hand. ²⁹My Father, who gave [them] to Me, is greater than all and no one is able to snatch [them] out of the Father's hand. ³⁰The Father and I are One."

³¹The Jews again took up stones to stone Him. ³²Jesus said to them, "I have shown you many excellent works from the Father. For which of these do you stone Me?" ³³The Jews answered him, "It is not for an excellent work but for blasphemy that we stone You, because You, being a man, make Yourself God." ³⁴Jesus answered them, "Does it not stand written in your Law,[g] 'I said, You are gods'? ³⁵If he called those gods, to whom the word of God came—and the Scripture cannot be broken—³⁶do you say to the One whom the Father set apart and sent into the world, 'You blaspheme,' because I said, 'I am the Son of God'? ³⁷If I am not doing the works of My Father, do not believe Me. ³⁸But I do [them], even if you do not believe Me, believe the works, in order that you may come to know and continue knowing that the Father [is] in Me and I [am] in the Father."

³⁹Therefore they tried again to seize Him, but He escaped out of their hand. ⁴⁰And He went away again across the Jordan to the place where John was at first baptizing, and He remained there. ⁴¹And many people came to Him and were saying, "John did no sign, but all the things John said about this man are true." ⁴²And many believed in Him there.

Chapter 11

Now a certain man was sick, Lazarus from Bethany, of the village of Mary and her sister Martha. ²It was the Mary[a] who anointed the Lord with ointment and wiped His feet with her hair, whose brother Lazarus was sick. ³So the sisters sent [word] to Him saying, "Lord, behold, he whom You love is ill." ⁴When He heard [it] Jesus said, "This illness is not to death but for the glory of God, that through it the Son of God may be glorified."

---

[f]An eight day celebration of the dedication of the temple by Judas Maccabeus, 164 B.C.

[g]Cf. Ps. 82:6.

[a]Cf. John 12:1-8.

[5]Now Jesus loved Martha and her sister and Lazarus. [6]When, therefore, He heard that he was ill, He remained two days in the place where He was. [7]Then after this, He said to the disciples, "Let us go into Judaea again." [8]The disciples said to Him, "Rabbi, the Jews were now seeking to stone You, and are You going there again? [9]Jesus replied, "Are there not twelve hours in the day? If a man walks in the day, he does not stumble because he sees the light of this world. [10]But if a man walks in the night, he stumbles because the light is not in him."

[11]He said these things and then further told them, "Lazarus, our friend, has fallen asleep, but I am going that I may wake him out of sleep." [12]At that the disciples said to Him, "Lord, if he has fallen asleep, he will get well." [13]But Jesus had spoken concerning his death, but those men thought that He had spoken concerning the sleep of resting. [14]So then Jesus told them plainly, "Lazarus died. [15]And for your sake I am glad I was not there, so that you may believe. But let us go to him." [16]So Thomas, called the Twin, said to his fellow-disciples, "Let us go also, that we may die with Him."

[17]When Jesus came, He found that Lazarus had already been in the tomb for four days. [18]Now Bethany was near Jerusalem, about fifteen stadia[b] away. [19]And many of the Jews had come to Martha and Mary that they might console them concerning their brother. [20]Now Martha when she heard that Jesus was coming, went to meet Him, but Mary continued sitting in the house.

[21]Then Martha said to Jesus, "Lord, if You had been here, my brother would not have died. [22]Even now I know that whatever things You ask God, God will give to You." [23]Jesus said to her, "Your brother will rise again." [24]Martha said to Him, "I know that he will rise again in the resurrection on the last day." [25]Jesus said to her, "I, Myself, am the Resurrection and the Life. He who believes in Me, even if he dies, he will live. [26]And everyone who lives and believes in Me will never die. Do you believe this?" [27]She said to Him, "Yes, Lord, I have come to believe that You are the Christ, the Son of God, the One who was to come[c] into the world."

[28]And having said this, she went away and called her sister Mary privately, saying, "The Teacher is here and He is calling for you." [29]As soon as Mary heard [it], she got up quickly and started to go to Him. [30]Jesus had not yet come into the village but He was still at the place where Martha had met Him.

[31]When the Jews who were with Mary in the house consoling her saw that she got up quickly and went out, they followed her, thinking she was going to the tomb to weep there. [32]When Mary came where Jesus was and saw Him, she fell at His feet, saying to Him, "Lord, if You had been here, my brother would not have died." [33]When Jesus saw her weeping, and the Jews who had come with her weeping, He was indignant in His spirit and was Himself troubled.

---

[b]Two miles.
[c]Promised one.

[34]He asked, "Where have you laid him?" They said to Him, "Lord, come and see." [35]Jesus shed tears. [36]The Jews then were saying, "Look, how He loved him!" [37]But some of them said, "Could not this man, who opened the eyes of the blind man, have caused this man also not to die?"

[38]Then Jesus, again indignant in Himself, went to the tomb. It was a cave, and a stone was lying against it. [39]Jesus said, "Take away the stone." Martha, the sister of the dead man, said to Him, "Lord, by this time there is decomposition; for he has been dead four days." [40]Jesus said to her, "Did I not say to you that if you will believe you will see the glory of God?" [41]So they took away the stone. And Jesus lifted His eyes upward and said, "Father, I thank Thee because Thou didst hear Me. [42]And I Myself knew that always Thou hearest Me. But for the sake of the crowd standing around I spoke, so that they may believe that Thou didst send Me."

[43]And having said these things, He cried out with a loud voice, "Lazarus, come out!" [44]The dead man came out, bound hand and foot with grave-cloths, and his face wrapped in a head-covering.[d] Jesus said to them, "Loose him, and let him go."

[45]Many, therefore, of the Jews who came to Mary and witnessed what He did, believed in Him. [46]But some of them went off to the Pharisees and told them what Jesus had done. [47]So the chief priests and the Pharisees called together the Sanhedrin and said, "What are we to do? This man is doing many signs. [48]If we let Him alone like this, all will believe in Him and the Romans will come and remove both our place[e] and our nation." [49]But a certain one of them, Caiaphas, being the high priest that year, said to them, "You do not know a thing about this. [50]You do not consider that it is to your advantage that one man should die for the people, rather than for the whole nation to be destroyed." [51]He did not say this of himself but, being the high priest that year he prophesied that Jesus was about to die in behalf of the nation, [52]and not in behalf of the nation only, but in order that He might also gather together into one the children of God that are scattered abroad. [53]Therefore, from that day they planned to kill Jesus.

[54]Now Jesus no longer went about publicly among the Jews, but went away into the country near the wilderness to a town called Ephraim, and there He remained with the disciples.

[55]Now the Jewish Passover was near, and many people went up to Jerusalem from the country before the Passover in order that they might purify themselves. [56]They were lookihg for Jesus and were saying to each other as they stood in the Temple precincts, "What do you think?—that He will not come to the festival at all?" [57]Now the chief priests and the Pharisees had given orders that if anyone should get to know where He was, he should disclose [it] so that they might arrest Him.

---

[d]*Soudarion.*
[e]Literally, "the place," meaning probably the Holy Place (the Temple).

Chapter 12

Six days before the Passover Jesus came to Bethany, where Lazarus was, whom Jesus [had] raised from the dead. [2]A supper was planned for Him there, at which Martha did the serving while Lazarus was one of those who reclined at [the] table with Him. [3]Then Mary took a pound of costly ointment of genuine nard, anointed the feet of Jesus and wiped His feet with her hair; and the house was filled with the fragrance of the ointment.

[4]But Judas Iscariot, one of His disciples—the one who was about to betray Him—said, [5]"Why was not this ointment sold for three hundred denarii[a] and [the money] given to poor people?" [6]He said this not because he cared about the poor, but because he was a thief, and had charge of the money bag, and he used to steal what was put in. [7]Then Jesus said, "Let her alone, in order that she may keep it for the day of My burial. [8]For you will always have the poor with you, but you will not always have Me."[b]

[9]A large crowd of the Jews learned that He was at Bethany, and they came, not only because of Jesus but also to see Lazarus whom He had raised from the dead. [10]But the chief priests decided to kill Lazarus also, [11]since it was because of Him that many of the Jews were leaving [them] and believing in Jesus.

[12]The next day the large crowd, who had come to the feast, upon hearing that Jesus was coming to Jerusalem, [13]took the branches of the palm-trees and went out to meet Him, and they kept shouting, "Hosanna! [c]Blessed is He who comes in the Name of the Lord,[d] even the King of Israel!"

[14]And Jesus found a young donkey and He sat upon it, just as it stands written, [15]"Stop being afraid, daughter of Zion! Behold, your King is coming, sitting on the colt of a donkey."[e] [16]At the time His disciples did not understand these things, but when Jesus was glorified, then they remembered that these things had been written about Him and they had done these things to Him.

[17]So the crowd that had been with Him when He called Lazarus out of the tomb and raised him from the dead kept testifying [to it]. [18]That was why the crowd went to meet Him, because they heard that He had done this sign. [19]So the Pharisees said to one another, "You see, there is nothing you can do. Look, the world has gone after Him!"

---

[a]See note on Matt. 18:28.

[b]Jesus' reply refers to His impending death and burial, which Mary seems to have anticipated.

[c]See note on Matt. 21:9.

[d]Cf. Ps. 118:26.

[e]Cf. Zech. 9:9.

²⁰Now among those who had come up to worship at the festival were some Greeks. ²¹They came to Philip, who was from Bethsaida in Galilee, and made a request of him, "Sir, we desire to see Jesus." ²²Philip came and told Andrew; and Andrew and Philip told Jesus. ²³And Jesus answered them, "The hour has come for the Son of Man to be glorified. ²⁴Truly, truly I say to you, unless the grain of wheat falls into the ground and dies, it remains itself alone. But if it dies, it produces much fruit. ²⁵The man who loves his life loses it, but he who hates his life in this world will keep it for life eternal. ²⁶If anyone serves Me, let him keep following Me; and where I am there also will My servant be. If anyone serves Me, the Father will honor him. ²⁷Now My soul is troubled, and what should I say? Father, save Me from this hour? But for this purpose I came to this hour. ²⁸Father, glorify Thy name!"

Then a voice came out of heaven, "I have both glorified [it] and I will glorify [it] again." ²⁹So the crowd that stood by and heard the voice said, "It thundered." Others were saying, "An angel spoke to Him." ³⁰Jesus answered, "This voice came not for My sake but for your sake. ³¹Now is the judgment of this world. Now the ruler of this world will be cast out completely. ³²And I, if I am lifted up from the earth, will draw all men to Myself." ³³He said this, signifying what sort of death He was about to die.

³⁴Then the crowd answered Him, "We ourselves have heard from the Law that the Christ remains forever. What do you mean by saying 'The Son of Man must be lifted up'? Who is this Son of Man?" ³⁵So Jesus said to them, "For a little time yet the light is among you. Walk while you have the light, so that darkness may not overtake you. He who walks in the darkness does not know where he is going. ³⁶While you have the light, believe in the light so you may become sons of light."ᶠ

After Jesus had said these things, He went away and was hidden from them. ³⁷Although He had done so many signs before them, they refused to believe in Him, ³⁸in order that the word of Isaiah the prophet might be fulfilled which he spoke, "Lord, who has believed our report? And to whom was the power of the Lord revealed?"ᵍ ³⁹For this reason they were not able to believe, for again Isaiah said, ⁴⁰"He has blinded their eyes and has hardened their heart, lest they should see with their eyes and perceive with their heart, and should turn, and I should heal them."ʰ ⁴¹Isaiah said these things because he saw His glory and spoke concerning Him.

⁴²But yet, even many of the Jewish leaders believed in Him; but on account of the Pharisees they did not confess [Him], lest they should be expelled from the synagogue. ⁴³For they loved the glory of men more than the glory of God.

⁴⁴But Jesus cried out and said, "He who believes in Me does not believe in

---

ᶠFilled with light.
ᵍCf. Isa. 53:1.
ʰCf. Isa. 6:9-10.

Me but in Him who sent Me. [45]and he who beholds Me beholds the One who sent Me. [46]I have come as a light into the world, in order that everyone who believes in Me may not remain in darkness. [47]And if anyone hears My teachings and does not keep them, I, Myself, do not condemn him. For I did not come that I might condemn the world but that I might save the world. [48]He who rejects Me and does not receive My sayings has one that condemns him: the very word which I have spoken, that will condemn him at the last day. [49]For I did not speak of My own direction but the One having sent Me—the Father Himself—has given a command what I should say and what I should speak. [50]And I know that His command is eternal life. What things therefore I, Myself, speak, just as the Father has said to Me, thus I speak.''

Chapter 13

Now before the festival of the Passover, Jesus, knowing that the hour had come for Him to leave this world [and go] to the Father, having loved His own people who were in the world, He loved them completely.[a] [2]The devil had already put it into the heart of Judas Iscariot,[b] the son of Simon, to betray Jesus. So during supper, [3][Jesus,] knowing that the Father had given all things into His hands, and that He had come from God and was going [back] to God, [4]arose from the supper and laid aside His outer garments, and wrapped around His waist a linen towel. [5]Then He poured water into the basin, and began to wash the disciples' feet and to wipe [them] with the linen towel which was wrapped around His waist.

[6]Accordingly, He came to Simon Peter, who said to Him, "Lord, are You going to wash my feet?" [7]Jesus answered him, "What I, Myself, am doing you do not know just now, but later you will know." [8]Peter said to Him, "You will never by any means wash my feet!" Jesus replied, "If I do not wash you, you have no part with Me." [9]Simon Peter said to Him, "Lord, not only my feet but also my hands and my head!" [10]Jesus said to him, "He who has been bathed has no need, except to wash his feet, but is completely clean; and you are clean, but not all [of you]." [11]For He knew the one betraying Him. That is why He said, "Not all [of you] are clean."

[12]When He had washed their feet, and taken His garments, and again reclined at [the] table, He said to them, "Do you know what I have done to you? [13]You call Me 'The Teacher' and 'The Lord,' and you speak correctly, for I am. [14]Therefore, if I, Myself, your Lord and Teacher, washed your feet, you, yourselves, ought to wash the feet of one another. [15]For I have given you

---

[a]Or, unto the uttermost.
[b]See note on Matt. 10:4.

an example, in order that just as I, Myself, did to You, you also should keep on doing. [16]Truly, truly I say to you, a servant is not greater than his lord, nor is an apostle greater than the one who sent him. [17]If you know these things, you are fortunate if you continue doing them.

[18]"I am not speaking about all of you. I know which ones I selected for Myself. But the Scripture must be fulfilled, 'He who eats of My bread has lifted up his heel against Me.'[c] [19]I tell you this now, before it happens, so that when it occurs you may believe that I am [He]. [20]Truly, truly I say to you, whoever receives anyone whom I send, receives Me, and he who receives Me, receives the One who sent Me.''

[21]Having said these things, Jesus was troubled in spirit and He testified and said, "Truly, truly I tell you that one of you will betray Me." [22]The disciples began looking at one another, being perplexed concerning which one He was speaking. [23]One of them, the disciple whom Jesus loved, was reclining on Jesus' bosom.[d] [24]So Simon Peter beckoned to him and said, "Ask who it is concerning whom He speaks." [25]He leaned back on Jesus' breast and said to Him, "Lord, who is it?" [26]Jesus, therefore, replied, "That man it is for whom I shall dip the piece of bread and give [it] to him." So He dipped the piece of bread in the dish and took it and gave it to Judas, [the son] of Simon Iscariot. [27]And after [Judas had received] the piece of bread, Satan entered into him. Therefore Jesus said to him, "What you are going to do, do quickly." [28]But none of those reclining at [the] table knew for what purpose He said that to him. [29]For some were thinking, because Judas had charge of the [money] bag, that Jesus said to him, "Buy what things we need for the feast," or "Give something to the poor." [30]Then that one took the piece of bread, and immediately went out. And it was night.

[31]Then when he had gone out, Jesus said, "Now the Son of Man has been glorified, and in Him God was glorified. [32]If God was glorified in Him, also God will glorify Him in Himself, and soon He will glorify Him. [33]Little children, I am with you yet a little [longer]. You will seek Me and, just as I said to the Jews, also I say to you now, Where I am going you cannot come. [34]A new commandment I give to you, that you keep on loving one another. Just as I have loved you, so also you should continue to love one another. [35]By this shall all men know that you are My disciples, if you keep manifesting love among each other.''

[36]Simon Peter said to Him, "Lord, where are You going?" Jesus answered, "Where I am going you cannot follow Me now, but you will follow Me later." [37]Peter said to Him, "Lord, why cannot I follow You now? I will lay down my life for You." [38]Jesus replied, "You will lay down your life for Me? Truly, truly I tell you, the rooster will not crow until you deny Me three times.

---

[c]Cf. Ps. 41:9.
[d]Very close to Jesus—a place of first honor.

Chapter 14

"Stop allowing your hearts to be troubled. Keep believing in God: keep believing also in Me. [2]In the house of My Father there are many dwelling places. If it were not so, I would have told you. As a matter of fact, I am going to make ready a place for you. [3]And if I go and make ready a place for you, I am coming again and I will take you along to Myself, in order that where I, Myself, am you may be also. [4]And you know the way [to] where I am going."

[5]Thomas said to Him, "Lord, we do not know where You are going. How can we know the way?" [6]Jesus said to him, "I, Myself, am the Way and the Truth and the Life. No one comes to the Father except through Me. [7]If you had known Me, you would have known My Father also. From now on you know Him and have seen Him."

[8]Philip said to Him, "Lord, show us the Father and we will be satisfied." [9]Jesus said to him, "For so long a time I am with you, and you have not known Me, Philip? He who has seen Me has seen the Father. How can you say, 'Show us the Father'? [10]You believe, do you not, that I am in the Father and the Father is in Me? The words which I, Myself, say to all of you I do not speak from Myself, but the Father who dwells in Me does His deeds. [11]Keep believing Me that I [am] in the Father and the Father [is] in Me, or else keep believing Me because of the works themselves. [12]Truly, truly I say to you, the man who believes in Me, the works that I, Myself, am doing, he also will do. Actually, he will do greater [works] than these, for I am going to the Father. [13]Whatever you ask in My name, this I will do, so that the Father may be glorified in the Son. [14]If you ask Me anything in My name, I, Myself, will grant [it].

[15]"If you love Me consistently you will keep My commands. [16]And I will request the Father and He will give you another Paraclete[a] in order that He may be with you forever—[17]the Spirit of truth, whom the world cannot receive, because it neither sees Him nor knows [Him]. You yourselves know Him, for He dwells with you and He will be within you.

[18]"I will not leave you friendless; I will come [back] to you. [19]Yet a little while and the world will see Me no longer. But you will see Me; because I, Myself, live you, too, will live. [20]In that day you will know that I am in My

---

[a]The Greek term, *parakletos*, means *called alongside*, or *summoned to one's aid*. It is used of one who appears in behalf of another in a court of justice, as intercessor or helper. It is used of the Holy Spirit in the Fourth Gospel here and in v. 26; 15:26; 16:7. In 1 John 2:1, *Parakletos* is used of Jesus Christ who is the believer's Advocate with the Father.

Father, and you in Me and I in you. [21]He who has My commandments and keeps them, that is the person who loves Me. And he who loves Me will be loved by My Father, and I, too, will love him and will reveal Myself to him."

[22]Judas[b]—not Iscariot—said to Him, "Lord, and what has happened that You are about to manifest Yourself to us and not to the world?" [23]Jesus answered him, "If anyone keeps loving me, he will keep My word; and My Father will love him, and We will come to him and make Our dwelling place with him. [24]He who does not love Me does not keep My words; yet the word which you hear is not Mine but the Father's who sent Me.

[25]"I have spoken these things to you while remaining with you. [26]But the Paraclete, the Holy Spirit, whom the Father will send in My name, He will teach you all things and will remind you of everything I, Myself, told you.

[27]"Peace I leave with you. My peace I give to you. Not as the world gives do I give to you. Stop allowing your hearts to be troubled, and do not let them be terrified. [28]You heard that I, Myself, said to you, 'I am going away: but I am coming [back] to you.'[c] If you loved Me, you would have rejoiced that I am going to the Father, because the Father is greater than I.

[29]"And now I have told you [this] before it happens, so that when it happens, you may believe. [30]No longer will I speak many things with you, for the world's ruler is coming but he has no power over Me. [31]Nevertheless, in order that the world may know that I love the Father I am doing just as the Father has commissioned Me. Rise, let us be going from here.

Chapter 15

"I, Myself, am the true vine and My Father is the vine-dresser. [2]Every branch in Me that does not bear fruit, He cuts away; every branch that bears fruit, He prunes in order that it may keep on bearing more fruit. [3]Already you are in a condition conducive to fruit-bearing[a] because of the word which I have spoken to you. [4]Remain in Me and I in you. Just as the branch cannot bear fruit of itself unless it remains in the vine, so neither can you unless you remain in Me. [5]I, Myself, am the Vine, you are the branches. He who remains in Me, and I in him, that one bears much fruit; because apart from Me you are not able to do anything.

[6]"Anyone who does not remain in Me is thrown outside as a branch and withers. And such branches are gathered and thrown into the fire and burned.

---

[b]This apostle is also called Thaddeus (Mark 3:18) or Lebbeus (Matt. 10:3). See also Luke 6:16; Acts 1:13.

[c]Cf. v. 18.

[a]Literally, "Already you are clean."

[7]If you remain in Me and My words remain in you, ask whatever you wish, and it will be done for you.

[8]"By this is My Father glorified, that you continue bearing much fruit and you will become [indeed] My disciples. [9]Just as the Father has loved Me, I too have loved you. Remain in My love. [10]If you keep My commands, you will remain in My love, just as I Myself have kept the commands of My Father and remain in His love.

[11]"I have spoken these things to you in order that My joy may be in you, and that your joy may be made complete. [12]This is My commandment, that you keep loving each other just as I have loved you. [13]No one has greater love than to lay down his life in behalf of his friends. [14]You, yourselves, are My friends if you keep doing what I command you. [15]No longer do I call you servants, for the servant does not know what his lord is doing, but I have called you friends, because I have made known to you all [the] things which I heard from My Father. [16]You did not select Me, but I chose you and appointed you that you should go and bear fruit and that your fruit remain, so that whatever you ask the Father in My name He may give you. [17]These things I command you, that you keep loving one another.

[18]"If the world hates you, remember that it hated Me first. [19]If you belonged to the world, the world would love its own. But because you do not belong to the world, and I, Myself, have selected you from the world, this is why the world hates you. [20]Remember what I said to you: A servant is not greater than his lord. If they persecuted Me, they will persecute you also. If they respected My word, they will respect yours also. [21]But they will do all these things to you on account of My Name, because they do not know the One who sent Me.

[22]"If I had not come and spoken to them, they would not be guilty of sin; but now they have no excuse for their sin. [23]He who hates Me hates My Father also. [24]If I had not done among them the works which no other man did, they would not be guilty of sin; but now they have both seen and hated Me and My Father. [25]But this fulfilled the word which stands written in their Law,[b] 'They hated Me without a cause.'[c]

[26]"When the Paraclete comes, whom I, Myself, will send to you from the Father—the Spirit of the truth who comes from the Father—He[d] will testify concerning Me. [27]And you are to testify because you have been with Me from the beginning.[e]

---

[b]See note on John 10:34.
[c]Cf. Ps. 35:19; 69:4.
[d]Emphatic pronoun.
[e]That is, from the beginning of Jesus' ministry, Cf. Luke 1:2.

Chapter 16

"I have told you these things in order that you may not be made to stumble. [2]They will expel you from [the] synagogues. Furthermore, a time is coming when anyone who kills you will think he is performing service to God. [3]And they will do these things because they have not known either My Father or Me. [4]But I have told you these things, so that when their time comes you may remember them, that I, Myself, told you.

"I did not tell you these things from the beginning, because I was with you. [5]But now I am going to Him who sent Me, yet not one of you asks Me, 'Where are You going?' [6]But because I have spoken these things to you, the sorrow has filled your hearts. [7]Nevertheless, I tell you the truth: It is to your advantage that I go away; for if I do not go away, the Paraclete will never come to you. But if I go, I will send Him to you. [8]And that One—when He comes—will convict the world regarding sin and regarding righteousness and regarding judgment. [9]In regard to sin, because they refuse to believe in Me. [10]In regard to righteousness, because I am going to the Father and you [will] see Me no more. [11]And in regard to judgment, because the ruler of this world stands condemned.

[12]"I have yet many things to tell you, but you are not able to bear them now. [13]But when that One comes—the Spirit of the truth—He will guide you into all the truth. For He will not speak on His own authority but what things He hears He will speak, and He will announce to you the things to come. [14]He will glorify Me, for He will take of that which is Mine and will declare [it] to you. [15]All things which the Father has are Mine. That is why I said that He takes from that which is Mine and will announce [it] to you.

[16]"A little while and you will no longer behold Me, and again a little while and you will see Me." [17]Therefore, some of His disiples said to each other, "What does He mean when He said to us, 'A little while and you will not behold me; and again a little while and you will see me'? and 'I am going to the Father'?" [18]So they were saying, "What is the meaning of His expression, 'a little while'? We do not know what He is talking about."

[19]Jesus knew that they wanted to question Him, so He said to them, "Are you inquiring with one another about the statement I made, "A little while and you will not behold Me, and again a little while and you will see Me'? [20]Truly, truly I say to you that you will weep and lament but the world will rejoice. You will experience grief, but your grief will be turned into joy. [21]When a woman is about to give birth, she has pain because her time has come; but when she brings forth the child she no longer remembers the distress because of the joy that a man has been born into the world. [22]So you, too, indeed are experiencing sorrow now, but I will see you again and your hearts

will rejoice, and no one will take your joy away from you. ^{23}And in that day you will not ask Me any question.^{a} Truly truly, I tell you, whatever you ask the Father, He will give you in My name. ^{24}Until now you have not asked anything in My name. Keep asking and you will receive in order that your joy may be increased more and more until it is filled completely.^{b}

^{25}"I have spoken these things to you in figurative language. The time is coming when I shall no longer speak to you in figurative language, but I shall announce to you plainly about the Father. ^{26}In that day you will ask in My name; and I do not tell you that I, Myself, will request the Father concerning you. ^{27}For the Father Himself, loves you, because you, yourselves, have reached a state of affection for Me and have come to believe that I came forth from alongside God. ^{28}I did come forth from the Father and I have come into the world; again I am leaving the world and am going to the Father."

^{29}His disciples said, "Well, now You are speaking plainly and using no figure of speech. ^{30}Now we know that You know all things, and there is no need for anyone to question You. For this reason we believe that You came forth from God."

^{31}Jesus answered them, "Do you now believe? ^{32}Listen, the hour is coming—as a matter of fact it has arrived—when you will be scattered, every man to his own interests, leaving Me alone; yet I am not alone, for the Father is with Me. ^{33}I have spoken these things to you in order that in Me you may continue having peace. In the world you will have distress; but keep encouraged, I, Myself, have overcome the world."

Chapter 17

After Jesus spoke these things, He lifted up His eyes to heaven and said, "Father, the hour has come. Glorify Thy Son in order that Thy Son may glorify Thee, ^{2}just as Thou didst give Him authority over all mankind, that He may give eternal life to all whom Thou hast given Him. ^{3}Now eternal life is this: that they might know Thee, the only true God, and Jesus Christ whom Thou hast sent. ^{4}I have glorified Thee on the earth, having completed the work that Thou hast given Me to do. ^{5}So now, Father, glorify Thou Me alongside Thyself with the glory which I used to have alongside Thee before the world existed.

^{6}"I have manifested Thy name to the men whom Thou didst give Me out of the world. They were Thine and Thou gavest them to Me and they have kept

---

^{a}The idea here may be either to ask a question, or to make a request.
^{b}Indicated by the Greek periphrastic perfect passive subjunctive.

Thy word. [7]Now they have realized that all things whatever Thou hast given Me are alongside Thee. [8]For I have given them the words Thou didst give Me, and they on their part received [them], and knew truly that I came from Thee, and they have believed that Thou didst send Me.

[9]"I pray for them. I pray not for the world, but for those whom Thou hast given to Me, for they are Thine. [10]And all who are Mine are Thine and all who are Thine are Mine, and I have been and continue to be glorified in them.[a] [11]And I am no longer in the world, but they are in the world and I am coming to Thee. Holy Father, keep them in Thy name[b]—the name which Thou hast given to Me—so that they may continue being one, even as we are. [12]While I was with them, I continued to keep them in Thy name which Thou hast given to Me, and I protected [them] and not one of them perished except the son of perdition, in order that the Scripture might be fulfilled. [13]But now I am coming to Thee, and these things I speak in order that in the world they may continually have My joy made complete within them.

[14]"I have given them Thy word. But the world hated them because they are not of the world, even as I Myself am not of the world. [15]I do not request Thee to take them out of the world but that Thou preserve them from the evil.[c] [16]They are not of the world, even as I Myself am not of the world. [17]Make them holy by means of the truth. Thine own word in its very nature[d] is truth. [18]"Just as Thou didst send Me into the world, I also sent them into the world. [19]And in their behalf I set Myself apart[e] in order that they also may go on being in the state of having been made holy in [the] truth.

[20]"I pray not only for these, but also for those who [will] believe in Me through their word, [21]in order that [they] all may go on being one even as Thou, Father, art in Me, and I in Thee, that they also may go on being in us, in order that the world may consistently believe that Thou didst send Me. [22]And the glory which Thou hast given to Me, I have given to them, in order that they may go on being one even as we are one, [23]I in them and Thou in Me, in order that they may continue in the state of having been brought to completeness in one, in order that the world may keep on knowing that Thou hast sent Me and hast loved them even as Thou didst love Me.

[24]"Father, I wish that those whom Thou hast given Me may go on being with Me, in order that they may keep beholding My glory which Thou hast given to Me, for Thou didst love Me before the creation of the world.

[25]"Righteous Father, although the world did not know Thee, nevertheless I have known Thee, and these men have known that Thou didst send Me. [26]And

---

[a]Referring to the disciples.

[b]The Father's name, i.e., His essential nature which is expressed in the incarnate Son.

[c]From the evil one (Satan); or from the evil thing.

[d]Indicated by anarthrous construction.

[e]Literally, "I make myself holy," "consecrate myself."

I made known to them Thy name, and will make [it] known, in order that the love with which Thou hast loved Me may go on being in them, and I in them.''

Chapter 18

Having said these things Jesus went out with His disciples beyond the Kidron valley, where there was a garden, into which He and His disciples entered. [2]Now Judas also, who was betraying Him, knew the place because Jesus had often met there with His disciples. [3]So Judas, having received the detachment of soldiers and Temple police both from the chief priests and the Pharisees, came there with torches and lanterns and weapons.

[4]Then Jesus knowing everything that was going to happen to Him, came out and said to them, "Whom are you seeking?" [5]They answered Him, "Jesus the Nazarene." He said to them, "I am He." Now Judas also, who was betraying Him, was standing with them.

[6]Now when He said to them, "I am He," they drew back and fell to the ground. [7]So He asked them again, "Whom are you seeking?" And they said, "Jesus the Nazarene." [8]Jesus replied, "I told you that I am He. If, therefore, it is I whom you want let these men[a] go their way,[b] [9]So that it was fulfilled which He spoke, "I have lost none of those whom You have given Me."[c]

[10]Then Simon Peter, who had a short sword, drew it and struck the high priest's servant and cut off his right ear. The servant's name was Malchus. [11]Then Jesus said to Peter, "Put the sword into the sheath. Shall I not drink the cup which the Father has given Me?"

[12]So the detachment of soldiers and their commanding officer and the Temple police of the Jews seized Jesus and bound Him [13]and led Him first to Annas, for he was [the] father-in-law of Caiaphas, the high priest that year. [14]It was Caiaphas who had advised the Jews that it was expedient for one man to die in behalf of the people.[d]

[15]Now Simon Peter and another disciple were following Jesus. And that disciple was known to the high priest, and went in with Jesus into the courtyard of the high priest; [16]but Peter stood outside the door. Then the other disciple, who was known to the high priest, went out and spoke to the maid in charge of the door, and brought Peter in.

---

[a]That is, the eleven disciples.
[b]Or, go home.
[c]Cf. John 17:12; 6:37.
[d]Cf. John 11:50.

[17]Then the maid-servant, who was in charge of the gate, said to Peter, "You are not one of this man's disciples also, are you?" Peter replied, "I am not." [18]Now the servants and the Temple police were standing [there]. They had made a charcoal fire because it was cold, and were warming themselves. And Peter was also with them, standing and warming himself.

[19]In the meantime the high priest[e] questioned Jesus about His disciples and about His teaching. [20]Jesus answered him, "I have spoken plainly to the world. At all times I have taught in [the] synagogue and in the Temple precincts, where all the Jews come together, and I have spoken nothing in secret. [21]Why do you question Me? Ask those who have heard Me, what I spoke to them. Certainly they know what things I, Myself, said."

[22]When He said these things, one of the Temple police who was standing near struck Jesus and said, "Is that the way for You to answer the high priest?" [23]Jesus answered him, "If I spoke wrongly, show evidence concerning the wrong. But if I spoke properly, why do you strike Me?" [24]Then Annas sent Him bound to Caiaphas the high priest.

[25]During all this, Simon Peter had been standing there warming himself. So they said to him, "You too are not [one] of His disciples, are you?" He denied [it], saying, "I am not!" [26]One of the servants of the high priest, being a relative of the man whose ear Peter had cut off, said, "Did I not see you in the garden with Him?" [27]Then again, Peter denied [it], and immediately a rooster crowed.

[28]Then they led Jesus from Caiaphas to the governor's palace. It was early morning, and they themselves did not enter into the governor's palace, in order that they might not be defiled but might eat the passover. [29]So Pilate came out to them and said, "What accusation do you bring against this man?" [30]They answered him, "If this man were not habitually doing evil, we would not have delivered Him to you." [31]Pilate then told them, "You take Him and judge Him according to your law." The Jews said to him, "For us it is not lawful to put anyone to death," [32]So that the word of Jesus was fulfilled which He spoke, signifying the manner of death He was about to die.[f]

[33]Then Pilate again entered the palace, and summoned Jesus and said to Him, "You—are You the king of the Jews?" [34]Jesus replied, "Do you say this of yourself, or have others told you concerning Me?" [35]Pilate answered, "I am not a Jew, am I? Your own nation and the high priests have handed You over to me. What have You done?"

[36]Jesus replied, "My kingdom is not of this world. If My kingdom were of this world, My servants would have fought to prevent Me from being

---

[e]Annas questioning about how Jesus chose His disciples and about the doctrines He taught.
[f]Cf. John 12:32-33.

delivered to the Jews. But as things are, My kingdom is not of this place."[g]

[37]Therefore Pilate said to Him, "So, You are [some kind of] a king?" Jesus replied, "You say[h] that I am a king. For this cause I was born, and for this cause I have come into the world, that I might bear witness to the truth. Everyone who is of the truth listens to My voice." [38]Pilate replied, "What is truth?"

When he had said this, he went out again to the Jews and said to them, "I find Him guilty of nothing at all. [39]But you have a custom that I should set free one prisoner for you at the Passover. Do you wish, therefore, that I release to you the King of the Jews?" [40]At this they shouted out again, saying, "Not this man, but Barabbas!" Now Barabbas was a robber.

Chapter 19

Then Pilate took Jesus and ordered Him to be whipped. [2]And the soldiers plaited a crown out of thorns and placed [it] upon His head and they threw a purple robe around Him, [3]and they marched past Him and kept saying, "Hail, King of the Jews!" And they kept striking Him with their fists.

[4]And again Pilate came forth outside and said to them, "Look, I am bringing Him out to you in order that you may realize that I find Him guilty of nothing at all." [5]Then Jesus came outside, wearing the thorny crown and the purple cloak. And Pilate said to them, "Behold the Man!"

[6]When the chief priests and the Temple police saw Him, they shouted, saying "Crucify Him!" "Crucify Him!" Pilate said to them, "Take Him yourselves and crucify [Him], for I do not find any guilt in Him." [7]The Jews answered him, "We have a Law, and according to that Law He ought to die, for He made Himself God's Son."

[8]Now when Pilate heard this word he was even more afraid. [9]He went again into the palace and said to Jesus, "Where do You come from?" But Jesus did not give him any answer. [10]So Pilate said to Him, "Do You refuse to speak to me? Do You not know that I have authority to release You, and I have authority to crucify You?" [11]Jesus replied, "You would have no authority at all against Me unless it had been given to you from above. For this reason he that delivered Me to you has [the] greater sin."

[12]Because of this Pilate kept seeking to release Him. But the Jews cried out, "If you release this man, you are not Caesar's friend. Whoever makes himself king speaks against Caesar."

---

[g]Literally, "from here."
[h]Cf. Matt. 27:11; Mark 15:2; Luke 23:3.

¹³So when Pilate heard these words, he led Jesus outside and sat Him down on [the] judgment-seat at the place called the Stone Pavement, or in Hebrew, Gabbatha.ª ¹⁴Now it was [the day of] preparationᵇ for the Passover, [and] it was about the sixth hour. Then he said to the Jews, "Look, your king!" ¹⁵Then these cried out, "Away with Him! Away with Him! Crucify Him!" Pilate said to them, "Shall I crucify your king?" The high priest answered, "We have no king but Caesar." ¹⁶Pilate then delivered Him over to them to be crucified.

So they took Jesus, ¹⁷and He went out, carrying the cross for Himself to the place which is called Skull, which is called in Hebrew, Golgotha, ¹⁸where they crucified Him, and with Him two others, one on each side and Jesus in the middle. ¹⁹And Pilate also wrote a title and put it on the cross. And it was written, JESUS THE NAZARENE, THE KING OF THE JEWS. ²⁰Now this title many of the Jews read, because the place where Jesus was crucified was near the city, and it was written in Hebrew, Latin, and Greek.

²¹Therefore, the chief priests of the Jews were saying to Pilate, "Do not write, 'The King of the Jews,' but that, "He said, 'I am King of the Jews.' " ²²Pilate answered, "What I have written, I have written."

²³So when the soldiers had crucified Jesus, they took His garments and divided them into four parts, to each soldier a part, [also] the tunic. But the tunic was without seam, woven from the top to the bottom.ᶜ ²⁴So they said to one another, "Let us not tear it, but let us cast lots concerning it to see whose it shall be," so that the Scripture was fulfilled, "They divided My garments among themselves, and over My clothing they cast lots."ᵈ So the soldiers did these things.

²⁵But there were standing alongside the cross of Jesus His mother, and His mother's sister, Mary the wife of Clopas, and Mary the Magdalene. ²⁶When Jesus saw His mother and the disciple whom He loved standing by, He said to His mother, "Woman, there is your son." ²⁷Then He said to the disciple, "There is your mother." And from that hour the disciple took her to his own home.

²⁸After this Jesus, knowing that all things had now been finished, in order that the Scripture might be fulfilled, He said, "I am thirsty." ²⁹A vessel was lying there full of vinegar.ᵉ So they put a sponge soaked in the vinegar on a hyssop stalk [and] held it up to His mouth. ³⁰Then when Jesus had taken the sour wine,ᶠ He said, "It has been finished [and remains in a state of completion]ᵍ. Then He bowed His head and yielded up His spirit.

ªAn Aramaic word which means elevation, ridge, or raised place.

ᵇFriday, the day of preparation.

ᶜLiterally, "woven from the top throughout."

ᵈCf. Ps. 22:18.

ᵉSee note at Matt. 27:48.

ᶠJesus had previously refused the drugged wine which was customary to offer criminals who were condemned to the cross. Mark 15:23; Matt. 27:34.

ᵍIndicated by *tetelastai*, perfect passive indicative, as in v. 28.

[31]Then the Jews because it was Preparation Day [and] in order that the bodies might not remain on the cross on the Sabbath, for great was the day of that Sabbath, requested Pilate to have the legs broken and [the bodies] taken away. [32]So the soldiers came and broke the legs of the first man and then of the other who had been crucified with Him. [33]But when they came to Jesus and saw that He was dead already, they did not break His legs. [34]However, one of the soldiers with a spear pierced His side, and instantly there came out blood and water.

[35]He who saw [these things] has given witness [to it] and his witness is true. And he knows that he is speaking [the] truth, in order that you too may keep believing. [36]For these things took place in order that the Scripture might be fulfilled, "A bone of Him shall not be broken."[h] [37]And again another Scripture says, "They shall look at [Him] whom they have pierced."[i]

[38]After these things Joseph of Arimathaea, who was a disciple of Jesus, but secretly because he was afraid of the Jews, requested Pilate for permission to take down the body of Jesus; and Pilate permitted [him to do so]. So he came and removed His body. [39]So then Nicodemus, who had first come to Him by night,[j] came bearing a mixture of myrrh and aloes, weighing about a hundred pounds. [40]Then they[k] took the body of Jesus and wrapped it in linen cloths with the spices, according to the Jewish burial custom.

[41]Now at the place where He was crucified there was a garden, and in the garden a new tomb, in which no one had ever yet been laid. [42]Because it was the Jewish [day of] Preparation, and the tomb was nearby, they placed Jesus there.

Chapter 20

Now early on the first day of the week, while it was still dark, Mary Magdalene went to the tomb and saw that the stone had been removed from the tomb. [2]She ran, therefore, and went to Simon Peter and to the other disciple whom Jesus loved, and said to them, "They have taken the Master out of the tomb, and we[a] do not know where they have placed Him!"

---

[h]Exod. 12:46; Ps. 34:20.

[i]Cf. Zech. 12:10.

[j]John 3:1ff.

[k]I.e., Joseph and Nicodemus. Mary Magdalene and Mary the wife of Clopas, and other disciples were present at or saw the burial. (Cf. Matt. 27:61; Mark 15:47; Luke 23:55).

[a]The plural verb indicates that Mary was not alone at the tomb. Cf. Matt. 28:1; Mark 16:1, Luke 24:10.

[3]So Peter and the other disciple went forth [from the city] and made their way toward the tomb. [4]And they were running, the two [of them] side by side. But the other disciple ran ahead more swiftly than Peter, and came first to the tomb. [5]He bent down and saw the linen wrappings lying; however he did not go in. [6]Then Simon Peter came along, following him, and went into the tomb; and he saw the linen wrappings lying, [7]and the headpiece which had been around His head, not lying with the linen cloths but apart, in the state of having been folded together in a place by itself. [8]Then the other disciple, who had arrived first at the tomb, also went in, and he saw and believed. [9]For they did not yet understand the Scripture that He must rise from the dead.[b] [10]Therefore, the disciples went home again.

[11]But Mary was standing outside the tomb weeping. And as she wept, she bent down and glanced into the tomb, [12]and she saw two angels clothed in white sitting one at the head and one at the feet, where the body of Jesus had been lying. [13]They said to her, "Woman, why are you weeping?" She said to them, "Because they have taken away my Master, and I do not know where they have laid Him."

[14]When she had said this, she turned around and saw Jesus standing [behind her] but she did not know that it was Jesus. [15]Jesus said to her, "Woman, why are you weeping? Whom do you seek?" She, thinking He was the gardener, said to him, "Sir, if you have carried Him away, tell me where you have put Him, and I will take Him away." [16]Jesus said to her, "Mary!" She turned and said to Him in Hebrew, "Rabboni!" which means "Teacher!"

[17]Jesus said to her, "Cease clinging to Me, for I have not yet ascended to the Father to stay.[c] But go to My brothers and tell them, 'I am going to ascend to My Father and your Father, and to My God and your God.' " [18]Mary Magdalene came and told the disciples, "I have seen the Lord!" and that He said these things to her.

[19]In the evening of that day, the first day of the week, even though the doors were locked where the disciples were, because they were afraid of the Jews, Jesus came and stood among them and said to them, "Peace to you!" [20]And having said this, He showed them His hands and His side. So the disciples rejoiced when they saw the Lord. [21]Then Jesus said to them again, "Peace to you!" Just as the Father has sent Me, I also am sending you." [22]After saying this He breathed on [them] and said to them, "Receive the Holy Spirit.[d] [23]If you forgive the sins of any, they [must already] have been

---

[b]Cf. Ps. 16:10; Luke 18:31-34.

[c]Implied by the Greek *anabebeka*, perfect tense. Cf. 16:7, 28; Luke 24:50-51; Acts 1:9-11.

[d]Cf. John 7:39.

forgiven.[e] If you retain [the sins] of any, they [must already] have been retained."[f]

[24]One of the Twelve,[f] Thomas called the Twin, was not with them when Jesus came. [25]So the other disciple said to him, "We have seen the Lord!" But he said to them, "Unless I see in His hands the mark of the nails, and put my finger in the mark of the nails, and put my hand in His side, I will never believe."

[26]After eight days His disciples were again inside the room and Thomas [was] with them. Jesus came, although the doors were fastened, and He stood among them and said, "Peace to you!" [27]Then He said to Thomas, "Bring your finger here and see My hands, and bring your hand and thrust [it] into My side; and stop disbelieving, but believe!" [28]Thomas answered Him, "My Lord and my God!" [29]Jesus said to him, "Because you have seen Me have you believed? Blessed are those who have not seen, and yet have believed."

[30]Now Jesus did many other signs in the presence of the disciples, which are not recorded in this book. [31]But these stand written in order that you might believe that Jesus is the Christ, the Son of God, and that by believing you may go on having life in His name.

Chapter 21

After these things Jesus manifested Himself again to the disciples at the Sea of Tiberias. Now He manifested [Himself] in this manner: [2]There were together Simon Peter, and Thomas called the Twin, and Nathaniel from Cana in Galilee, and the sons of Zebedee, and two others of His disciples. [3]Simon Peter said to them, "I am going fishing." They said to him, "We ourselves are going with you." They went forth and entered into the boat, but in that night they caught nothing.

[4]When early morning came, Jesus stood on the shore. However, the disciples did not know that it was Jesus. [5]Then Jesus said to them, "Fellows, you have not caught anything, have you?" They answered Him, "No." [6]So He told them, "Cast the net to the right of the boat and you will find [something]." So they cast [the net as He said], and no longer were they able to drag it [in] because of the multitude of the fishes.

---

[e]Perfect indicative passive. The Greek perfect tense expresses completed action, the results of which remain. See note at Matt 16:19

[f]Reference is made of the apostles, though Judas had betrayed the Lord and later hung himself.

[7]Then that disciple whom Jesus loved said to Peter, "It is the Lord!" When Simon Peter heard that it was the Lord, he girded himself with his upper garment—for he was wearing only a waist-cloth—and leaped into the sea. [8]But the other disciples came in the little boat, for they were not far from the land, but about three hundred feet, dragging the net with the fishes.

[9]As soon as they stepped off on the shore, they saw a heap of burning coals set and a fish lying upon it, and bread. [10]Jesus said to them, "Bring some of the fish you have just caught." [11]Simon Peter went aboard and dragged the net to the land, full of large fish, one hundred and fifty-three; and although there were so many, the net was not torn.

[12]Jesus said to them, "Come, have breakfast." None of the disciples was bold enough to ask Him, "Who are You?" for they knew that it was the Lord. [13]Jesus came and took the bread and gave [it] to them, and the fish likewise. [14]This [was] now [the] third [time that] Jesus was manifested to the disciples after He was raised from the dead.

[15]So when they had eaten breakfast Jesus said to Simon Peter, "Simon, son of John, do you love Me more than these?"[a] He said to Him, "Yes, Lord, You know that I have affection for You." He said to him, "Keep feeding My lambs." [16]He said to him again a second time, "Simon, son of John, do you love Me?" Again, Simon answered, "Yes, Lord, You know that I have affection for You." Jesus said to Him, "Keep being a shepherd to My little sheep." [17]Jesus said to Simon the third [time], "Simon, son of John, do you really have affection for Me?" Peter was grieved because Jesus had said to him the third [time], "Do you have affection for Me?" and he said to Him, "Lord, You know all things, You know that I [do] have affection for You." Jesus said to him, "Keep feeding My little sheep. [18]Truly, truly I say to you, when you were younger, you used to fasten your belt and walk around where you wished. But when you grow old, you will stretch out your hands and another will dress you and will carry [you] where you do not wish [to go]." [19]He said this signifying by what kind of death he was to glorify God. And having said this, He said to him, "Keep following Me."

[20]Peter turned around and saw the disciple, whom Jesus loved, following—the one who at the Supper also leaned on His breast and said, "Lord, who is the one who will betray You?" [21]So when he saw him, Peter said to Jesus, "Lord, but what about him?" [22]Jesus told him, "If I will that he remain until I come, what is that to you? You keep following Me."

[23]So this report spread among the brothers that this disciple would not die. But Jesus did not say to him, "He will not die," but "If I will that he remain until I come, what is that to you?"

[24]This is the disciple who bears witness to these things, and who has recorded them, and we know that his testimony is true.

---

[a]Or, more than you love these things?

[25]And there are also many other things which Jesus did which by their very nature if they should be recorded one by one, I suppose the world itself could not contain the books that would be written.